Poland Under Martial Law

A report on Human Rights by the Polish Helsinki Watch Committee

First published in Polish by the Polish Helsinki Committee, Warsaw.

© 1983 English Edition by the U.S. Helsinki Watch Committee.

Distributed in Europe by the International Helsinki Federation for Human Rights

Printed and bound in the United States of America.

Cover Design: Charles H. Gabriel

TABLE OF CONTENTS

ACKNOWLEDGMENTS... i

PREFACE by Leszek Kolakowski............................. ii

A NOTE ON THE POLISH HELSINKI WATCH COMMITTEE by
  Catherine A. Fitzpatrick............................... vi

LETTER FROM THE TEMPORARY COORDINATING COMMITTEE
  OF SOLIDARNOSC... ix

INTRODUCTION... 1

I.   LEGAL AND EXTRALEGAL MECHANISMS OF LEGALITY
      IN THE PEOPLE'S REPUBLIC OF POLAND (PRL).......... 9

II.   THE IMPOSITION OF THE STATE OF WAR IN
      LIGHT OF POLISH AND INTERNATIONAL LAW............. 37

      A.   The Effect of Martial Law on the Legal
           System of the PRL............................ 37

      B.   Regulations on Martial Law and the Inter-
           national Obligations of the PRL............. 46

III. LEGISLATION UNDER THE STATE OF WAR............... 58

      A.   Legislation on Labor Unions................. 58

      B.   Legislation on Proceedings Against
           Individuals Refusing to Work and the PRL's
           International Commitments................... 63

      C.   Legislation on Special Legal Regulations
           During the Suspension of the State of
           War... 72

IV.   THE REPRESSIVE ROLE OF PROPAGANDA................ 78

V.   THE COURTS AND THE PUBLIC PROSECUTOR'S OFFICE
      UNDER THE STATE OF WAR........................... 87

      A.   Penal Regulations Under Martial Law......... 87

B.   Judges, Prosecutors, and Attorneys
Under Martial Law............................   94

C.   The Authorities' Guidelines on Penal
Policy....................................... 104

VI.   PENAL PROCEDURES DURING THE STATE OF WAR:
INVESTIGATIONS, TRIALS, SENTENCES, MISDEMEANOR
COURTS.. 106

A.   Investigations............................... 107

B.   Detention.................................... 108

C.   Interrogations............................... 112

D.   Investigations and Trials Inspired by the
Secret Police (SB)........................... 127

E.   The Prosecutor in the Investigation
Process...................................... 129

F.   Misdemeanor Courts........................... 169

VII.   PRISON CONDITIONS AND THE STATUS OF POLITICAL
PRISONERS... 174

VIII.   INTERNMENT CAMPS.................................. 189

A.   Categories of Internees...................... 191

B.   Camp Regulations............................. 193

C.   Living Conditions............................ 196

D.   Repressions of Internees..................... 200

E.   Quantitative Data............................ 204

F.   Suspension of the State of War............... 206

IX.   BEHAVIOR OF POLICE AND MILITARY DURING STRIKES
AND STREET DEMONSTRATIONS........................... 207

A.   Strikes...................................... 207

B.   Street Demonstrations........................ 216

C.   The Fate of the Arrested Following Street
Demonstrations............................... 227

        1. Circumstances of Arrest................ 227

    D. Subsequent Fate of the Arrested............ 230

        1. Summary Proceedings in Misdemeanor
           Courts.................................. 231

    E. Jurisdiction of Misdemeanor Courts
        Dealing with Demonstrations of May 3,
        August 31, and November 11, 1982, in
        Warsaw...................................... 232

        1. Court Trials Under Accelerated
           Procedures............................. 246

        2. Court Cases Under Summary Procedures..... 247

X.   REPRESSION OF WORKERS........................... 249

    A. The Right to Work Under the State of War
        and Its Implementation...................... 250

    B. Verification................................ 258

        1. Administrative Offices.................. 258

        2. Polish Radio and Television............. 261

    C. Repression of Workers Who Participated
        in Strikes and Protests..................... 262

    D. The Secret Police and the Worker............ 271

    E. The Assumption of Secret Police and
        Militia Functions by the Management
        and Other Professionals..................... 275

    F. Methods of Action, Threat of Punishment..... 277

XI.   REPRESSION OF THE PRESS......................... 282

XII.   HIGHER EDUCATION IN POLAND ONE YEAR AFTER THE
      IMPOSITION OF MARTIAL LAW....................... 290

    A. Background: Higher Education Between
        August 1980 and December 1981............... 290

    B. Legal Regulations on Education During the
        State of War................................ 293

    C. Unofficial Interference by Authorities in
        Academic Institutions......................... 307

    D. Education Under Martial Law: Schools........ 310

    E. Repression of High School and University
        Students in Connection with Protest
        Actions....................................... 316

SUMMARY... 322

GLOSSARY.. 325

ACKNOWLEDGMENTS

The English translation of this report was edited by Catherine A. Fitzpatrick, Irena Lasota, and Sonia Sluzar.

The assistance of the J. Roderick MacArthur Foundation in publishing this report is gratefully acknowledged.

We would like to thank the following individuals and organizations who generously donated their time and efforts in translating and providing technical help in the publication of this report:

Andre B. Blaszczynski
Committee in Support of Solidarity (New York City)
Irena Dubicka
Anna Findeisen
Friends of Solidarity (Washington, DC)
Eva C. Jedruch
Maria Kaminska-Gornikiewicz
Ted Kontek
Barbara Kwasnik
Tadeusz Morawski
Krzysztof M. Munnich
Iwona Oksiuta
Barbara Sikora
Solidarity and Human Rights Association (New York)
Solidarity International, Inc. (Connecticut and New York)
Solidarity Support Committee of Western Massachusetts
Bohdan Struminski
Studium (North American Study Center for Polish Affairs, Canada and U.S.)
Support of Solidarity (Boston, MA)
Jerzy Thieme
Bozena Warchol
Thomas Warchol
Jerzy Warman
Bohdan Wasiutynski
Elizabeth Wasiutynski
Wojciech Wasiutynski
Anna Wroblewska

The entire text of this report in the original Polish, including more than 500 pages of appendices not included in the English edition, is available from Instytut Literacki, 91 Avenue de Poissy, Mesnil-le-Roi, 78600-Maisons Laffitte (S. et O.) FRANCE.

A limited number of copies of an English translation of the appendices may be available upon written request from CSCE, House Annex 2, Rm. 3281, Washington, DC   20515.

-i-

PREFACE

Hardly anything can be added to this concise, dry and objective report. The description of Polish "martial law" prepared by people in underground Solidarnosc - in light of general human rights principles and the Polish Constitution - makes any commentary unncessary. Does one have to prove that political murder, torture, arbitrary mass arrests, blackmail and similar accomplishments of Polish socialism do not represent any great progress in the history of human rights? But there is one side of the affair that perhaps merits special attention. That is the basic normality of a state of emergency under the communist regime.

One occasionally hears the remark: "the number of those murdered, tortured, beaten and imprisoned on political grounds in Poland during martial law was still smaller than in various other countries, for example, in Latin America." That may be. It is hard to calculate the numbers of victims for such comparisons, since despotic regimes are at least accomplished in one area: they are good at concealing the extent of persecution. In any case, such calculations offer no great consolation to young Grzegorz Przemyk who was tortured to death in a Warsaw militia station last May, probably to give his mother - and thereby all mothers and fathers - an emphatic warning: "Keep quiet, otherwise not

only you but your children may be killed". (The mother's
"crime" was that she had been active in a church aid center;
a few days later she herself was attacked in church by
"unknown assailants").

Be that as it may, the number of corpses says little
about a political system. The range and cruelty of the acts
of repression naturally have not remained at a constant level
throughout the history of Poland and other communist states.
Depending on various circumstances, they may sometimes change
for the better or the worse. The essential characteristic of
these states is that the principle must never be violated,
according to which the governing powers (responsible to no
one) are completely free to determine the form and extent of
repression. Genocide, mass relocations and routine torture
are not constant features of communist governments: they are
used when necessary. Lawlessness is a natural feature of the
system. All attempts to reestablish legal autonomy, even to
a limited extent - for example Czechoslovakia in 1968 or
Poland during the period of Solidarity - are necessarily, and
rightly, regarded as subversive: they attempt to give
society partial control over the governing powers. They are
in essence anti-communist.

You are severely beaten by the police on the street or
in a factory because of a suspicion - warranted or
unwarranted. Then you are taken to court and all of the

policemen bear witness that you have attacked them. Are you sick and frail? So what - you have assaulted four heavily armed men on the street. That's what they say. The judge believes them. Are they not officials of a progressive system? Or perhaps he doesn't? He can and will be removed from office in a few days and the prosecuting attorney will appeal to a higher court. Do you want to publicize your case in the papers? That is impossible. The press is either in the hands of the government or censored by it. During "martial law," as well as before it, there were countless cases of this sort.

In brief: the accusor, the judge, the prosecutor, the police and the executioner are united in one. In ideological language, this is called "the political and moral unity of the socialist people."

Is it conceivable that a communist system will someday reestablish a degree of legal autonomy? Yes, under the condition that it ceases to be a communist system - in a historical sense as well as with respect to its ideological self-determination.

"Martial law" was, however, by no means insignificant in the history of law enforcement under communism. The governing powers felt compelled to be open about lawlessness for the first time. There had always been censorship of letters. The word "censorship", however, did not exist in official jargon. Now, for the first time, people received

letters that were officially stamped as "censored". he
tapping of telephones had always been practiced. Now, for
the first time, the population was warned about it. There
had always been arbitrary arrests. But for the first time,
these were announced. The lifting of "martial law" is really
a normalization: that is, a return to normal lawlessness.

Leszek Kolakowski
Translated by Boria Sax

A Note about the Polish Helsinki Committee

In November 1981, the U.S. Helsinki Watch Committee published Prologue to Gdansk, a report on human rights in Poland prior to the emergence of Solidarity. The report was written by the Polish Helsinki Committee, which was established in Warsaw in September 1979 by members of KOR, the independent Committee for Social Self-Defense. At that time the Polish Helsinki Committee had to work underground.

But by November 1980, when the Polish Committee's report was presented at the opening of the Helsinki review conference in Madrid, its work was open within Solidarity's network. A new era had begun in Poland. The report itself seemed mainly a historical record of past lawlessness.

In December 1981, however, Polish authorities imposed martial law in an effort to suppress Solidarity. Human rights activists throughout the world assumed that Helsinki monitoring in Poland had been forcibly ended. Zbigniew Romaszewski, founder of the Polish Helsinki Committee and Solidarity's Intervention Bureau, an editor of Prologue, and a member of Solidarity's National Coordinating Commission, was forced underground. He was eventually arrested in August 1982 and sentenced in January 1983 to four and a half years of imprisonment for operating Solidarity's clandestine radio station. He is now awaiting trial on another indictment, together with ten other Solidarity leaders and advisors, charged with attempting to overthrow the Polish state.

In February 1983, however, we learned that a new Helsinki Committee with different personnel had been created in Poland, and had prepared a report on violations of the Helsinki Accords under martial law, a summary of which was presented in March to the Madrid conference. The new Helsinki monitors wish to remain anonymous. They are represented in the West by Jakub Karpinski in New York. The report, entitled "Human and Civil Rights in the Polish People's Republic During the State of War (December 13, 1981 - December 31, 1982)" is the report we publish here under the title Poland Under Martial Law.

Poland Under Martial Law is sad testimony that the brutal repression described in Prologue was reinstated and reinforced during the state of war in Poland. It is now institutionalized, so that, although martial law has been lifted, most of its features have been incorporated in the Polish regime's apparatus of coercion.

The Polish Helsinki monitors work under constant threat of searches, interrogations, and arrests. At great personal risk, they have collected, compiled, and corroborated the testimonies of numerous victims of the martial law regime. Unfortunately, for fear of government reprisal, they cannot be named here, but their work has been authenticated by

It is our hope that the publication of their research will serve as a reminder that, in the words of Solidarity, "there is no peace without social justice."

Catherine A. Fitzpatrick

Staff Director, Soviet and East
   European Affairs
U.S. Helsinki Watch Committee

December 1983

TO THE CONFERENCE ON SECURITY AND
COOPERATION IN EUROPE

January 30, 1983

We consider it our civic duty to monitor our country's
compliance with the Helsinki agreements and international
conventions on human and civil rights. Therefore, we submit
this report to reveal the extent of lawlessness as practiced
by the authorities of the People's Republic of Poland.

This report does not reveal all the cases of violations
of law in Poland. Many such cases are being covered up by the
authorities and the security apparatus, and the evidence is
being destroyed. Repression against all forms of independent
activity and prosecution of union officials prohibit
gathering, verification and documentation of human rights
violations and lawlessness. As these difficulties are
overcome, we will supplement this report with additional
information. In case we are arrested, our effort will be
continued and the reports to follow will be signed by eminent
and respected members of our society.

We trust that this report will serve the cause of peace
and security in Europe, since there is no peace without social
justice.

                    Temporary Coordinating Commission
                    NSZZ SOLIDARNOSC

                    Zbigniew Bujak (Mazowsze region)
                    Wladyslaw Hardek (Malopolska region)
                    Bogdan Lis (Gdansk region)
                    Jozef Pinior (Dolny Slask region)
                    Eugeniusz Szumiejko (member of the
                        National Commission Presidium)

The Polish-language original of this report with an English summary
was presented to the Helsinki Review Conference in Madrid in March
1983 by Jerzy Milewski, Executive Director of the Coordinating
Office Abroad of NSZZ Solidarnosc.

INTRODUCTION

The Polish People's Republic (PRL) is party to the basic
international agreements pertaining to human rights: the
International Covenant on Civil and Political Rights and
the International Covenant on Economic, Social and Cultural
Rights (1977); the Conventions of the International Labor
Organization (ILO) (including No. 29 [1958]; No. 87 [1956];
No. 105 [1958]; and No. 111 [1961]) and the UNESCO convention on discrimination in education (1964). The Polish government also signed the Final Act of the Conference on Security
and Cooperation in Europe (Helsinki, 1975). Thus the state
authorities of the Polish People's Republic undertook an
obligation under international law to act in accordance with
the signed agreements as well as to recognize those rights
which protect its citizens against certain defined actions by
state bodies.

However, political and legal guarantees of human rights
and fundamental civil liberties have not yet been instituted in
Poland. The lack of such guarantees is part of the specific
feature of the political system created in Poland after
World War II.

According to Art. 40 of the International Covenant on
Civil and Political Rights, each participating state is obliged
to submit reports to the Human Rights Committee on the
"measures they have adopted which give effect to the rights

-1-

recognized" in the Covenant. We do not know whether the government of the Polish People's Republic prepared such a report covering the period during the state of war. In keeping with the commonly practiced PRL tradition of not revealing many important documents published abroad to Polish public opinion, the content of such a government account, if it exists, was not made accessible to the press or other forms of public communication in Poland.

For these reasons, documentation on the observance of human rights in the Polish People's Republic should be collected, analyzed and presented to international organizations as a citizens' effort, independent of the work undertaken in this regard by the state and beyond the reach of administrative constraints.

This study contains material pertaining to the state of war, i.e., the period beginning December 13, 1981, and ending December 31, 1982.

The problem of human rights observance in the PRL was already the topic of a work prepared by a group of authors independent of the state authorities. In 1980, members of the Polish Helsinki Committee founded in the late 1970s prepared Document No. 1: On the Observance of Human and Civil Rights in the Polish People's Republic.*

---

*This report was published in English in 1981 by the U.S. Helsinki Watch Committee under the title: Prologue to Gdansk.

In this work, which was available to international institutions and the Polish public, the authors presented material on the period 1976-1980. Incidents of human rights violations were presented in Document No. 1 together with an analysis of the characteristics of the political system which contributed to a lack of legal security for its citizens.

The cutoff point for Document No. 1 was July 1980, when the massive strike movement broke out and spread throughout Poland.

Our work is not a continuation of Document No. 1. We are a different group of authors and are active under different circumstances. The material we are presenting here does not cover documentation on violations of human rights between August 1980 and December 13, 1981, although it does include several examples of violations of human rights from that period. Needless to say, the scope and extent of repressive actions undertaken by the authorities before December 13th were much smaller than during the state of war.

Our work is composed of two parts. Part One consists of general material (Chapters I through IV) and analysis of various types of abuses and repressions (Chapters V through XII). Part Two has been omitted from the English edition of this report. It contains documentation and commentary on the issues covered in Part One.

Chapter I describes mechanisms within the system

conducive to the practice of violating human rights during various periods of the history of the PRL. This chapter also comments on the situation in Poland between August 1980 and December 1981.

Chapter II analyzes the legal regulations of the state of war in the PRL in the context of the international legal norms by which Poland is bound. The question is considered as to whether the way in which the state of war was introduced was compatible with national law. The legal consequences of the decree proclaiming the state of war are discussed.

Legislation adopted by the Sejm (parliament)of the PRL during the state of war is analyzed in Chapter III in the context of international law and particularly of Poland's international legal obligations pertaining to human rights. Items examined from this viewpoint include: the Oct. 8, 1982 act "On Labor Unions;" the Oct. 26, 1982 act "On Measures Against Persons Shirking Work;" and the Dec. 18, 1982 act "On Special Legal Regulations During the Period of the Suspension of the State of War."

Chapter IV deals with the repressive functions of propaganda. This includes defamation of social organizations (in particular the Independent and Self-Governing Trade Union Solidarnosc) and of individuals held in pre-trial detention, in penitentiaries, and in internment centers. The situation of those who are defamed and deprived of the right to defend themselves constitutes a separate class of human rights violations.

Chapters V through XII analyze in turn the issue of penal repression, the problems of internment centers, the situation in the prison system and in military penal camps, the repressive actions of military and police forces during strikes and protest activities, repression in the workplace, the role of security forces in the work environment, and repression of youth, academics, artists, and journalists.

The selection of materials, the method of preparation, and the form of this study were significantly shaped by the conditions under which it was undertaken.

Under the state of war in Poland, the apparatus of coercion became more active and received new prerogatives (searches of passersby, tapping of telephone conversations, etc.) and was not subjected to any restraint. Consequently, much effort was required to organize this work in such a way as to shield participations against imprisonment and the materials against confiscation.

Another difficulty was the lack of reliable data from official sources. Although the official media provided almost daily accounts of arrests, indictments, trials, and convictions, these accounts nevertheless were intended primarily to serve various propaganda purposes.

Statements by government spokesmen and representative of

the highest authorities manipulated statistics and gave
descriptions of the humane treatment of interned and
imprisoned individuals which were intended to reassure. This
occurred particularly before protest actions scheduled by
Solidarnosc. The authorities threatened to use "all
available means at the disposal of the disciplinary organs."
Contradictions, gaps, and completely arbitrary criteria for
the selection of data characterizes the quantitative
information available from official sources about arrests,
trials, internments, and fatalities. Information pertaining
to many types of repression was not published at all. For
example, there are no official data on dismissals from
employment for activity in Solidarnosc, even though this
type of repression affected thousands of workers. As a
result, it is not possible to use official sources in
preparing any sort of a complete record of the violations of
human rights under the state of war.

Information about repression was gathered by persons
operating independently of the authorities (in regional and
enterprise-level units of underground Solidarnosc, in
clandestine independent publishing operations, and others.
These persons struggled with difficulties similar to those
experienced by the authors of this work. While utilizing
these materials, we were cognizant of their shortcomings and
limitations. We sought to have trustworthy information by

comparing data received from different sources and by
omitting many reports whose reliability was difficult to
establish.

We interviewed victims of repression, ex-internees, and
persons released from prisons, as well as those dismissed
from work for labor-union activity.

As a consequence, the final result of our efforts is not
free of shortcomings, gaps, and faults, including those of an
editorial nature.

There is a shortage of statistical reporting. The
figures we have presented are not a complete tabulation of
violations in a given category; the numbers represent the
lower estimates for the data available. Evidence for
the number of those arrested, convicted and the interned is
fragmentary.

When presenting specific cases of repression based on
accounts related by persecuted individuals (verbal accounts,
written statements smuggled from detention and prison), the
basic problem was the need to present the original document
in such a way as not to subject people to reprisal by the
authorities, leading to further repression and persecutions.
Thus, in many instances we decided to provide documents while
omitting data that could lead to the identification of
individuals. The original documents are in the possession of
the team which edited this work. In many cases, the victims

themselves decided to make public information about abuses.

The state of war in Poland was formally suspended on December 31, 1982. However, the legislative act on special regulations during the period of suspension of the state of war, other recently enacted legislation, and especially the actual behavior of the PRL authorities at the onset of 1983, do not promise hope of increased legal security for citizens in the near future.

In presenting to international bodies this material on human rights violations under the state of war in Poland, we are aware of the limitations and difficulties in enforcing international legal obligations by the PRL on the part of states who are parties to these international agreements. All the same, we are convinced that the exposure of abuses and transgressions against human rights is an obligation and a right of all who possess reliable information on this subject.

Furthermore, we are convinced that even the limited means at the disposal of international bodies can have an influence in bringing about an improved observance of human rights in our country.

CHAPTER I

LEGAL AND EXTRALEGAL MECHANISMS OF

LEGALITY IN THE PRL

One cannot explain violations of human rights in the
Polish People's Republic simply by citing incidents or facts.
The lack of legal security for citizens and of an
institutionalized and effectively functioning system to protect
of human rights in the PRL derives from the political system
shaped in Poland after World War II. This system was not based
on the people's right to self-determination (see Art. I of the
International Convention on Economic, Social and Cultural
Rights), but was imposed on Poland from outside.

Taking advantage of the military protection of the
Soviet Union to realize their plans for sociopolitial change
and the creation and consolidation of new constitutional and
legal forms, the political forces which assumed power in
Poland in 1945 were forced to apply continuous repressive
pressures on society. It is clear that the scope, intensity
and nature of that pressure were modified by factors
prevailing in a given period.

In the years 1944-1948, political terror was aimed primarily against active opponents of the system, who resisted
with armed as well as legal, political methods. Attacks
against legal part of the activities (such as the crushing

of the Polish populist party) was characteristic, as was
the use of terror against randomly selected individuals.

In the years 1949-1955, after crushing the organized
forms of resistance, terror became the fundamental element of
a policy aimed at destroying all social ties not controlled
by the authorities, changing social consciousness, crushing
resistance to collectivization of agriculture, liquidating
the influence of the Church, and making the articulation of
socieal aspirations impossible.

Repression by the security apparatus and by a completely
submissive judicial system was greatly intensified during
these periods. The authorities' actions were largely
outside the law. Penal regulations were, however, adapted to
fit the situation. The regulations in force provided for
very severe punishment of minor infractions and for special
proceedings which virtually ruled out legal defense.

After 1956 (an arbitrary date since many changes had
started earlier), a new phase began, much different from the
previous ones. The new leadership group under Wladyslaw
Gomulka was able to obtain a certain legitimacy for its power
(as exemplified by the the 1957 elections) after it
had formulated a new policy and partially implemented it.
Terror was no longer the basic component of policy. While
repressive pressure on society was not relinquished, the
purpose of that pressure was confined mainly to the

prevention of independent political activity. Exhausted by
the tragedies experienced since 1939, and assured of relative
improvement in its economic and sociocultural fate, society
did not manifest any marked aspirations in that direction.

In the first few years after 1956, the potential for
applying terror was limited at least in part by a degree of
autonomy for the judiciary. One should also mention that
amnesty was declared in 1956 and that so-called
rehabilitation proceedings allowed for the release of most
prisoners who had been sentenced during the terror.

Nevertheless, apart from the transfer of many cases to
civil courts, the legal status did not change until 1969,
i.e., severe regulations from the previous period were still
in force. It would also be difficult to speak of new,
permanent political guarantees for the observance of the law
There was no implementation to speak of in the
domain of human and civil rights. The standard penalty for
so-called "dissemination of false information" was three
years in prison; this penalty was applied against all critics
of the authorities who attempted to express their views
publicly. There remained also an area where mass terror was
not suspended. In the sphere of economic activity, a
so-called "organized crime-mania" led to the use of draconian
penalities, including capital punishment, for actual but also
for alleged economic crimes. Since these penalties

were applied largely, according to the personal views and grudges of Gomulka, one can clearly see how shaky and unsound the foundation was for not applying terror in other spheres. Characteristic of this period was a narrowing in the range of tolerance (significant turning points occurred in 1963 and 1968) and an intensification of repressive policy. This was accompanied, among other things, by the growth of the role of police organs in the system of rule. The possibility of using terror was realized in 1968, during the so-called March events. Repressive measures were then targeted at students and intellectuals.

Terror reigned on a much greater scale in December 1970. The events which occurred in the northern cities of Poland overwhelmingly illustrate the argument that there was a complete lack of protection of even the most basic civil rights in Poland. Gomulka's fall from power cannot be considered a direct consequence of these events, much less a reaction of the political system to this bloody pacification. This pacification was never totally rejected by the new authorities, its course and consequences were never exposed and the perpetrators never punished. Of course, an association was formed in the public consciousness between the terror used by Gomulka and his fall along with the installation of a new ruling clique. The new group had to reckon with this view since it wanted to obtain and keep a semblance of social trust. However, although there were some positive results, a stronger safety mechanism did not evolve. In contrast to 1956, the issue of legality and civil rights did not become a matter for serious public discussion, and was not included among the demands of society that the new authorities promised to satisfy.

After 1970, the credibility of the authorities was based on assurances by Gierek's team that there would be economic reform and some opportunities in the purely personal prospects of citizens. Politically, these were confined to certain measures (rapidly abandoned), such as providing opportunities to criticize and announcing an increased public order. This was understood to mean an intensified campaign against crime but could also have been a warning against attempts to organize independent political actions. These announced intentions were implemented in the so-called "law-and-order" campaign, when men were forced to cut their hair even though long hair was fashionable.

Initially, there were no signs of change in the area of civil rights. While it is true that in 1971, political prisoners were released before serving out full sentences, at the same time, members of the "Movement" ("Ruch") group were given sentences of up to seven years. There were also instances of less well-known political trials. The authorities' misuse of the militia and SB was increasing and prison conditions were worsening. The practice of holding

so-called "citizen conversations," became endemic, i.e.,

people who had expressed critical opinions were summoned for

interrogation and pressure was brought to bear on them.

A particularly drastic way of violating the law was the

trials in which persons were sentenced for acts other than

the ones they had committed. An example is the case of the

Kowalczyk brothers. They blew up an assembly hall at the

Advanced Pedagogical Academy (WSP) in Opole, a crime which is

punishable by up to ten years in prison. However, since

their act was politically motivated, it was judged to be

particularly dangerous. Therefore they were tried on a charge

of attempting to assassinate public officials and given a

death sentence and 25 years of imprisonment respectively. The

Council of State then exercised the right of clemency. A

similar development occurred with the participants in a

Warsaw prison riot who were tried on a charge of attempted

murder (this brought a sentence of 25 years).

In 1976, a real wave of abuse occurred during the

demonstrations against food price increases in Radom and

Ursus. Beatings, forced testimony, and long sentences

for crimes never committed were characteristic in that year.

At the same time, events took place which were to change the

political image of Poland. Independent groups, previously

active in a campaign against amending the Constitution,

became engaged in a program of active aid to the repressed

and, in September 1976, formed the Workers' Self-Defense

Committee (KOR), an independent institution which was to

coordinate and initiate activities in defense of the regime's

victims. The authorities responded with persecution (48-hour

arrests, beatings, scare tactics, dismissal from work, etc.)

but refrained from major confrontation (an attempt was made

in the spring of 1977, but was quickly abandoned.) The KOR

campaign was successful in that it resulted in both the

release of those sentenced after the June 1976 events and in

the significant development of autonomous institutions having

a variety of programs and methods of action, but unanimously

appealing to principles expressed in the Covenant on Civil

and Political Rights.

It would be a mistake to conclude that this tolerance of

sorts by the authorities (consisting merely of refraining

from making arrests) meant real achievement of human in

Poland. Repressions continued even so, although in a milder

form. Anyone who decided to exercise the human rights to

which Poles were formally entitled by Poland's ratification

of the human rights Covenants at the end of 1977, as well as

by the PRL Constitution, had to reckon with repression (even

though that repression did not befall everyone). It is still

difficult to explain exactly what motivated the authorities

to relinquish the most drastic sanctions against independent

activities. Undoubtedly, a considerable influence was
exerted by the Western campaign on behalf of human rights,
conducted in conjunction with the signing of the Helsinki
Accords and later by President Carter's policy. It is clear
that such influence on the situation in Poland was possible
thanks only to the exist-ence of economic ties, credit, and
other connections. Edward Gierek's international ambitions
also played a role in this regard. However, it is difficult
to determine whether these were the only reasons.

The very special status of activists and independent
activity in Poland in the late 1970s has to be examined in a
broader context. Nothing or almost nothing changed in the
observance of civil rights in other aspects of life. The
repressive practices described earlier continued (a partial
documentation is contained in Document No. 1 of the
Helsinki Committee). There is no evidence to claim that
real legal and political guarantees were created that could
substantially change the status of citizens of the PRL.
Repeated arrests of the major activists, and the trials on
fabricated charges of people who participated in independent
movements, demonstrated the unsoundness of the authorities'
practices. The ratification of the previously cited
conventions should also be seen in this context. It created a
positive impression on the West, but was of little direct,
practical significance. That is how social conditions

appeared on the surface. However, more dramatic changes were taking place in social consciousness. A qualitative difference was emerging in the thinking of various social groups due to ongoing independent activity, information about world-wide campaigns in defense of human rights, and finally, assurances by the authorities that these rights would be respected. A new, attractive opportunity was opening up for many people: the possibility of expressing social aspirations not by questioning the entire system but by appealing to declarations made by representatives of that system.

The enrichment of social consciousness through the knowledge of human rights covenants had an undoubted influence on the intensification of a critical attitude towards reality. These conventions provided a high standard for comparison. A sense of entitlement to certain rights grew, as did a feeling of power - thanks to international support. The events of August 1980 reinforced this new sense of possibility. The demands presented at that time by the workers not only went beyond economic aspirations but also created a new political outlook which, on the one hand, surpassed whatever experience had been gained up to that point, and on the other hand, did not question the realities of time and place. One cannot overestimate the role that the new awareness of rights played in the shaping of that perspective. This pertains to agreements dealing with socio-economic issues as well as those encompassing political and human rights. In questioning both political authority and the practices of the system (but not the system itself), the August 1980 Agreements arose from a concept of public life largely derived from international law. Awareness of the existence of that law also had great significance in the shaping of determined yet prudent actions on the part of the workers.

After August 1980, a new era of Polish history began. Workers' strikes on the coast and in other regions of Poland ended with the signing of the agreements with the authorities in Gdansk, Szczecin and Jastrzebie, the birth of Solidarnosc and Rural Solidarnosc, and the growth of autonomy in other organizations, labor unions and associations. These events are processes were occurring against the background of an economic crisis whose size, scope, and causes became the object of public discussion in all parts of society. As a result, civil activity became emanicipated in Poland on a massive scale and expressed itself in a strong reform movement. The main impetu in the reform movement was directed at creating institutions and legal guarantees which would lead to the creation of publi control over the hitherto arbitrary state Party rule, whose organs would then act in conformity with the law and would respect civil rights. Solidarnosc was the leading force for reform. The labor union took on many functions which are normally carried out by other organizations. There were two reasons for this. The first was the union's power and its seemingly unquestioned legality. A great variety of activities to which the authorities objected or could have objected were thus included in the union's framework. In this way it was possible to avoid a threat or at least the feeling of a threat. The second reason was the popularity of the union itself, of its leaders and advisors, which kindled hopes for the resolution of other problems as well.

The focus of public attention on Solidarnosc should not, however, mask the fact that, during the 15-month period, a large number of union and non-union organizations was formed which introduced a new quality in the country's public life, and in the rights and opportunities of individuals. Among these organizations were those that included among their goals the defense and development of human rights. One example is the Association of Polish Journalists, actively seeking freedom of expression; another is Patronat, an association with pre-war traditions of aiding prisoners.

Freedom of expression is not simply, or even primarily, a matter of law. Even before legislation was enacted (actually, after September 1980), the range of freedom was expanded for the censored Polish press, although there was regression and it was not uniform throughout the entire country. Great differences cropped up among the various voivodships. Even more significant was the emergence of a union news network which was exempt from censorship, yet which had an immense circulation. Finally, independent publications already in existence were able to develop and expand their circulation with much greater freedom than before (although not without hindrances, confiscations, etc.)

The significant freedom to organize was accompanied by diminished harrassment of opposition activities (with the exception of the Confederation for Independent Poland – KPN – whose activists were severely repressed during this time). Forty-eight hour arrests now occurred very infrequently, and were rare for a period of time. This permitted the expansion of independent political activity. The term "independent" is used here intentionally. The adjective "oppositionist," applied frequently to denote activists, is not used in this text since the activists never intended to seize power but rather wanted to make it impossible for the authorities to return to past practices, and thus control their power. Civil rights concerns had a leading role in these activities. Also, they became unquestionably both a fundamental part of the widespread set of attitudes which motivated people to take an active part in political events, and a basic component of the vision of the publicly desired form of social order. The best example of this was the unusually widespread, vehement, and determined public reaction to the illegal acts committed by the authorities in Bydgoszcz in March 1981. The scope of social protest went beyond the framework of Solidarnosc, since it even encompassed a significant part of the Polish Communist Party The program adopted at the First Congress of Solidarnosc as well as the amendments to the statute which extended the organization's tasks in defense of its members' human rights, demonstrate the continuous presence of this idea in the mass social movement. It had a large role in the rebirth of the legal community. After a short period of relative autonomy, the justice apparatus was again subordi-nated to the party in the 1960s, and the situation did not change much under Gierek. This pertained to the public pro-secutor's office, the courts, and to a certain degree, to the bar as well. The latter had the most freedom, due specifically to its lack of a decision-making power. While it was true that the bar was controlled by the Party administration, and its members in the bar could be repressed, nevertheless the independent stance of several defense attorneys was tolerated particularly in the 1970s (previously, repression occurred more often). Defense lawyers were also allowed at political trials.

The situation was much more complex in the case of judges. A judge was theoretically independent in the sphere of his jurisdiction, yet was actually subordinate to the judicial administration. The changed situation in the whole country prompted a type of rebirth in the legal community. A specific feature was the special role of civil rights cases. This was manifested in the activities of both the Solidarnosc judges and public prosecutors, and of the pre-1980 professional union of jurists. Such parallel action was typical. A common expression of these aspirations was the attempt to change the judicial system so as to make it impossible to use the judicial administration to limit the independence and autonomy of judges. A distinct change in attitude took place whereby anything that was incompatible with an independent judiciary but which had been considered normal up to this time was rejected. A sense of dignity in the legal profession increased as judges came to be treated as officers of the law and not of the authorities, in accordance with democratic tradition. A similar process took place in the prosecutor's office, albeit with more difficulty and on a much smaller scale. This was due to the dissimilarities between these institutions, as well as to the fact that there were more individuals in the latter who were associated with the state of affairs brought into question in August 1980.

Things were somewhat different with the bar. The ferment which took place there was, on the one hand, quickly channeled into work on new legislations, and on the other, revealed itself in the lawyers' participation in Solidarnosc activity and other public initiatives.

The situation of the apparatus of coercion has to be considered separately. Shielded by an immunity of sorts and economically privileged, this apparatus basically constituted a secure base for the authorities. And yet, even there, significant developments took place. These changes pertained only to the militia - relatively the least privileged, sheltered and socially-isolated - which had a difficult and often dangerous job to perform. For these reasons society's aspiration found an echo in the militia: a union was to be formed for the militia that was not to be part of Solidarnosc. These attempts were suppressed, yet undoubtedly were a sign of potential for change even in that apparatus.

The changes described here greatly reduced the degree to which the apparatus for administering justice was at the political service of both the central and local authorities. Yet, their control was not entirely destroyed. The court administration remained at the disposal of the authorities; it continued to be possible to arrest people and try them on dubious charges even though this became more difficut and

required a more frequent referral of cases to the most
submissive body, the Supreme Court.

Now we come to the position adopted by the authorities.
Internally divided and undergoing a profound moral-political
crisis, the power centers counterracted the reformist
aspirations of a self-organizing society with various
resistance and defense tactics. The ruling elite could not
accept the shape of the reform process and the ways of
realizing it. Typical of the authorities' resistance to
reform were the difficulties they created over a new law
which would extend and safeguard civil liberties. Despite
the involvement and genuine efforts of many representatives
in the Sejm, this highest legislative body remained at the
service of the power center which clearly did not want the
proposed changes. During a time when a great variety of
citizens' initiatives developed, the net record of
legislative achievments by the Sejm was rather skimpy. Its
sole major achievement was a new law on the press,
publications, and theatrical performances, although its
regulations are still far from those principles which
constitute the basis for international agreements regarding
freedom of expression (see Art. 19 of the International
Covenant of Civil and Political Rights). The Sejm did not
introduce anything new in the penal code provisions upon
which the citizens' legal security is based. It is

significant that the Sejm did not undertake any work relating

to its own organization - for example, regulating the process

of recalling representatives or filling vacancies in the

Sejm.

The authorities did not undertake any publicly

discernible reforms of the form and function of the

institutions composing the apparatus of coercion (e.g., the

SB). Apart from the military, this was the only part of the

administration which was never subjected to official

criticism. It was consistently stated by the authorities,

even during negotiations with Solidarnosc regarding legality,

that human rights were and are respected in Poland. Although

the term human rights was used, it is characteristic that it

did not find its way into the language and become part of the

Polish Communist Party's so-called "renewal" program. The

"renewal" was a kind of alternative to the reformist ideas

which evolved from spontaneous public activity. The program

adopted at the IXth Congress of the Polish United Workers'

Party demonstrated this particularly well. Rhetoric on the

topic of legality was abundant, yet it was understood as a

situation in which laws are observed by citizens (law

understood to mean directives from the authorities) and by

state agencies alike. In this interpretation, contrary

to its origin and meaning in democratic countries, the law

becomes relative and ceases to function as a measure for

evaluating the state. The authorities' stance was not, of course, limited to verbal expressions.

Throughought the whole period of Solidarnosc activity, the criminal and security police violated the law. For the most part, these violations did not constitute an organized plan of action, yet it is most significant that the perpetrators were not held liable for their actions despite published information on such incidents in the labor union press. The situation intensified after the summer of 1981, when the Polish United Workers' Congress Party was held. This questioning began to take on the appearance of an organized campaign. New investigations of independent publication, posters, etc. were continually initiated at the Congress. The faction oriented toward a confrontation won and the rights and freedoms already gained by society came into question and arrests were made often (for short periods of time since the courts were overturning decisions made by the public prosecutors). An unusually vehement propaganda campaign atacked everyone who made use of existing freedom. However, the authorities were no longer able to change the situation in the country by simply undertaking a harsher course of action. The judicial apparatus and, to a certain degree, the prosecution apparatus, were not fully submissive. It was necessary to take Solidarnosc as well as society's solidarity and resistance into account.

Under these conditions, there were two possibilities for
the authorities: either to rely completely and openly on
their only remaining support, the army and the police, or to
work out a new legitimacy by reaching a genuine agreement
which would be based on the recognition of human
rights and, in practice, would mean the introduction of
reforms and legal guarantees. These would have greatly
expanded the authorities base, but would also have required
far-reaching changes. As is well-known by now, the first
solution was chosen. While publicly declaring their desire
to find a political solution, the authorities simultaneously
used provocative and intimidating propaganda in the mass
media. Finally, despite all declarations and assurances
to the contrary, they abandoned the search for political
solutions and took the path of crushing the reformist
aspirations of society by force when they declared a state of
war on December 13, 1981.

The imposition of the state of war proved that the
authorities interpreted the complex mosaic of society's
behavior and aspirations, the widespread rebirth of civic
initiative, and the people's awakening to participation in
public life, as an immense danger to their own position and
influence, and also as a dangerous attempt to fundamentally
question the habitual ways of wielding power. As a
consequence of the imposition of the state of war, all the

characteristics of the political system of the PRL that made it impossible to respect human rights were magnified. This led to the violation of human rights on a scale not seen in Poland since the Stalinist era.

We have reviewed the methods used by the PRL authorities in applying repressive measures on society in various periods preceeding the imposition of the state of war. Despite the lack of conditions for instituting democracy after 1945, aspirations toward the creation of a democratic social order guaranteeing respect for human rights were never extinguished in Poland. In that context, the conflict between the authorities and society became overt in many periods in the history of the PRL (in 1956, 1968, 1970, 1976, 1980, and during the state of war). Still, understanding the geopolitical limitations of Poland, society basically did not question the fundamental principles of the political system, but only demanded reform of the system, limitation of lawlessness on the part of various apparatuses of power, and the restoration civil rights.

What are the principal features of the legal-political system in the PRL which played an important role in blocking reformist tendencies in society and which are a constant source of illegality?

The primary feature of the system in the PRL is that it is not based on a concept of law characteristic of democratic systems, viz., where the law both limits the arbitrariness of authority and prevents license on the part of the citizenry. In Poland, laws are strictly instrumental. The law is primarily a means of for authority to obtain compliance. As a consequence, the promulgated rights of the citizens are meaningless since there are no specific duties on the part of the authorities, and citizens' duties are not accompanied by true rights of defense against the authorities' decisions.

The PRL Constitution is a prime example of this particular concept of the law. It does not provide for a division of power, whereby the organs of the authorities would check and supplement each other. In a formal sense, the supreme authority is the Sejm and its Council of State. The Sejm has full legislative power and controls the government and the judiciary. Arts. 8 and 20 of the Constitution state that in its policy the Sejm is guided by the "interest of the Polish nation" and "the realization of the nation's law, which is the expression of the interests of the working people." The principle of representation is also acknowledged in the Constitution: "The working people govern the state through their intermediary - by means of their representatives to the Sejm of the PRL and to national councils who are chosen in general election..." (Art. 2).

In reality, the Polish United Workers' Party is the only political force that controls the constitutional mechanism guaranteeing influence over decisions pertaining to the composition of the Sejm. Polish United Workers' Party. This stems from the principle of the leading role of the communist party ("the leading social political force in the building of socialism is the Polish United Workers' Party" - Art. 3) as well as from the provision that the Party "...along with the Populist Party and the Democratic Party constitute the foundation for a National Unity Front" (Art. 3). The "Front" is a "common arena of activity for social organizations." Art. 100, which states that "candidates for representation are nominated by political organizations active in urban and rural areas," is an empty declaration since we know already from the previously-cited articles what is the "foundation" of the "Front." A common feature of the above constitutional provisions is a declarative facade which suggests that the PRL is a country that does not have conflicts or even conflicting aspirations and political interests, and that at the same time carefully guarantees the political interests of only one distinct group -the Polish United Workers' Party.

Constitutional chapters concerning legislation demonstrate the nature of the law in the PRL. The Sejm passes laws (Art. 20 par. 3), while the Council of State passes decrees which have the power of law when the Sejm is not in session (Art. 8) and which are ratified by the Sejm.

However, the Constitution does not provide for a process to ratify these decrees, nor for a situation in which they are not ratified. On the basis of legal acts and in order to implement them, the Council of Ministers gives orders and adopts resolutions, while the ministers issue orders and regulations (Artile 41 and 42). There are no provisions or limitations in the Constitution to which the normative power of the executive is subject, nor are there provisions defining more closely the nature of the executive norms. Thus acts passed with the force of legislative decree, in reality have only as much legal force as the laws on the basis of which they are passed. Art. 62 provides that judges are to be exclusively governed by the statutes. Ordinances, resolutions and regulations are nevertheless an integral part of the legal system and are based on the statues. In practice then, judges are responsible for applying executive acts on par with laws, without the right to control their legality, i.e., conformity with the law. Placing the judges in such a position greatly limits the scope of their jurisdiction. Each regulation, no matter how trivial, introduced by the lowest administrative body becomes an obligatory "law" for the judges.

The most essential matter in the proper functioning of the judiciary is the issue of the judges' independence. Art. 58 of the Constitution recognizes the autonomy of judges, yet Art. 60 gives the Council of State the right to appoint and call them. This regulation, then, undermines the principle of autonomy embodied in the tenure of judges. According to the laws in force in the PRL, judges can be transferred to a different court "for the good of the dispensation of justice or the authoritative position of judgeship," and they can be promoted and rewarded according to the decisions of the judicial administration. Officials of the latter (court presidents) are appointed by the Minister of Justice, while the Council of State makes appointments to the Supreme Court.

On the other hand, the public prosecutor's office in the PRL enjoys an immense range of independence and privileges. In accordance with Art. 64 of the Constitution, "the General Prosecutor of the PRL guards the people's legality and secures respect for civil rights." As a result, there is a linkage here, in one institution and in one person, between the duties of combatting crime and defending citizens' rights. The General Prosecutor is independent of the government and is responsible to the Council of State. In practice, this means that the prosecutor's function is highly politicized.

Constitutional provisions pertaining to the process of instituting legislation, to the judges and to the office of public prosecutors, have their effect in the public perception of the law. The dominant belief in Polish society

is that the law is an instrument of the authorities and is
manipulated by them. Polish citizens sense that the law is
mainly a norm of the executive. The difference between the
law and an act by the authorities has been erased in practice
and in social consciousness, while the understanding of the
concept of law as embodying inalienable rights of the people
has been eliminated from the language of the law.
Inalienable and natural human rights do not have superior and
absolute value in the PRL Constitution. From the way in
which the articles pertaining to human rights are formulated
it is obvious that these rights are based on the will of the
PRL, i.e., that they are given to the people. Examples:

- Art. 69 - "The Polish People's Republic, in
  preserving the achievements of the working
  people, strengthens and extends citizens
  rights."
- Art. 82, Paragraph 1 - "The Polish People's
  Republic ensures for its citizens the freedom
  of conscience."
- Art. 82 - "The Polish People's Republic
  ensures for its citizens the freedoms of
  speech, press, assembly, rallies, marches and
  demonstrations.
- Art. 87 - "The Polish People's Republic
  ensures for its citizens personal immunity."

Some of these constitutional provisions require the

-33-

following commentaries:

- Art. 69 makes civil liberties contingent on the ability of the PRL to preserve the achievements of the working people.

- Art. 82 elicits questions concerning the State's methods of ensuring freedom of conscience for its citizens.

- Art. 83 is a declaration incompatible with statutes regulating the exercise of rights specified in the declaration.

According to the Constitution, the freedoms of expression, press, and assembly are unlimited. The law on censorship therefore is contradictory to the Constitution, as are regulations on administrative control over gatherings, rallies and demonstrations. In practice, the executive regulations on permits for meetings and marches cancel the freedoms provided in the Constitution. In reality, the PRL has secured only for itself the freedom of holding gatherings or rallies.

The PRL Constitution also contains provisions concerning social and economic rights. In this area, there are no formulations such as: "The Polish People's Republic ensures..." in the articles relating to these rights (to work - Art. 68; to rest - Art. 69; to health care - Art. 70;

and to education - Art. 72). Nevertheless, with respect to these particular matters, such obligations on the part of the state are necessary. Such, we believe, were the intentions of the authors of the International Covenant on Economic, Social and Cultural Rights, which is an integral part of the Universal Declaration of Human Rights, ratified by the PRL in 1977.

The emptiness and vagueness of the formulations concerning citizens' rights and liberties in the PRL Constitution is further demonstrated by the typical omission of points which must be stipulated in such fundamental legislation. First of all, the Constitution has no legally institutionalized guarantees of such basic civil rights as the right to compensate for damages unjustly incurred by the citizen at the hand of State bodies, the right to freely choose the place of one's residence, the right to form associations and unions without prior permission of State bodies, the right to go to court to determine damage or loss, or the right to freely leave and return to one's country. The PRL Constitution contains detailed statutes which, to a great degree, are over and above what is customarily in the constitutions of democratic countries. However, the catalogue of civil rights in the PRL Constitution does not include the right to express opinions in the framework of the legal constitutional order; the right to exercise freedom of speech on the radio and television, or the right to strike. These features of the Constitution have great significance for the cause of implementing human rights. The Constitution forms the legal framework for the socio-political life of the country. The PRL Constitution contains many declarations on the topics of democracy, legality and civil rights, yet at the same time, it establishes governmental arbitrariness and also creates the possibility that the detailed elaborations in subordiate legal acts could contradict the stated principles. The results are the arbitrariness of the continually expanding police apparatus in the PRL: mechanisms allowing for repression of Polish citizens by groups representing the special interests of even the lowest levels of authority; obliteration of the criteria for dividing responsibility for decisions among various agencies and hierarchies; and lack of established norms regulating relations between the authorities and the citizens. All these and other manifestations of a threat to human rights in the PRL have their origins in the constitutionally sanctioned, political-legal system of this state.

CHAPTER II

THE IMPOSITION OF THE STATE OF WAR IN THE LIGHT

OF POLISH AND INTERNATIONAL LAW

In this chapter we will discuss the problem of the
compatability of the introduction of the state of war with
the norms of national and international law, as well as the
legal consequences of the state of war decree.

A. The Effect of the Imposition of Martial Law on the Legal
System of the Polish People's Republic

Poland's 1952 Constitution (amended in 1976) provides
for the possibility of introducing the state of war.
According to Art. 33, decisions concerning the state of war
passed by the Sejm and when the Sejm is not in session - by
the Council of State. On December 12, 1982, the Council of
State issued four decrees:

1. Decree on the state of war.

2. Decree on specific courses of action in case
of violations and misdemeanorss while the state
of war was in effect.

3. Decree on the transfer of cases of specific
violations to the jurisdiction of military
courts and on changes in the structure of
military courts and of military units under the
PRL Prosecutor for the duration of the state
of war.

-37-

4. Decree on pardon and amnesty for certain

   infringements and violations.

Yet Art. 31 of the Constitution states that the Council of State can issue legally valid decrees only between sessions of the Sejm. Nowhere does the Constitution state that the Council of State can issue decrees while the Sejm is in session.

The decrees of December 12, 1981, were issued by the Council of State while the Sejm was in session, on a day between its deliberations. Therefore, the issuance of the decrees by the Council of State was contrary to the Constitution. According to the legality, state bodies must act not only strictly according to the law, but also by observing the regulations of the law. Breaking these legal rules means that the decrees issued by the Council of State have no legal force. Consequently, one must question the legality of the other legal acts relating to the state of war, whose validity is based upon the legal force of the above decrees.

The provisions of the imposition of the state of war permitted the assumption of power in Poland by the so-called Military Council of National Salvation (WRON). These provisions led to changes in the existing legal system of the PRL. In most general terms, these changes encompassed:

   (1) The annihilation of civil rights defined in the

       Constitution and in international agreements

and regulations, particularly the inviolability of the person, the right to privacy of the home and mail, the right to organize, freedom of speech, press, assembly, rallies, marches and demonstrations.

(2) The suspension of heretofore existing rights in the workplace (militarization of the workplace, allowing the authorities to arbitrarily impose working conditions on citizens.

(3) The authorities' ability to impose on all citizens the duties of national and civil defense of the country described in the statues (as in the event of a regular war).

(4) The authorization of the President of the Council of Ministers and of Voivods to issue any regulations affecting order which they deem necessary (these are in effect the same rights granted to military commanders in wartime).

(5) Injunctions were issued concerning personal movement, both with regard to time (curfew) and place (travel to any place other than that of permanent residence was prohibited).

(6) Any person over the age of three had to carry identity documents on his person.

(7) In cases where permission was obtained to travel from one place to another, the person in possession of the permit was obliged to register at the place of destination within 12 hours.

(8) Travel to places near the borders required special permits.

(9) The prohibition of tourism and nautical sports on the coast, both in inland and coastal waters.

(10) The prohibition on attending cultural, recreational or sports events.

(11) Suspension of the right to strike or hold protest actions.

(12) Suspension of trade union activities and other organizations and associations as well as the dissolution of others as NZS and SDP were dissolved.

(13) The seizing of assets of many organizations, chief among them Solidarnosc.

(14) Suspension of the activities of workers' self-management groups (many leaders of these groups were interned, others were arrested and sentenced following sham trials).

(15) The censorship apparatus was given the

power to in effect destroy many publications,

aside from this, a number of other publica-

tions were simply closed down.

(16) All institutions providing services were

placed under specific supervision and security

measures. These regulations applied even to

the use of typewriters in many institutions.

(17) All mail was subjected to censorship.

(18) In the early period, all telecommuncations

were cut off (the consequence of this action

proved particularly tragic; the effects of the

January floods were enormously aggravated,

while the inability to telephone for an

ambulance caused fatalities).

(19) Following the reopening of telecommunications,

all telephone conversations were subject to

control by the militia (wiretapping).

(20) All sport and hunting weapons and all amateur

radio transmitter equipment were confiscated;

the sale of certain chemicals such as rat

poison and insecticides was forbidden.

(21) The wearing of Solidarnosc and other emblems

was prohibited. In many cases, disciplinary

committees imposed fines of 5,000 zlotys for

wearing such buttons.

(22) In so-called extraordinary circumstances (the definition of which was unusually broad and imprecise) the militia, the army and other military groups were empowered to use coercive force, including chemical disabling agents, water cannon and firearms. Art. 26, par. 3 of the decree states that decisions regarding the use of force shall be made by the Minister of Defense or the Minister of Internal Affairs, but in par. 4, immediately following, it is stated that such decisions may be made even by a unit or sub-unit commander.

(23) All persons between the ages of 15 and retirement age can be forced to perform assigned work.

(24) A worker may be obliged to work seven days a week with one day per month holiday.

(25) The director of a place of work may order a 12-hour work day.

(26) Vacation time is a total of 12 days a year.

(27) Farmers may be compelled to supply specified products to the government.

(28) The authorities may seize an individual's living quarters and assign them to another

person, or assign an additional person to
those quarters. (In Cracow there were
instances in which the apartments of people in
hiding were seized and assigned to others).

(29) All real estate considered necessary by
the government may be expropriated.

(30) Transactions in personal bank accounts (both
zlotys and foreign currency) were first
blocked and then limited.

(31) The authorities may halt and limit partially
or completely the functioning of communication

(32) installations, including mail and telephones.
The authorities may wholly or partially
prohibit the transportation of people and
articles, by road, rail, air and water.

(33) The authorities may prohibit (wholly or
partially) the movements of motor vehicles.

(34) All ordinary citizens may not cross national
frontiers.

The above regulations are not exhaustive. Other will be
discussed in subsequent chapters.

Beginning with December 13, 1981, the military-police
authorities began behaving against citizens in a way not
controlled by any regulations or regulated only partially.
This included coercion of citizens to submit and sign loyalty

oaths. The texts of such declarations varied for different regions of the country and for different social groups (students, journalists, teachers, etc.). If a person refused to sign such a declaration, the most frequent consequences were internment, dismissal from work, and the threat of the so-called "wolf's ticket" [a form of black-listing]. The threat of a "wolf's ticket" was most frequently used against employees in the judicial administra-tion and other government agencies. In February, the authorities thought of a plan to force internees (as it turns out, they had in mind top Solidarnosc leaders) into political emigration. Internees were forced to sign requests to emigrate; otherwise, they would be detained indefiniately. When this did not work (top Solidarnosc leaders refused to sign the request to leave the country) this method was dropped. Requests to emigrate were signed by almost all internees belonging to the so-called "pacification" movement, that is, by people on the margins of society.

People were dismissed from their jobs on a mass scale and in a variety of ways. (This will be discussed in Chapter X.)

The first weeks after the imposition of the state of war were characterized by even more methods of oppressing the people. Some examples: radio and television programming was restricted to broadcasts of a military nature; activities in elementary, secondary and higher educational institutions were suspended; newspapers were not printed. On the streets of some cities, e.g., Warsaw and Cracow, so-called civil defense patrols were stationed next to the militia and the military. These were supposedly worker activists of the PZPR [party], but most likely they were members of the SB. This lasted a very short time, until the Christmas holidays. Since the sale of gasoline was suspended, very few cars were on the streets. Mostly militia and military vehicles were to be seen (automobiles, armored vehicles).

The changes in the legal system presented above -results of the initial illlegal act of the Council of State in issuring decrees contrary to constitutional regulations -signified not only the introduction of new temporary strict laws disciplining society, but also the actual abolition of law as a factor controlling the actions of the authorities. This pertained especially to human, but not only to them. The Law had proved to be dangerous -not for society but for the authorities. Martial law was directed not only against Solidarnosc and society but also against all the workers in the government apparatus who rejected the principle of submissiveness in favor of the principle of legality. One could rebut this statement by saying that the regulations of martial law did not contain rules establishing the omnipotence of the authorities, that a series of limitations was retained. Such an interpretation would be wrong. True, there were limitations, but their essence was to concentrate decision-making in the upper echelons of the administration. For example, no one can be kept in jail for more than 48 hours without an arrest warrant or a decision on internment. In practice this means that a neighborood militia command cannot hold a citizen under arrest without a decision by the public prosecutor or the voivodship militia commander. But on that level, depriving a citizen of freedom is at their discretion.

Even more dangerous than the degree of arbitrariness possible under the state of war decree is the complete abolition of all control mechanisms. They were always weak, but under the state of war the advantage of the bureaucracy over the citizens became so enormous that all control became impossible. The only thing a citizen could hope for under the state of war was the good will of a functionary in organs of justice or administration.

B. Regulations on Martial Law and the International
    Obligations of the Polish People's Republic.

Let us now review martial law regulations in the context of international legal norms to which Poland subscribes.

The legality of state the of war in the light of international law can be judged by the International Covenant on Civil and Political Rights, to which Poland is a party. Art. 41 of this Covenant states:

> In time of public emergency which threatens
> the life of the nation and the existence of
> which is officially proclaimed, the State
> Parties to the present Covenant may take

measures derogating from their obligations
under the present Covenant to the extent
strictly required by the exigencies of the
situation, provided that such measures are not
inconsistent with their other obligations
under international law and do not involve
discrimination solely on the ground of race,
color, sex, language, religion or social
origin.

Did any exceptional public danger threaten the existence

of the nation in the period before December 12, 1981 in

Poland?

In Chapter I of this report, we tried to outline the

situation in the country before imposition of the state of

war. In addition, we would like to point out:

- There were no armed demonstrations, nor armed

  acts of terror in Poland.

- There were no organized attempts on the lives of

  any representatives of authority.

- There were no organizations that

  were planning a violent coup or similar acts

  that could possibly substantiate the theory

  about the existence of a threat to the life of

  the nation.

Later events proved that the only organization planning a

coup by force against the existing legal order was the PRL

authorities - more precisely, a part of the

political leadership, the military and the police.

Official declarations by the authorities about a threat

to the existence of the nation were always very vague. The

proclamation by WRON on December 13, 1981, states that Poland is threatened by a "mortal danger," that "the country is on the brink of civil war," that "preparations for a reactonary coup are evident, that the threat of terror may lead to the spilling of blood." The authorities did not present to the public, either before or after December 13, any convincing proof of preparation for a coup. The authorities did not initiate any legal steps against the instigators or organizers of the alleged coup, since such groups did not exist, either in Solidarnosc or any other independent citizens' organizations. It was a fact however, that the PRL authorities found themselves in a position politically isolated from society and delayed the introdution of reforms. They did not want further changes or genuine control over their actions. They did not trust the law or the Polish courts; they defended their group interests and fostered tensions in order to be able, with the help of extraordinary means, to free themselves from the need to engage in dialogue and to publicly furnish proof of illegality in the activities of other social forces.

Art. 4 of the Covenant on Civil and Political Rights envisions the existence of specific circumstances and conditions which must be convincingly demonstrated by the state proclaiming emergency or the state of war.

The PRL authorities did not provide such proof. Instead, they stressed the sovereign character of their decision and merely complied with the conditions formally (i.e. official proclamation) and informing the Secretary General of the United Nations. Even so, a nation's sovereignty and the concommitant freedom to enter into international agreements do not imply that these may be selectively observed. This is exactly what happens when our country fulfills only partially those obligations pertaining to the imposition of a state of emergency mandated by the Covenant on Political and Civil Rights.

Art. 4, sect.1 of the Covenant allows a conditional suspension of obligations arising from this agreement, provided that such a suspension does not conflict with other obligations under international law. As a result of the imposition of the state of war, the PRL has violated the international law embodies in the ILO Conventions to which the PRL subscribes. The imposition of forced labor under the state of war may serve as an example of this.

Art. 29 of the December 12, 1981 state of war decree, states that "the Council of Ministers may, by way of an ordinance, introduce the universal obligation to work, for all who have reached the age of 15 who have not reached the age of retirement." In executing the decree, the Council of Ministers issued an ordinance (Legislative Journal No. 32/81, sect. 187) on mandatory work for all men aged 18-45 during the state of war. None of the international agreements entered into by the

PRL allows for forced labor as a result of the imposition of a state of war or a state of emergency. Moreover, this mandatory work requirement decreed by the Council of Ministers was for the purpose of economic development, which is contrary to Art. 1b of Convention No. 105 of the ILO. The wording of the Council's order testifies to its intention by stipulating that the executors of the decree shall direct workers to those establishments which report a need for workers. It is also necessary to consider whether the states of emergency foreseen in the agreements which would exempt such work requirements from being defined as forced labor, are indeed applicable to Poland during the time of the state of war.

In general, such situations may be divided into four categories: military service, serving a court-imposed sentence, the ordinary duties of citizens, and those sudden and extraordinary events which threaten the existence of a nation. Only the last category might possibly be applicable to Poland. Even so, this was not the case, nor is it now, since there was no extraordinary danger of a life and death situation threatening the country at the end of 1981 and the beginning of 1982. Since such circumstances were not present, the government had other appropriate services at its disposal (or these could have been organized), which would have made compulsory work unnecessary. Unless, of course, as was the case in Poland, the aim was to harass a segment of the population.

For the sake of clarification, let us add that Art. 4,
sect. 1 of the Covenant on Political and Civil Rights allows
for the suspension of adherance to its stipulations (that is,
for instance, the temporary imposition of a mandatory work
requirement) in a given country "in time of public emergency
which threatens the life of the nation" and this danger has
been "officially proclaimed". Such a suspension, however, in
accordance with Art. 4, sect. 1, may not violate a country's
"other obligations under international law". In the case of
Poland, such "other obligations" are two ILO Conventions (No.
29 and 105) which make no provisions for their suspension.

Moreover, Art. 4, Sect. 1 of the Civil and Political
Rights Covenant states that any suspension of the observance
of its provisions (among others, Art. 8, Sect. 3 on forced
labor) permitted only "to the extent strictly required by the
exigencies of the situation." This means that it is not
permissible to institute forced labor in cases of political
unrest, or to suspend the right to organize in the event of a
sudden epidemic. In no way did the situation in Poland after
December 13, 1981, require such compulsion. In conclusion,
the imposition of a universal mandatory work requirement in
the PRL during the state of war was in all respects contrary
to Poland's international legal obligations.

Poland's violation of international law during the
state of war is also exemplified by the suspension of
the right to organize. Poland is a party to ILO Convention

No. 87, which deals with freedom of association and union rights, and to ILO Convention No. 98 which guarantees the right to organize and bargain collectively (both ratified by Poland on December 13, 1956).

These conventions were violated by Poland following the state of war decree. Art. 1 of Convention No. 98 states that workers "should have appropriate safeguards against all discriminatory acts which have as their goal the violation of the freedom to organize in the workplace," and particularly against those acts which make membership in a trade union a condition of employment. In direct contradiction of this Convention, on December 17, 1981, Gen. M. Janiszewski, head of the Council of Minister's office, ordered on December 17, 1981, dismissal of all workers in the government administration who stated that they would not leave the ranks of Solidarnosc.

Next, Art. 2 of Convention 87 states that "workers and employers without distinction whatsoever shall have the right...to join organizations without previous authorization," of their own choosing. The rights concerning the forming and functioning of unions were suspended by the state of war decree.

In regards to the above-mentioned example of Convention No. 87 alone, the question must be asked, whether the PRL has the right to temporarily suspend the observation of this regulation, even in the event that an actual danger threatening the existence of the nation justified the imposition of a state of emergency.

The Polish authorities answer this question affirmatively, quoting Art. 4, sect. 1 of the Political and Civil Rights Covenant, while passing over in silence that section of the article which requires that measures introduced during a state of emergency not violate other (than those in the Covenant) international legal agreements entered into by the given country. Just such another agreement is ILO Convention No. 87. The suspension of freedom of association as a result of the state of war decree violates the resolutions of Convention No. 87 as well as the conditions of Art. 4, sect. 1 of the Covenant.

It should be emphasized at this point, that both in the preparatory work on Conventions No. 87 and 98, and in the actual text of these agreements, there is no provision for their suspension. Certain conventions of the ILO, typically those addressing work hours, clearly provide for the possibility of suspension. The lack of such clauses in Convention No. 87 clearly testifies to the intentions of the parties to this Convention to rule out the suspension of its observance.

Despite accusations by the Polish authorities that a political campaign is being waged against them in the ILO they are are well aware that they have violated Convention

No. 87. In a declaration at an ILO session (cited in the

official press) Polish officials stated that "the government

of the PRL intended to return to full compliance" with this

Convention.

The next important consideration on martial law in

Poland is the indefinite internment of persons based on the

decisions by administrative authorities.

Art. 9, sect. 1 of the Covenant on Civil and Political

Rights guarantees that "no one shall be subjected to arbitary

arrest or detention." The concept of "arbitrariness" is

understood to include, among others, those administrative

decisions which deprive a person of freedom. Moreover, Art.

9, sect. 4 of the Covenant states that "anyone who is

deprived of his liberty by arrest or detention shall be

entitled to take proceedings before a court, in order that

such court may decide without delay on the lawfulness of his

detention and order his release if the detention is not

lawful". Art. 5 of the European Convention for the Protection

of Human Rights has a similar resolution.

According to Art. 4, sect. 1 of the Covenant (and Art.

15 of the European Convention) the observation of these

regulations may be suspended if there is an "extraordinary

public danger threatening the life of the nation." Moreover,

such a condition is necessary for the suspension of certain

other regulations of the Covenant, among them Art. 9. Given that such conditions were not present in Poland in December 1981, the suspension of the observance of the regulations was equivalent to a violation of the Covenant. Even if we hypothetically accept the position of the Polish authorities and agree that such a threat did in fact exist, we must still question whether deprivation of freedom by administrative authority does not violate other international legal agreement and also whether such means, strictly speaking, were appropriate for the exigencies of the situation described in Art. 4, sect. 1 of the Covenant.

Beside the Covenant on Civil and Political Rights, Poland has no other internatonal obligations on this issue. One may have serious doubts, however, that the internments were an appropriate response to the demands of the situation in Poland. The hitch is that, unlike the European Convention, the Civil and Political Rights Covenant makes no provision for a procedure that would result in a binding decision by an international body. In view of this weak enforcement system in the Covenant, we may refer to the practices of the European Convention for the Protection of Human Rights (to which Poland is not a party) where the issue of administratively ordered internments is handled by two bodies: the European Commission and the European Court of Human Rights.

The issue of internment arose in 1957 with the announcement of special legislation and the use of internment in the Republic of Ireland, as well as in Great Britain (especially Northern Ireland) in 1971. By analyzing Arts. 5 and 15 of the European Convention, the Commission and the Court reached the decision that in both instances, a public danger threatening the life of the nation did in fact exist (that is, the special emergency legislation was valid, and the means used, that is, internment, were deemed appropriate to the needs of the situation.)

The use of administrative internments in that situation was a result of the activities of the Irish Republican Army (IRA). In justifying their decision, the Commission and the Court stressed that the IRA was an illegal, underground, armed and terrorist organization using political murders and bombings of public places, during which bystanders are killed. In the proceedings before the Commission and the Court, it was further stressed that the civil courts had enormous difficulties in proving the terrorist activities of accused, and that potential witnesses in those cases were intimidated by the IRA.

When the situation in Northern Ireland and the Republic of Ireland is compared to the actual state of affairs in Poland, the illegality of the internments of union members, people in the arts, and others is made evident. It must be emphasized once again that even though the PRL authorities were dealing with legal organiza-tions and activites, they did not avail themselves of normal legal means to prevent any potential violations of the law. Internment is a means disproportionate to the potential threat and inappropriate to the requirements of the situation. It is hard to believe that union members, acting legally, posed such a threat to the safety of the country that it was not possible to prove this against them in a civil court and that one of the basic human rights had to be violated. There is no doubt that internment by administrative decision is nothing but a means of political repression, applied against those who cannot reasonably be accused of breaking the law.

In light of this, internment is a legal means which is not appropriate to the requirements of the situation. As such, it violates the conditions of Art. 4, sect. 1 of the Covenant on Civil and Political Rights.

CHAPTER III

LEGISLATION UNDER THE STATE OF WAR

A. Legislation on Labor Unions

Although never officially acknowledged, the real reason
for the imposition of the state of war on December 13, 1981,
was to destroy the independent and self-governing labor
unions and particularly "Solidarnosc." In the judgment of
the authorities, the resolute actions of these unions,
undertaken for the purpose of carrying out democratic changes
both in union activity and in other areas of public life,
threatened the entire political system in the PRL.

After the imposition of martial law, the destruction of
the existing union structures took place in two stages.
First, the activity of all labor unions was suspended by the
state of war decree of December 12, 1981. Activists and
Solidarnosc members were subjected to persecution and
harassment. The second stage was the dissolution of existing
unions by the passage of a new bill on labor unions. This
took place on October 8, 1982.

The bill on labor unions as passed by the Sejm contains
restrictions that violate both the human rights conventions
and other international agreements and conventions ratified
by the PRL. This is especially true of ILO Convention No. 87
concerning freedom of association and protection of the right
to organize (voted on June 17, 1948, in San Francisco), as

Convention No. 98 concerning the application of the
principles of the right to organize and of collective
bargaining (voted on June 3, 1949 in Geneva). The PRL
ratified both of the conventions on December 14, 1956
(Legislative Journal No. 29/58, Pt. 125). Neither of them
was applied in practice, nor was reflected in domestic law.

According to Art. 8, sect. 2 of ILO Convention No.
87, national legislation should not violate the guarantees of
this convention, nor can it be so applied as to violate these
guarantees. The Sejm's labor bill of October 8, 1981 (L.J.
No. 32/82 Pt. 216) violates the fundamental guarantees
contained in this Convention.

Art. 2 of the convention states that "Workers and
employers, without distinction whatsoever shall have the
right to establish and, subject only to the rules of the
organization concerned, to join organizations of their
choosing without previous authorization." The right to form
union organizations may be limited by domestic law only with
respect to the military and the police (Art. 9, Sect. 1).
Other additional restrictions are contained in ILO Convention
No. 151, dealing with service in the government. This
convention allows for the possibility of domestic laws
limiting the freedom to form and join unions of "high-level
employees whose functions are normally considered as

policy-making or managerial" or of "employees whose duties are of a highly confidential nature."

The regulations presented specify precisely the groups of people who do not have full freedom to form or join labor unions.

The drafters of the labor bill have seemingly forgotten the regulations contained in the conventions which were, after all, ratified by the PRL and have introduced further restrictions contrary to accepted commitments. Art. 16 of the bill reads that, "other provisions describe the principles of representing workers of state agencies, the courts and the prosecutor's office, the state's economic administration, the organs of state control and the state labor inspection." The regulations published in this cateogry to date provide either for membership in a specific labor union designated by the legislation or for workers' councils only for certain categories of workers.

Further restriction contradicting ILO Convention No. 87 are found in Art. 53, sect. 4 of the labor bill. According to the provisions of this article, "In the transition period, until December 13, 1984, one union will function in a given workplace," while the relevant resolution of Convention No. 87 guarantees workers the right to form unions at their own discretion. The designation of a transition period does not justify the violation of the convention.

Allowing only one union organization to function in a
given workplace also violates the provisions of Art. 8, sect.
1a of the International Covenant on Economic, Social and
Cultural Rights adopted on December 16, 1966, in New York,
which states that everyone has the right to form labor unions
of their own choosing.

The labor bill also prohibits the formation of
cross-workplace union organizations (until December 31,
1983). Only organizations comprising workers of a single
workplace are allowed during this period.

Another significant limitation is also contained in Art.
8 of the bill controlling the joining of international labor
organizations, such as federations, confederations, etc..
This article permits joining such organizations solely "for
the purpose of representing the professional and social
interests of its members in the international community and
acting to strengthen the international solidarity of the
working class as well as promoting progress and social
justice." Such a formulation constitututes interference with
the substance of union activity and encroaches on the freedom
of union activities guaranteed by ILO Convention No. 87. An
even more flagrant violation can be seen in Art. 3, sect. 2
of the Council of State resolution regarding guidelines and
methods for forming unions in workplaces. This regulation
defines precisely the manner in which a name should be given

to a union. The purpose of such a detail is to eliminate the possibility that the word Solidarnosc appear in the name of a labor union.

A few comments regarding the dissolution of labor unions. According to Art. 4 of ILO Convention No. 87, employees and employers' organizations shall not be dissolved or suspended by administrative authority. A dissolution can only be ordered by the courts after hearing evidence. The manner in which labor unions that were already in existence prior to the enactment of the bill of October 8, 1982, were dissolved represents a serious violation of this convention. The dissolution was simply enacted by Art. 52 of the bill on trade unions.

Particularly important, in all legal regulations relating to labor unions, are the rules on strikes. Art. 3 of ILO Convention No. 87 provides that labor organizations may formulate their own statutes, including conditions for conducting strikes. In light of this convention, Art. 38, sect. 1 of the labor bill is an unacceptalbe interference in union liberties. It states that a strike may be called by union officials only after ratification of the strike through secret ballot by a major of the employees (including non-union members) and its approval by the management. interpretation is supported by statements issued by the ILO Committee for Union Liberties as well as the Commission of

Experts on Compliance with ILO Protocols and Conventions.

These are examples of only the most important restrictions that -in spite of previous international commitments -were put into effect by the PRL authorities e under the recently enacted labor bill.

B. Legislation on Proceedings Against Individuals Refusing to
    Work and the PRL's International Commitments.

On October 26, 1982, the Sejm enacted a bill dealing with proceedings against individuals who avoid work. This bill violates international agreements previously ratified by the PRL. The PRL is party to the International Covenant on Economic, Social and Cultural Rights adopted at the UN on December 16, 1966 and ratified by the PRL in 1977 (Legislative Journal No. 38, items 167-170). Poland is also party to ILO Convention No. 29, adopted in 1930, on forced or compulsory labor (ratified June 23, 1958 - Legislative Journal No. 20/1959, item 122) as well as ILO Convention No. 105 of 1957, on the abolition of forced labor (also ratified in 1958 - Legislative Journal No. 39/1959, item 240).

The idea that Parliament should enact such a bill as well as the content of the published draft make it clear that, from the beginning, there was no intention to adhere to the norms of international law to which the PRL is bound. Confirmation of this is found in a statement by Maria

Regent-Lechowicz, Deputy Minister of Justice, who publicly stated that "we are currently working on a formulation that would not be explictly inconsistent with ratified conventions." In drafting the bill, the government acted in bad faith, with full knowledge of the impact of its actions on existing international obligations.

How do the regulations contained in this bill relate to the provisions of the international agreements mentioned above?

Art. 1 of the bill requires that all citizens between the ages of 18 and 45, who are not working or studying for a period of at least 3 months and who are also not registered with an employment office and seeking work, must report to the regional government agency and explain the reasons for their unemployed/non-student status. The names of these individuals are kept in a special register. Certain categories of people are exempt from this regulation.

The bill stipulates that those who fail to respond to a summons and do not provide appropriate justification are subject to imprisonment for up to 3 months and a fine of 20,000 zlotys. The punitive sanctions, therefore, are aimed only at those who do not abide by the regulations (and a few others), not at all the unemployed. This approach represents the greatest "accomplishment" of the legislators in bypassing international agreements by which the PRL is bound. It is not difficult to see that this resolution gives the citizen a choice between two alternatives: either find a job or report to the government agency and become entered in the register; otherwise, face imprisonment or fine as well as inscription in the register.

Art. 6, sect. 1 of the International Covenant on Economic, Social and Cultural Rights states that the signatories recognize "the right of everyone to the opportunity to gain a living by work which he freely chooses or accepts." This resolution, as well as others in the International Covenant on Civil and Political Rights and ILO Conventions No. 29 and 105, requires the abolition of forced labor. According to Art. 2, sect. 1 of Convention No. 29, compulsory or forced labor is "all work or service which is exacted of any person under the menace of any penalty and for which the said person has not offered himself voluntarily."

Both of the Covenants describe in detail those situations in which work performed under the threat of judicial or administrative penal measures does not constitute compulsory labor. It should also be noted that, under certain circumstances, the obligation to work cannot be equated with compulsory labor. For example the ILO and the European Convention for Protection of Human Rights and Fundamental Freedoms (Poland is not a party to the latter) do not always define as compulsory labor the administrative measures requiring graduates of higher educational institutions to work before and during their course of studies. In such cases, the administrative measures are considered to be an instrument of a rational employment policy. In the bill we have been discussing there is no evidence that the demands of proof of employment or the administrative register have anything to do with a policy of national employment.

What then is the purpose of the verifications and registrations?

On the one hand, it is an indirect method of forcing people to work; on the other, it creates the framework for repression and harassment of individuals who, for political reasons, find themselves unemployed. One can suspect that in the latter situation, this bill will be scrupulously enforced. The bill goes into effect on January 1, 1983. At this point, there is insufficient evidence to determine how these regulations will be enforced.

The requirement to report and explain one's status, which amounts to registration, leaves no choice but to get a job or expose oneself to the sanctions. It is, in effect, a stigmatizing, repressive tool limiting the freedom of chosing employment. This regulation, therefore, is in conflict with international agreements to which the PRL is bound.

The bill violates these agreements in yet another way. It provides for the introduction of the obligation to work on public projects which, in itself, is compulsory labor. According to the bill, this type of forced labor will apply only to those persons administratively registered as "individuals consistently shirking their work responsibility." The register, therefore, is a direct instrument of compulsory labor and, consequently, is an instrument of illegality.

Some additional words on this subject. According to Art. 13 of the bill, "individuals entered in the register may be required to perform work for the benefit of the public in cases of natural disaster or emergency resulting in serious menace to the welfare and normal existence of most or part of the population." Art. 15 states, in turn, that "the total time devoted to performing work for the public benefit by individual persons cannot exceed 60 days per year."

The objective of international agreements signed and ratified by Poland is to eliminate compulsory labor, regardless of its purpose or form. Art. 1, par. 1 of ILO Convention No. 29 states that every member of the ILO, "undertakes to eliminate forced or compulsory labor in all its forms." On the basis of par. 2 of this article, compulsory labor can be used only in the transitional period and must conform to the standards and guarantees provided for in the convention. Art. 1, par. 3 states that the transitional period should not exceed five years from the time the convention was ratified.

The official position of the PRL authorities is that the bill is in compliance with Convention No. 29 since the mandatory labor provided for under this bill is limited to services benefiting the general public, it applies only to individuals between the ages of 18 and 45, and the total time for performing such services does not exceed 60 days per year. These conditions are contained in the convention, but they apply only to the transitional period. The PRL authorities seem to overlook the fact that the ultimate goal of these international agreements is the total abolition of compulsory labor. It is this responsibility that the PRL accepted upon ratifying the agreements. Art. 13 of the bill is not in compliance with international law because of the very fact that it provides for the establishment of compulsory labor. It may be asked whether the situations to which Art. 13 refers are not analogous to situations defined in the international agreements where circumstances are described under which work enjoined by law is not considered to be compulsory or forced labor.

Art. 8, par. 3 of the International Covenant on Civil and Political Rights states:

(a) No one shall be required to perform forced or compulsory labor;

(b) The preceding sub-paragraph shall not be held to preclude in countries where imprisonment with hard labor may be imposed as a punishment for a crime, the performance of hard labor in pursuance of a sentence to such punishment by a competent court;

(c) For the purpose of this paragraph, the term "forced or compulsory labor" shall not include:

    i. Any work or service, not referred to in subparagraph (#b), normally required of a person who is under detention in consequence of a lawful order of a court, or of a person during conditional release from such detention;

    ii. Any service of a military character and, in countries where conscientious objection is recognized, any national service required by law of conscientious objectors;

    iii. Any service exacted in cases of emergency or calamity threatening the life or well-being of the community;

    iv. Any work or service which forms part of normal civil obligations.

Art. 2, par. 2 of ILO Convention No. 29 states:

"Nevertheless, for the purposes of this Convention, the term

"forced or compulsory labor" shall not include:

(a) Any work or service exacted in virtue of compulsory military service laws for work of a purely military character;

(b) Any work or service which forms part of the normal civic obligations of the citizens of a fully self-governing country;

(c) any work or service exacted from any person as a consequence of a conviction in a court of law, provided that the said work or service is carried out under the supervision and control of a public authority and that the said person is not hired to or placed at the disposal of private individuals, companies or associations;

(d) any work or service exacted in cases of emergency, that is to say, in the event of war or of a calamity or threatened calamity, such as fire, flood, famine, earthquake, violent epidemic or epizootic diseases, invasion by animal, insect or vegetable pests, and in general any circumstance that would endanger the existence or the well-being of the whole or part of the population;

(e) minor communal services of a kind which, being performed by the members of the community in the direct interest of the said community, can therefore be considered as normal civic obligations incumbent upon the members of the community, provided that the members of the community or their direct representatives shall have the right to be consulted in regard to the need for such services.

ILO Convention No. 105 supplements the above resolutions, stating in Art. 1 that:

Each member of the International Labour Organization which ratifies that Convention undertakes to suppress and not to make use of any form of forced or compulsory labor –

(a) as a means of political coercion or education or as a punishment for holding or expressing political view or views ideologically opposed to the established political, social or economic system;

(b) as a method of mobilising and using labor for purposes of economic development;

(c) as a means of labor discipline; as a punishment for having participated in strikes;

(d) as a means of racial, social, national or

religious discrimination.

An analysis of these articles leads to the conclusion that compulsory labor "in cases of emergency or calamity threatening the life and welfare of most or part of the population" on the surface on appears to be in compliance with the pertinent resolutions of the Conventions and the Covenants. These resolutions deal with the normal duties of all citizens and do not justify employment verification and registration of unemployed individuals or forcing a group of persons to work who, have been pre-selected in advance. The resolution from previously cited international agreements cannot, therefore, be invoked as justification for the regulations mentioned above. Furthermore, ILO Convention No. 29 permits compulsory labor in the transitional period only and solely for individuals of the male sex (Art. 11, par. 1), while the bill provides for compulsory labor for both men and women.

The bill also violates another international agreement. Maintaining registers on individuals of the female sex serves the additional purpose of registering and repressing prostitutes. This violates Art. 6 of the 1950 Convention on the Suppression of the Traffic in Persons and the exploitation of prostitutes (ratified by the PRL in 1952 Legislative Journal No. 41, sect. 278) which prohibits the maintenance of a special registry on individuals engaged in or suspected of prostitution.

All of the above arguments confirm the fact that the bill is in violation of the PRL's obligations with respect to international law.

C. Legislation on Special Legal Regulations in the Period of the Suspension of the State of War.

This bill introduces in Poland a new legal situation not foreseen by the Constitution. The Constitution provides for a state of war but does not provide for a suspended state of war. These two legal regulations: of a state of war and of a suspended state of war differ significantly in their potential consequences, but little in their actual consequences. The majority of regulations limiting the freedom of the citizens in various spheres of private and public life were not introduced directly by the state of war decrees, but rather were contained in the delegation of powers to various state agencies, especially to the Minister of Internal Affairs. In the majority of cases, these delegated powers were not used and they specifically ceased to be binding at the time of suspension of the state of war. The actual significance of many regulations is therefore small, the more so since there exists the constant possibility that the state of war might be re-imposed.

The bill also introduced changes in the regulations

which had been applied throughout the entire period of the state of war. Those changes in particular concern internment, which has been replaced by military service in special camps. The right to suspend organizations administratively has been also lifted, with the provision that this will not become effective in practice until six months after the suspension of the state of war. Meanwhile, the authorities have full power to liquidate those societies, associations, social and trade organizations that will not conform entirely to their will.

The propaganda role of the suspension of the state of war is well illustrated by the fact that Art. 1, par. 1, sect. 4 of the law restores the right to stike. This is totally illusory in view of the bill on trade unions passed on October 8, 1982.

The bill on suspension of the state of war contains a number of new legal ramifications. Some of them are to be binding only in times of the suspension of the state of war; others have been incorporated permanently into Polish law.

From the standpoint of human rights, two groups of norms are significant: the one concerning the labor law and the one concerning penal law and penal procedures.

As to the labor law, the bill introduced far-reaching limitations on the freedom of the employee to terminate employment unilaterally. According to Art. 2, par. 1 of the

bill, those working in militarized establishments, which have
been demilitarized during the suspension of the state of war,
may dissolve their contract only by the mutual agreement of
both parties, that is , of employee and employer. Par. 3 of
the same article allows the Council of Ministers to extend
these provisions to enterprises involved in operational
programs and for national defense; and in case of natural
disasters and also in order to fulfill international
agreements. In this way the above restrictions were extended
to workers in almost all of the the key industries. Leaving
one's job without the permission of the employer brings on
the same consequences as outright abandonment of a job, that
is, difficulties in finding new employment, limitations on
salary and vacations.

Art. 5, in turn, introduced an extension, unacceptable
from the point of view of the basic principles of labor law,
of reasons for terminating the work contract with the
employee without prior notice, through the employee's fault.
According to that regulation, participation in an unlawful
strike, protest action or gathering on the premises of the
establishment or outside it, is treated as a serious breach
of the basic duties of the employee and cause for the
dissolution of the work contract without previous notice,
through the employee's fault.

Thus, repression against the labor force may be applied

for activities totally unrelated to the fulfillment of duties
and to the employee-employers relationship. That regulation
goes further in its repressiveness than the corresponding
regulations of the state of war decree.

Art. 5 of the bill also imposes on university
authorities the duty of expelling students participating in
an unlawful strike or protest action, or gathering on the
premises of the school or outside it. In such cases, the
disciplinary measures provided by the higher education law
are no longer applicable.

In the area of penal law and penal procedure, the
regulations on suspension of the state of war retained the
institution of summary trials and the extension of the
authority of military courts, considerably limiting, however,
the range of their application. This change should not be
overrated.

During the state of war, the tribunals often desisted
from summary trials, while the average military judge did not
demonstrate greater repressive inclinations tha a civilian
judge. The changes may, in some cases, result in lower
sentences, but on the whole, the situation remains
essentially the same. The opponents considered particularly
dangerous by the authorities will still be tried in military
courts by carefully selected panels of judges. The political
trial has become a routine, daily fare for the justice

system. According to the intentions of the authorities, this is the way things will remain in the future. This intent is clearly indicated by the changes introduced into the penal code and the code of penal procedure. The procedural change is that the prosecution or the court can now have access to correspondence, parcels or tapped telephone conversations when their contents have any bearing on the trial in process. Informing the defendant of this fact may be delayed for a time "necessary for the good of the cause." (Art. 13 of the bill). This regulation in effect abolishes the privacy of correspondence and telephone conversations. Information obtained by these means constitutes proof in the case being tried. Violation of the privacy of correspondence and telephone tapping took place even before the penal code changes, as part of the basic operating procedures of the security forces (SB). But previously, materials so obtained could not be used, without infraction of procedural norms, as evidence in ongoing trials.

Art. 12, par. 3 of the bill introduced into the penal code a new category of political crime, providing that "whoever undertakes activities aimed at causing public disturbances or unrest is subject to the penalty of deprivation of freedom for up to three years" (Art. 252 (a) of the penal code). Until now, the penal code did not contain such a broadly defined paragraph, although the penal laws of other socialist countries have provisions such as "anti-Soviet agitation." The purpose of such formulations is to allow prosecution of any person critical of the government. In Poland this function was fulfilled for a long time by a clause on dissemination of false information, variously interpreted by the authorities according to the needs of the moment. Today, given the changed political situation in the country, this proved insufficient. This issue was addressed on December 13, 1982 by Kazimierz Barcikowski, Secretary of the Central Committee of the Polish United Workers' Party, during a session of the Sejm: "The draft of the bill also adds regulations to the penal code and to the code of penal procedure. The intention of these changes is to increase the effectiveness of the fight against enemy political activity..."

The practical application of these new penal regulations is still not known, but as can be seen from the above quotation, the intentions of the authorities are plain.

In summary, the conclusion may be drawn that the suspension of the state of war is a new form of the same method of governing, which started on December 13, 1981, - a method based on a continuous violation of human rights.

CHAPTER IV

THE REPRESSIVE ROLE OF PROPAGANDA

Although Solidarnosc was not given access to radio or television, it managed to break the government monopoly on information. Solidarnosc issued hundreds of publications, such as the weekly Solidarnosc newspaper, distributed nation-wide, and numerous office and factory newsletters. These publications were generally beyond the censors' reach. The existence of these independent channels of information and opinion seriously influenced the government-controlled media, forcing it to adhere to the truth and restrain its aggressive propaganda. Every obvious lie was immediately exposed by the independent media.

Thus the frustration caused by the propaganda of the martial law period was even greater. This propaganda was not concerned with what was really happening, but with political expediency. For example, from the outset, the propaganda described the relief felt by the entire nation and its support for the military. This was a patently false representation of the true feelings of Polish society.

The thesis of popular support for the government was based on the following fallacious arguments:

- the workers' protest of August 1980 was just, but afterwards the trade union movement was taken over by small groups of people who led it and used it for their own political ends, contrary to the interests of the workers.

- these people, as well as all opposition activists, do not act independently on their own convictions, but according to instructions from foreign centers seeking to destroy Poland.

Solidarnosc and other independent associations were presented as a mindless herd without an opinion of its own, easily manipulated by politicians. The union's leaders were accused of criminal intentions. According to Col. Wojciech Zukrowki, a pro-government writer, Solidarnosc leaders who "...on the backs of the workers wanted to climb up and run Poland like a hereditary estate, intended a bloodbath for the communist authorities and their supporters." (Zolnierz Wolnosci, December 16, 1981). A sequel to that theme was the accusations that underground Solidarnosc, during the martial law period, was involved in terrorist activities. In particular, before every demonstration called for by the union, television broadcasts would show arsenals of weapons that the police had allegedly found and confiscated from underground activists. After a while, the more observant television viewers noted that it was always the same arsenal that was being shown.

The second crime supposedly planned by the union leadership was the precipitation of an outbreak of civil war and bloodshed. According to the authorities, the leadership

-79-

came close to achieving this goal, and the expression "on the

brink of a precipice" started to crop up very often in the

propaganda texts of the first few months of the martial law

period. While Solidarnosc was denied a voice, the worst,

most fantastic lies and insinuations were hurled at it. At

the same time, the military regime was presented as savior of

the nation.

> In the autumn of 1981, the developments were
> clearly leading our country to the brink of a
> precipice. Let us recall that the state's
> mechanisms were ceasing to function,
> disorganized by the crisis, paralyzed by the
> opposition. The economy was falling apart.
> The rifts in society were deepening, often as
> a result of irrational causes. Constant
> conflicts, protest actions, strikes for minor
> reasons, and incitement to hatred were
> bringing about psychological disaster. The
> crisis got out of control, the necessary
> reforms could not be implemented, appeals and
> attempts at national reconciliation went
> unheeded. Let us say it outright - we were
> threatened by civil war. (Piotr Rzadca "From
> the Brink of the Precipice," Trybuna Ludu June
> 12-13, 1982).

> The steady injection of anarchy into our
> country's life, the breakdown of law and
> order, total blocking of administrative
> action, served the leaders of
> counter-revolution in intensifying the mood of
> discontent and destructiveness. Social
> demagogery, a leaflet-and-poster campaign
> saturated with the poison of hatred for the
> authorities, lies, creating new, blank spots
> in the history of our nation - these were the
> weapons used on a massive scale. Over the
> past few weeks, combat groups have been formed
> of selected individuals who are aggressive and
> at odds with the law. These groups shielded
> the activities aimed at lawful order and
> legality. Their conduct was patterned on
> methods used before in history by extremist

movements, methods of psychological and
physical terror. (Col. Zdzislaw Rozbicki,
Zolnierz Wolnosci, January 2-3, 1982).

Demands were made for the reform of the prison
system, supposedly based on humanitarian
grounds. In fact, this had a different aim, to
give impetus...to prison breakouts. Because
such people, who would avoid serving full
prison sentences for crimes, could reinforce
the counterrevolutionary forces and
considerably spread destructive activity.
Then, at the time of the decisive upheaval
against the socialist state, they could stand
at the head of the counterrevolutionary
forces. (Col. Marian Nowinski, Zolnierz
Wolnosci, January 20, 1982).
The time between the notorious Radom
conference, and the meeting of the
Solicarnosc National Committee in Dagnsk
became in practice one of activity by combat
units based on fascist methods...these facts
finally unmasked the faces of the
trouble-makers and reinforced my belief that
the ideologues of Solidarnosc learned from
fascist models." (Bronislaw Kruszewski,
Zolnierz Wolnosci).

Apart from such libel, the propaganda machine praised

the military authorities for having put an end to the terror

supposedly created by Solidarnosc and - in the same breath

- for decreasing the number of ordinary crimes, murders, and

robberies. News of arrests of Solidarnosc activists were

always accompanied by news of arrests of ordinary criminals.

Attention was constantly paid to the fact that martial law

reduced the frightening growth of crime. Meanwhile it was

said that critically endangered public safety was an

immediate consequence of the anarchy in public life brought

about by Solidarnosc.

The people who presumably were trying to cause civil war in Poland were called Solidarnosc by the propaganda extremists. This meant the opposition, KOR activists (Committee for the Defense of the Workers), members of KPN (Confederation for Independent Poland). All these people were supposedly under orders of "command centers from abroad" from which they were said to be receiving instructions and material assistance. Some of them were alleged to be outright spies.

Often, and almost daily leading up to demonstrations called for by underground Solidarnosc, one could read in the press or see on television "all the truth" about people who were being denied the chance to respond to the lies levelled at them. A grotesque example of this was a television program in August 1982, in which Karol Modzelewski was accused, among other things, of undemocratically preventing other people from expressing their views. At that time Karol Modzelewski was interned in prison, so putting him before television cameras for the democratic purpose of allowing him to defend himself would have been no problem.

KOR was accused of being a mafia. KPN was claimed to be chauvinistic. Zbigniew Romaszewski was accused of having sent the Helsinki Report to the West (an act which made him a spy).

Everybody else was accused of intending to take power, and of accepting money from "Western agents". A thesis was advanced about an "anti-socialist coup" said to be prepared by the "enemies of socialism from KPN and KOR, by extremist members of Solidarnosc and reactionary Church elements." (Jan Sobczak, Zolnierz Wolnosci, January 9-10, 1982). These were the people, along with "specific Zionist groups aiming to antagonize Polish society" that had supposedly been "assigned roles" by "foreign agents" some years earlier. "All this was arranged and agreed upon much earlier by the special branch of the NATO states specializing in psychological warfare." (Col. Jozef Godyk, Zolnierz Wolnosci, February 23, 1982).

With respect to certain people, libels and insinuations were mixed with common insults. These were union and opposition activists whom the government wanted to make particularly odious in the eyes of society, but who were denied any opportunity to respond. Anything went. In an article on the women's internment center in Goldapia (Gazeta Wspoltzesna, April 2-4, 1982) Dionizy Sidorski wrote that the women interned there were ugly, old, and unattractive, and from innuendos in the text, it appeared that they were also greedy, aggressive, and sloppy.

Andrzej Slowik, a Solidarnosc leader in the Lodz region,

was called a political vampire by Henryk Prawda in Glos
Szczecinski of January 21, 1982.

After seven members of KSS-KOR (Committe for Social
Self-Defense) were charged by the prosecutor with preparing
to overthrow the system by force, Trybuna Ludu printed a
series of articles in which members of KOR were accused of
almost every crime: corruption ("green banknotes became
ordinary, daily currency for people such as Kuron or
Michnik"); intent to destory Poland ("plainly speaking, it
was a conspiracy of a few against the masses. Society's
outcasts against soceity itself. And primarily a subversive
initiative coordinated with foreign certers... An overall
Western inspiration advised the "commandos" to incite and
aggravate the tension in Poland by increasing social
discontent, by disseminating confusion ... A subversion of
the nation, an atomization of society, and above all, open
civil war: it was to cause - starting with Poland - a
conflagration in the entire socialist community").

Kuron was accused of giving 60 newspaper interviews
during the time of Solidarnosc and Michnik allegedly gave 34
interviews. (A journalist from Trybuna Ludu suggested that
these were false statements inciting unrest.) They were
accused of intending to destroy the Polish United Workers'
Party; of having ties to revisionists, anarchists and
terrorists (Michnik); of participating in "the ideological

aggression of NATO against Poland"; of being anti-Polish and
of having suicidal mania ("leading to self-destruction, KOR
was gaging where the American Masters wished to take Poland
in the name of their own interests); of nurturing the Beria
tradition ("people like Michnik wanted at all cost to regain
the power lost by their fathers"); of forming military mafias
(" numerically small but well-trained KOR cadres together
with their regional operational assignments.") Finally, they
were accused of intending to overthrow the system by force.
The accusation is in the prosecution's indictment, which has
not yet been proven in court. (See Ignacy Krasicki, "Against
the State, Against Poland"; "Deep Go the Roots"; and "Toward
Self-Destruction", three articles published in Trybuna Ludu
on September 14, 20 and 22, 1982, respectively).

Another issue is the cooperation of television with the
SB. Films were broadcast that had been made with a camera
hidden during police interrogations. This happened at least
three times on national programs.

The first time was in the summer of 1982, after a
demonstration on Victory Square in Warsaw, near the Primate's
cross. The camera showed young men who had been caught
there. They were very frightened, and were not so much
interrogated as humiliated and forced to make demeaning
statements of repentence. Although shown with their eyes
covered by a black band, information about their places of
work was supplied. In September 1982, after the major

demonstrations of August 31, 1982, two women who had been

detained for paying fines at the misdeamenor court (for

people caught during the protests) were shown on television

and one of them was identified by her place of work and

occupation.

Adam Borowski, a member of the Social Assistance

Commission for the Mazowsze Region and Solidarnosc leader at

his enterprise was shown on television while he was being

interrogated by the police. From jail, he sent the following

statement to the underground press:

> I declare that I have never taken part in any
> television program. I was filmed without my
> permission or knowledge by a hidden camera
> during interrogation by the militia and a
> dubbed statement was inserted into the film.
> I intend to sue on grounds of defamation. The
> information that I was referring to Z.
> Romaszewski is false. (Adam Borowski, Warsaw,
> Odolansk Street 14, Apt. 5.)

CHAPTER V

THE COURTS AND THE PUBLIC PROSECUTOR'S OFFICE

UNDER THE STATE OF WAR

A. Penal Regulations Under Martial Law

Throughout the history of the PRL, the prosecutor's office and the courts have been used to suppress a society that has been insubordinate to the undemocratic government imposed upon it from outside. Penal codes, formulated according to the needs of a particular moment, have paralyzed the free expression of opinions that differed from the official norm.

The architects of martial law assigned leading roles to the prosecutors and the courts. They viewed them as instrumental in the process of intimidating society, which had since August 1980 been carrying out a bloodless revolution, or, as Jadwiga Staniszki put it, "a self-limiting revolution."

The martial law decree of December 12, 1981, (Legislative Journal No. 29, December 14, 1981, Item 154) and other regulations associated with it, introduced considerable changes into the legal system and penal procedures for the duration of martial law. These changes derived directly from the martial law decree, from the decree on special procedures in cases of offenses or violations during martial law, (published on December 12, 1981, Legislative Journal, No. 29,

December 14, 1981, item 156), and from the decree

transferring jurisdiction over certain crimes to military

courts, changing the nature and procedures of military courts

and military sections of the public prosecutor's office for

the period of martial law (Legislative Journal, No. 29,

December 14, 1981, item 157). The martial law decree

introduced or increased criminal prosecutions in the

following instances:

(1) continuation of activities by a member of a suspended association, trade union or organization (Art. 46, sect. 1) - imprisonment from 3 months to 3 years.

(2) organizing or leading a strike or protest action (Art. 46, sect. 2) - imprisonment from 3 month to 5 years.

(3) appropriating or using a motor vehicle for or during a strike or protest action (Art. 46, sect. 3) - imprisonment from 3 months to 3 years; and, in case when the vehicle is public property (Art. 46, sect. 4) - from 3 months to 5 years as well as a fine.

(4) inducing another person by means of physical force, unlawful threats, or deception, to participate in a strike or protest action, or to refrain from starting or performing work (Art. 45, sect. 5) -imprisonment from 3 months to 5 years.)

(5) destroying, damaging or disabling a factory or machinery, or making these impossible or difficult to operate properly in order to organize a strike or protest action (Art. 46, sect. 6) -imprisonment from 1 to 10 years and a fine.

(6) activities advantageous to the enemy or prejudicial to the interests of public safety or the defense of the PRL, or an ally of the PRL (Art. 47, sect. 1) - imprisonment from 3 to 15 years.

(7) dissemination of false information which can cause public disturbance or unrest (art. 48, sect. 1) - imprisonment from 6 months to 5 years.

(8) dissemination of information with intent to weaken the defense readiness of the PRL and which could weaken this readiness (art. 48, sect. 2) - imprisonment from 1 to 8 years.

(9) preparing, gathering, storing, transporting, carrying, or mailing in order to disseminate writings, printed materials, recordings or films containing false information which could produce public disturbance or unrest, or of information which could weaken the defensive readiness of the PRL (art. 48, sect. 3) - imprisonment from 3 months to 5 years; and if the action is executed by using printed material or other mass communication means (art. 48, sect. 4) - from 1 to 10 years.

(10) failing to inform the prosecution promptly about crimes, listed in points 7,8, and 9, their circumstances and the location of the perpetrators (art. 48, sect 5) - imprisonment from 6 months to 5 years.

The "crimes" listed in the decree, presented here in abbreviated form, clearly indicate the main goal of the new, special penal code: to crush opposition to and dissatisfaction with, the new reality which was to have begun on December 13, 1981, which was to mean a radical change from the political and judicial situation prevailing in the period of "anarchy" between August 1980 and December 1981. In order to ensure effective action in the intended direction, the decree on special procedures introduced summary trials before civil and military courts throughout the country. These summary trials were conducted in the majority of cases involving offenses against the martial law decree, as well as for serious offenses, described in the penal code as being against the fundamental interests of the PRL, such as treason (Art. 122 of the penal code); overthrowing the state (Art. 123); espionage (Art. 124); terrorist attack (Art. 126); sabotage and subversion (Art. 127); against public order, e.g. dissemination of false information detrimental to the interests of the PRL (Art. 271, par. 1); and defamation or degradation of the Polish nation, the PRL, its political system or governing bodies (Art. 270, par. 1).

We do not mention ordinary criminal offenses here. The purpose of summary trials, regardless of where or by whom they are introduced, is to speed up the process of sentencing - usually in order to institute political repression. The basic characteristics of this method of "dispensing justice" are:

(1) shortening the investigation period to a minimum and shortening all the phases of the trial including the sentencing;

(2) eliminating appeals by allowing for an overturn of the verdict only by special reviews or re-trials;

(3) raising penalties above the limit set by law and introducing special penalties, e.g. introducing the death penalty where it was not stipulated in the regular code.

According to the decree, summary trials may be ordered
by the public prosecutor or by the court in cases where, in
their opinion, a serious danger to society exists. The
investigation period was shortened to 15 days and, in
particularly complicated cases, with permission of a higher
prosecutor's office, to 30 days. The citzens' factor -the
assessors [jurors] - was eliminated from the courts. The
courts conducting summary trials (namely, the voivodship,
regional military and various armed forces courts) are
comprised of three professional judges.

Irrespective of the type and duration of the sentences
prescribed by the penal code, at the summary trials the court
can impose sentences of 25 years imprisonment or the death
penalty, or imprisonment for not less than 3 years, unless a
higher penalty is indicated by the code. The court can also
sentence a person to the loss of civil rights or it may decide
to make the sentence public. In cases to be judged in summary
trials, the accused is always placed under temporary arrest.

The decree on special procedures also introduced changes
in existing simplified and summary procedures described in the
penal code, by extending the range of application and special
regulations during the trials.

The summary procedure differs from other methods of
conducting trials in that it allows a person to be tried
immediately after arrest on the charge of having committed a

crime. The person arrested is brought before a court within 48 hours after the arrest, and the trial begins immediately.

Procedures before and during the trial are minimal, and the rights of the accused are limited. Such limitations, allowed in summary trials, preclude a full investigation and, therefore, have a negative impact on the decisions of the court. The summary procedure was used particularly often during martial law at trials conducted as a means of repression after mass street demonstrations.

The decree of December 12, 1981, transferred many kinds of cases from the jurisdiction of civil courts to military courts. Among them were cases against persons accused of damaging the fundamental interest of the PRL, or the public order, as well as Art. 47, sect. 1, and Art. 48 of the martial law decree. The jurisdiction of the military courts was also increased because of the miliarization of factories and enterprises of vital significance to the economy.

For example, from the metallurgy and machinery industry alone, 129 of the biggest factories were militarized. The militarized factories and enterprises were listed in an unpublished resolution, Number 9/81, of the Committee for National Defense on December 12, 1981.

According to regulations of November 21, 1967, on the obligation to defend the PRL, (Legislative Journal, No. 18 of November 18, 1979, item 111) persons on duty in a militarized unit (i.e., in a militarized factory) are subject to regulations applicable to soldiers on active duty in time of war or mobilization. In cases of a prolonged or persistant refusal to work, as well as in cases of refusal to fulfill a work related order of a superior -individuals could be sentenced to a minimum of 2 years' imprisonment or even to death.

The penalties for absenteeism were: from 1 to 2 days - disciplinary action; from 3 to 14 days - court action if the management of the factory advised so; more than 14 days - obligatory court action initiated by the prosecutor's office. Many such cases occurred particularly in the Katowice and Rzeszow regions, although they occurred in other regions as well. As a rule, summary trials were held. There were a few court actions against persons refusing to obey orders given by a supervisor. For example:

> The Warsaw Voivodship Military Court sentenced Leszek Witowski, an employee of the Automated Press Factory, to one year and six months in prison.

> For the same crime,the Cracow Military District Court sentenced Stanislaw Dyleg for refusal to return to his job as supervisor, which he had before becoming a paid employee of the Solidarnosc factory committee, to four years' imprisonment and three years' loss of civil rights.

> The Navy Military Court in Gdynia sentenced Irena Kwiatkowska, an employee in the Transbud factory, to five years of prison for not executing the orders of the manager in the militarized factory.

B. The Judges, Prosecutors and Attorneys Under Martial Law

After August 1980, a significant number of judges
(approximately 900 from among 3,000 in the entire country)
joined Solidarnosc. Their chief aim was to create a new
model for the justice system that would correspond to t he
needs of society. Their priority was to obtain institutional
guarantees for judges' independence, such as judicial
autonomy, tenure and immunity. Some of these prerogatives
already existed in Polish law, but it was necessary to modify
them and, above all, put them into practice. Several drafts
of proposed changes in existing law were written, including
one of the functioning of courts.

Solidarnosc's program concerning the legal profession
was generally accepted. As a result, an uprecedented event
took place in November 1981. Candidates for a judgeship at
the Warsaw Voivodship Court were elected. The largest number
of votes was cast for Dr. Stanislaw Rudnicki, Supreme Court
Judge and the candidate supported by Solidarnosc. In the
first days of martial law, Judge Rudnicki was removed from
office and his judge's license was revoked by the Council of
the State, on the grounds that "his performance as a judge of
the court of the PRL was not guaranteed." This is very
indicative. For the majority of judges, Stanistaw Rudnicki
embodied the highest professional and moral standards, but
for the State authorities, he did not possess the necessary
qualification to be judge.

For the majority of judges in Poland, the imposition of martial law was a shock. The judges, the entire "system for dispensing justice," were to become the prime executioners of the martial "law". All legal guarantees to defend the autonomy of judges and the agreements signed in the post-August period by the representatives of the judicial body and the Ministry of Justice were suddenly deprived of all meaning.

After December 13, 1981, violations of the basic guarantees of judges' autonomy - which had occurred before - - took place with increasing frequency.

On December 18, 1981, a conference for voivodship court judges was held at the Ministry of Justice. At this conference, representatives from the Committee for National Defense, a judge of the military section of the Supreme Court, Col. Henryk Kostrzewa, outlined an explicit verification program for judges. Its chief criterion was their union affiliation.

During the period of martial law until December 1982, about 40 judges (17 by January 24, 1982; 23 by March 10, 1982) were removed by the Council of State from their judgeships because of "the lack of a guarantee of the lawful performance of judicial duties in the PRL." The last case occurred in November 1982. None of these judges was given an opportunity to appeal the recall. The Council of State's decisions did not give grounds other than the aforementioned legal formula.

Several dozen judges resigned from the bench during the first months of martial law or retired early. Thus, the judges with the most experience, and the highest respect of their colleagues, left the judiciary, for example Judge Kazimierz Barczyk from Cracow, Judge Kazimierz Strzembosz from the Warsaw Voivodship Court, Judge Jozef Wlekiera from Olkusz.

> On the night of December 12-13, the immunity of Judge Jozef Lubieniecki was violated when he was interned. He was from the regional Labor and Social Security Court in Olsztyn, and was a member of the National Coordinating Commission of Judicial Employees of Solidarnosc. He was dismissed from his position only following his internment. The Council of State's Decision Nr. 112/81 concerning this case was dated December 24, 1981. By ordering his internment, the Olsztyn Voivodship Militia Commander violated Art. 49, par. 1 of the bill on the judiciary which establishes the immunity of judges.
>
> Jozef Lubieniecki filed a complaint, with the military prosecutor's office of the Olsztyn Garrison. On August 31, 1982, the latter refused to initiate an investigation because of "the negligible public damage of the act." Further complaints were unsuccessful as well. On October 13, 1982, the military prosecutor for the Warsaw District issued a decision that an appeal be rejected (Po. Nadz. II 256/82), because "the decision of the regional commander in Olsztyn was formally and legally violating the law only at the moment of its issuing and during the next 11 days.... Taking into account the time when this decision was made -the first day of martial law -and the accompanying difficulties in properly applying unfamiliar martial law regulations, no decision could be made other than the one already taken."
>
> Another judge, Wojciech Soinski from

Szczecin, was interned in May 1982. This time
the internment was preceded by a decision of
the Council of State to dismiss him from his
judgeship. The internment occurred, however,
withing the two-month notice period.

In March and April, 1982, agents of the
Military Internal Services (LSW) harassed two
judges from Bydgoszcz: Dzierzykraj-Lipowicz
and Siderkiewicz, both Solidarnosc members.
Their apartments were searched, and they were
detained and interrogated several times. One
Judge's life was threatened. The Bydgoszcz
Commander demanded in a letter to the
presiding judge of the Bydgoszcz Voivodship
Court that both judges be dismissed from their
judgeships. In view of such treatment, both
of them resigned, effective May 1, 1982.

In the same period, Judge Hubert Blaszczyk,
vice president of the Swiebodzin Voivodship
Court, had his immunity violated when he was
arrested on the charge of being active in
underground Solidarnosc. In June 1982, the
Wroclaw District Military Court in Zielona
Gora sentenced him to four years in prison and
three year's loss of civil rights.

From the outset of the state of war, the court
presidents conducted talks with judges and court employees
who were Solidarnosc members. During these talks, the judges
were told to submit written or oral resignations from the
union. The first series of such talks took place in Cracow
on December 30-31, 1981. Members of unions other than
Solidarnosc were not called for these talks.

Those who demanded such declarations and those who were
asked to submit them were well aware of the illegality of
such requirements. According to information published by the
Minister of Justice in March 1982, 137 judges refused to

resign from Solidarnosc. (Those who had already been
recalled or forced to resign from the bench are not included
in this number). At that time, the Minister announced that
the verification had been completed. In spite of this, after
several weeks, in the second half of May 1982, similar talks
with the judges and court employees were resumed. They were
told that refusal to resign from Solidarnosc would result in
their removal from the bench. Such talks reoccurred after
every period of unrest in the country.

And there were other forms of pressure:

> One of the judges of the Regional Court in
> Wyszkow was summoned to the militia precinct
> to sign the loyalty oath.

> In Bialystok, the judges were brought into
> court buildings at Maria Curie-Sklodowska
> Street on a holiday and were threatened not
> only with their removal from office, but with
> immediate internment as well. At the time,
> the building was cordoned off the by ZOMO.

There were also cases of disciplinary proceedings
against some judges because of their rulings. Such was the
case of Judge Mikolaj Kwiatkowki of the Regional Appeals
Commission on Labor Relations in Warszawa-Srodmiescie.

> At the beginning of September 1982, the
> president of the Warsaw Voivodship Court asked
> the Minister of Justice to recall Judge
> Krzysztof Kaube. Forty judges of the Warsaw
> courts petitioned for a review of this
> decision. On September 29, 1982, all the
> judges who signed this petition
> were requested by the court president to
> declare whether they indeed signed the
> petition, to state the reasons for their
> action, and to affirm that they were familiar

with the content of the petition. The judges
who signed the petition were reprimanded, and
the division chiefs among them were removed
from their positions. They were: Hanna
Bajer, Ryszard Bulacinski, Teresa Heming, Anna
Hertman, Maria Jankowska.

Immediately after December 13, 1981, public prosecutors

were subjected to similar scrutiny and purges in order to get

rid of those who, in the eyes of their superiors, were

"politically unreliable" and could not be depended on to

discharge their duties according to the requirements of

martial law.

> Stefan Sniezka, Olsztyn deputy prosecutor and
> a member of the Presidium of the National
> Coordinating Commission of the Prosecutor's
> Office Employees Section of Solidarnosc, was
> interned. He was held from December 13, 1981
> to December 23, 1982 in various internment
> camps called "isolations centers" by the
> authorities.

On December 14, 1981, several prosecutors resigned from

their posts in protest against the impostition of martial

law. Others were forced to resign, while still others were

fired under the terms of par. 13 of the Bill on the

Prosecutor's Office which speaks of the lack of guarantees

that the prosecutor will lawfully perform his duties. The

authorities claimed that they reached their decisions after

talks held on December 14 and later with the prosecutors.

These talks were held with Soldiarnosc members and the

prosecutors were later to have negative attitudes toward

signing one of the many versions of the loyalty oath.

There were adequate reasons to assume that these decision were made regardless of a person's formal attitude towards the loyalty oath. Some prosecutors were fired from office without being asked to sign any declaration. All were removed from prosecution duties effective December 14, 1981, and were given notices and "special holiday" from December 14, 1981 until the end of the notice period. The apartments of some of the prosecutors persons were searched by the militia.

Prosecutor J. Arciszewski of the regional prosecutor's office in Warsaw's Mokotow District refused to take part in summary trials. Several other prosecutors in various parts of the country made similar decisions.

On August 26, 1982, at the meeting of the Board of the General Prosecutors of the PRL, it was stated that "the prosecutors and administrative cadres of prosecution -- with very few exception -- can be relied upon to fulfill the constitutional duties of the prosecutor's office." This opinion was based on the mid-year personnel review which was conducted from a political and ideologial perspective.

Attempts to shape the justice system according to the wishes of the martial law authorities did not leave the bar unaffected. Nearly 20 defense attorneys were interned - some of them removed from ongoing court proceedings where they defended people arrested for martial law violations.

In mid-January 1982, attorneys K. Glogowski
and Grabowski of Lodz were interned. The
former was the defense attorney for Ryszard
Kostrzewa who was tried for organizing a
strike in the Anilana-Polenil textile factory
in Lodz and sentenced on December 31, 1981 by
the Voivodship court in Lodl. In the
internment decision, the Lodz Voivodship
Militia Commander stated that Attorney K.
Glogowski "instigates unrest by publicly
questioning in court and elsewhere the legal
grounds for the decision to impose martial law
by the Council of State decree, thus making it
difficult to attain the goals set by the
Military Council for National Salvation, and
therefore propagates despotism for which he is
liable to internment."

In March 1982, the Minister of Justice issued a secret

instruction, demanding that judges report all cases where

defense attorneys questioned in court the legal grounds for

the imposition of martial law.

On May 12, 1982, two days before Jerzy
Dluzniewski, president of the Solidarnosc
factory committee at the J. Marchlewski
Textile Industrial Works, was sentenced by the
Lodz Voivodship Court, his defense attorney,
Andrzej Kern, was interned.

Attorney Piatkowski, defending Mariusz
Przybylski who was sentenced by the Opole
Voivodship Court, was interned in June 1982,
just before the case was to be presented to
the Supreme Court. The court appointed an
attorney for the case.

Attorney Kiziel of Lodz was interned as a
consequence of the defense he had conducted.

Other repressive actions were also used against defense

attorneys who were deeply committed and who courageously

defended the accused:

The Minister of Justice asked that

disciplinary action be taken by the Warsaw Bar
Association against attorneys
Tadeusz de Virion and Piotr Andrzejewski
because of their alleged "misuse of freedom of
speech in defense speeches" during the trial
of Tadeusz Pacuszk and others charged with
organizing a strike at the Institute of
Nuclear Research in Swierk near Warsaw. The
disciplinary action was eventually dropped.

In 1982, Warsaw attorneys sent two petitions
to the Sejm, demanding that women be freed
from internment and that all political
prisoners be given amnesty. Each of these
petitions was signed by several dozen
attorneys. In December 1982, these lawyers
were called in for interrogation to the Office
of the Security of the Bar at the
Militia in Warsaw, which is a new section of
the SB and is headed by a lieutenant. The
interrogations took place in the SB building
on Okrzeju Street in Warsaw. Some of the
attorneys who were interrogated are: Anna
Sobocinska-Lorenc, Elzbieta Kumaniecka,
Misgier-Chojnacka.

After the trial of Wladyslaw Frasyniuk at the
Wroclaw Voivodship Court, his defense
attorneys, Henryk Rossa and Stanislaw Afenda,
were twice seized at their offices on November
24-25, 1982, and taken to the Wroclaw
Voivodship Militia Headquarters, where SB
agents interrogated them for several hours on
subjects closely related to their defense of
Frasyniuk.

They were treated similarly after the trial of
Piotr Bednarz in the same court. The
interrogations of lawyers took place between
sessions of that trial. A consequence, one of
Piotr Bednarz's defense attorneys withdrew
from the case. Attorney Stanislaw Afenda was
once again interrogated. It is known that
attorneys' apartments were searched, for
example, Attorney Krzystof Pieniewicz's
apartment.

In late December 1982, the pension owned by
attorney Piotr Andrzejewski was burned down in
Wladyslawown.

Around that time, "unknown perpetrators" set
fire to the entrance of the apartment of
attorney Wladyslaw Sila-Nowicki.

Various methods are thus being used against those members

of the bar who try - within the framework of the present legal

system - to conduct a defense in political trials. The purpose

of such actions is to limit the defendant's right to defense,

and of course, to intimidate as many attorney's as possible,

thus to eliminating the best defense attorneys - even if only

temporarily - from the justice system.

B. The Authorities' Guidelines on Penal Policy

In October 1980, the first post-August political crisis

- the so-called "registration crisis"- occurred in the country

because of the struggle over the legal registration of

Solidarnosc. At the General Prosecutor's Office in Warsaw, a

meeting of prosecutors was held with Lucjan Czubinski, then

General Prosecutor of the PRL. At the meeting, he raised

several issues which indicated the general approach of the

authorities toward the new social movement, and the strategy

which ultimately lead to December 13, 1981. The General

Prosecutor stated that he was giving several months, at the

most, half a year to the Solidarnosc activists and then

indictments would come fast and furiously. A little more time

was granted but, after December 13, there was a deluge of

indictments.

The Military Council for National Salvation (WRON)

outlined in its proclamation the rules of prosecution and

punishment for offenses against the order stipulated by the

state of war decree:

> Persons found guilty of actions against the
> interests of the socialist state and the
> workers will be punished with full severity,
> with all available means and prerogatives
> arising from martial law... Society and the
> state cannot tolerate any longer the liberties
> of subversives, instigators, and adventurers.
> Instead, the implementation and observance for
> the decisions of the legal authorities and
> state organs, discipline, law and order have
> to be ensured.

"Let no one count on weakness and indecision," added

General Jaruzelski in his speech on December 13, 1981. "The

Military Council will assume conditions for the relentless

intensification of the struggle against crime."

On September 1, 1982, the day after the August 31

protests, Tadeus Skora, Deputy Minister of Justice, sent a

telex (No. 102/82) to all the Polish courts in which he

stated:

> I emphasize that the greatest efficiency in
> court actions is the order of the day, which
> also necessitates a review of the current
> application of penal policy in cases of a
> political nature. There is a need for change
> in the application of penalties for such
> crimes by taking into account the degree of
> threat to the security of the country. All
> those who did not draw appropriate conclusions
> and who disturb public law and order, should
> be treated with the full severity of martial
> law. The degree to which their actions
> contribute to public danger increases
> significantly and this fact has to be clearly

reflected in all sentences given by the courts.

Sylwester Zawadzki, Minister of Justice, in a speech to criminal trial judges on October 6, 1982, in Warsaw stated:

One cannot look at verdicts from the point of view of an expert on criminal law -each sentence is seen by society as a weapon in the struggle. Mild sentences are treated as a boycott of the authorities. If acquittal is viewed as a sign of the weakness of the authorities, this has to be taken into account. A humanitarian who disregards reality may cause serious damage. Who can guess how many more accidents - similar to those that occurred in the Wujek coal mine or in Lubin - would happen had it not been for martial law.

These are the words of the chief of "justice," a university professor of law.

The demands of the authorities on the judiciary were presented clearly and directly.

CHAPTER VI

PENAL PROCEDURES DURING THE STATE OF WAR:

INVESTIGATIONS, TRIALS, SENTENCES, MISDEMEANOR COURTS

One of the chief forms of terror used by the authorities
against society was judicial repression. Included in this
category are investigations, trials, sentencings, and the use
of misdemeanor courts to deal with infractions. The state of
war decree introduced new categories of infraction and
provided for horrendous sanctions.

A critical element of the terror brought about through
the courts was the engendering of a general sense of
insecurity in society. There was no need for evidence to
determine guilt; often suspicion was sufficient. Sometimes,
however, especially in administrative proceedings, even
suspicions were irrelevant. The severity of sentences of
people found guilty of the same infractions in similar
circumstances differed drastically, depending on the time and
place of the trial. When a person decided to become active,
he was unable to predict whether the sentence for any given
action would be a few months or 10 years. But one could also
be tried and sentenced without being active.

It is still too early to determine accurately the number
of people affected by specific types of repression. One can

assume, however, that several thousand people -certainly around 4,000 - were subjected to investigations and trials for political activity. The number of people who were dealt with by misdemeanor courts is much larger. The total number of people sentenced to jail for political activity is estimated at about 30,000.

A. Investigations

In cases dealing with infractions against the state of war decree and political infractions of the penal code, the investigation was formally conducted by the city or voivodship militia commands. In some special cases, the investigation was conducted by the Office of Investigation of the Ministry of Internal Affairs.

Supervision over the investigations was provided by the regional, voivodship, or general prosecutor, respectively. The militia also conducted investigations in cases where military courts had jurisdiction. These cases were supervised by the military garrison prosecutor, and on rare occasions, the military district prosecutor.

Nevertheless, oversight of the prosecutor's investigations was often only a formality, since all decisions critical to the case were made by the SB. Some cases were subjected to detailed supervision. For example, the investigation of Radio Solidarnosc, involving Zbigniew Romaszewski and others, was conducted by a group from the office of investigations of the Ministry of Internal Affairs, under the direction of Lt. Col. Dr. Mieczyslaw Faliszewski, under the formal supervision of the Warsaw Military District Prosecutor, as well as the supervision of the Deputy Minister for Internal Affairs, Gen. Stachura, Chief of the SB.

With minor exceptions, Internal Military Security forces limited themselves to cases clearly dealing with military infractions and with people who were militarized in various ways.

A short description follows of some of the investigative methods - detention, interrogation, searches - which emerges from the documents in our possession.

B. Detention

The short-term, (maximum 48 hours), legally permissible detention is one of the militia's chief methods. It continues to be used without any effective external control. Oversight of the legality of detention formally belongs to the prosecutor. In reality, this is limited to meaningless periodic controls of the so-called militia detention books, whose entries usually do not contain any serious irregularities but are far from truthful. Detention is especially abused for purposes having nothing to do with what is classified as "pursuit of a criminal" or "dispension of justice." Before August 1980, detention and searches were the usual ways in which the political opposition was harassed.

According to penal regulations, detention was allowed when someone was caught red-handed or apprehended following a chase after a crime, or for infractions - (when provisions for summary trials before misdemeanor courts were imposed) - or in cases where a justified presumption existed that the person had committed the crime and might go into hiding or destroy evidence of the crime. Under the state of war, detention was also allowed for the purpose of internment. A review of this type of detention is to be found in other sections of this report. A person detained by the militia or SB does not have the right to appeal the detention, nor the right to compensation for unlawful detention. The Polish penal code departs in this instance from provisions of the International Covenant on Civil and Political Rights. Art. 9, par. 4 of that Covenant states:

> Anyone who is deprived of his liberty by arrest or detention shall be entitled to take proceedings before a court, in order that such court may decide without delay on the lawful-ness of his detention and order his release if the detention is not lawful.

And further, in par. 5:

> Anyone who has been the victim of unlawful arrest or detention shall have an enforceable right to compensation.

Of course these articles make sense only when the court is independent.

Some of the detentions, except for criminal cases, were directly related to cases involving decree and non-decree political violations. There were many detentions unrelated to any ongoing investigations. They were only intended to harass and intimidate certain individuals and their associates, and to prevent them from engaging in activities disliked by the authorities. There were also detentions for the duration of protest actions planned by underground Solidarnosc.

During the 48-hour detentions (which were sometimes less), militia or SB conducted informal, pseudo-interrogations, without keeping a record. They insisted that the detainee sign various declarations of submission to the military authorities, or promises to abstain from alleged activities against the state, without producing evidence to suggest that the detainee conducted such activities. Cooperation with the SB was also suggested to the detainees.

A very large number of 48-hour detentions took place immediately before planned protest actions. In these instances, detention served a preventative and repressive purpose. Detentions were often accompanied by beatings upon arrest, en route to, and upon arrival at, the precinct.

Those detained during protest actions often had to pass

through the so-called "health paths" [two rows of militia men

clubbing the victim]. This is described in more detail in

Chapter VII, which deals with repression used at times of

mass protest actions, when beatings at the moment of

detention and directly afterward were the rule.

The perpetrators of the beatings remain unpunished!

Investigations, even when they are initiated, are, as a rule,

closed "because the perpetrator cannot be found" or "due to

insufficient evidence that a violation was committed."

There are also modifications to that rule.

> Jan Sniega, a teacher at School No. 8 in Glogow,
> was beaten at the local militia precinct and
> forced to sign a certificate that he had been
> properly treated by the militia. J. Pasana,
> an employee of one of the factories in
> Tarnowskie Gory, was detained after a mass at
> the Katowice Cathedral on October 19, 1982,
> and beaten in the local voivodship militia
> command. He was warned before his release not
> to file any complaints. On that day, about a
> dozen people were treated in similiar
> fashion.

When complaints by the victims are filed with the

prosecutor or militia, often no formal actions are undertaken

except for a few explanatory motions. A receipt is provided

for the complaint submitted, which admits that the facts

described in the complaint did in fact take place. For

example, Maj. A. Maciejewski, Warsaw Militia Commander, wrote

the following in response to the complaint of a father whose

son was brutally beaten during detention in 1982:

> I wish to apologize sincerely to you for the
> unpleasantness concerning the detention of
> your son ... It was impossible, unfortunately,
> to determine who the militiaman was who allowed
> the blatant infraction of the rules of conduct
> with detained persons ...

C. Interrogations

The chief evidence in criminal proceedings are the

statements of witnesses and the testimonies of the suspects.

In order to obtain testimonies that would serve the interests

of the investigators in cases when there is a suspect but no

evidence, the interrogators often obtain statements or

explanations by physical or psychological pressure. A method

commonly used by the militia and SB is to obtain the desired

statement through beatings - more or less painful, more or

less sophisticated.

> At the Oswiecim Militia Command, a
> person under interrogation was beaten on the
> back with a truncheon by one militiaman and by
> another on the legs and arms. The person
> fell, and was raised from the floor by a
> truncheon pushed into his mouth. This was
> repeated as long as the militiamen were able
> to lift the victim.

> At the same command, a more original method
> was used on Janusz Goldynia, born 1958, a
> worker in an Oswiecim chemical plant, detained
> on February 28, 1982, and sentenced on March
> 31, 1982, by the Warsaw Military District
> Court in session in Krakow under Art. 46,
> sect. 1-2 and Art. 48, sect. 1-2 of the
> decree, and Art. 286 of the Criminal Code, to
> one year in prison. Janusz Goldynia was
> beaten and burned with an iron during
> interrogation. The militiamen were trying to

force him to confess his activities and reveal
those of other people.

On January 13, 1982, despite poor health (he
was recovering from a heart attack), Jerzy
Mnich, a worker at the Manifest Lipcowy Coal
Mine, was detained and then arrested. He was
accused of organizing and leading a strike
immediately after the imposition of the state
of war. He was taken directly from the
hospital to the Katowice Militia Command
on Lompy Street and interrogated. During the
interrogation he was severely beaten. The
interrogator forced him to kneel on a
footstool while his hands were handcuffed to
the bars of the window high above him. In
this position, he was beaten with truncheons
on the soles of his feet. Gas was sprayed
in the direction of his eyes from a hand
dispenser a short distance away.

The prison doctor diagnosed a burned retina in
one eye and progressively deteriorating
eyesight. He spent a few months in the
hospital, and is currently classified as a
group III invalid since he is partially
blind.

On March 6, 1982, Stanislaw Matejczuk, a
student at KUL (Catholic University in
Lublin), was beaten during interrogation. He
was later sentenced by the Warsaw Military
District Court to six years of prison. During
his detention he was so badly beaten that he
had to be brought on a stretcher to his first
interrogation. Thereafter, he was
interrogated daily for two weeks from 3:00
a.m. to 1:00 p.m. He was kept under arrest at
the militia precinct and then under
investigative arrest at Rakowiecka Street
Prison in Warsaw.

From reports by persons subjected to
interrogation during investigative arrest on
Lakowa Street in Wroclaw, it is known that
during interrogation, a person was tightly
strapped with belts to a hard board while a
bowl was placed upside down under his spinal
cord. This method is very painful and can

cause paralysis of the arms and legs. It does not, however, leave any visible traces.

Also, in Wroclaw, 24-year-old Wojciech Swirski of 83 Stalowa St., apt. 16, an employee of the Installation Works Company charged with taking part in the August 31, 1982 demonstration, was beaten during interrogation. As a result, he seems to be suffering from spinal cord damage and partial paralysis.

Also beaten during interrogation were:

Piotr Kochmaniewicz, of 123 Armii Czerwonej, in Chorzow, philosophy student at Warsaw University, was arrested on December 14, 1981, and sentenced on December 29 by the Warsaw District Military Court to two years of prison for putting up flyers in public places.

Edward Stanczak, born 1959, of 67 Koszykowa Street in Warsaw, researcher at the Higher Pedagogical School in Dzestochowa, arrested on May 5, 1982.

Mateusz Wienzbickio, born 1954, of 15 Rembielinska Street in Warsaw, philosophy student at Warsaw University, arrested February 5, 1982.

Slawomir Siwinski, born 1961, of 13 Klonowa Street in Jaworzno, a worker in the Komuna Paryska Coal Mine, arrested on December 18, 1981.

Andrzej Kreciszewski, a worker at the Lenin Shipyard in Gdansk, was beaten and forced to admit to atacking a militiaman during the December 7, 1981 demonstrations in Gdansk.

Anna Michalska, a former employee of the Children's Home in Sieborowice, was beaten during interrogation at the Cracow Voivodship Command on Mogilska Street.

On June 17, 1982, during interrogation at the Warsaw Militia Command, Marek Rasinski, one of those charged in the Radio Solidarnosco trial, was beaten until he lost consciousness.

Some of the defendants in the trial at the
military court in Elblag from June 21 through
July 5, 1982, testified to having been beaten
during the investigative interrogations. L.
Golarz and D. Kucharski were beaten on the
head with a truncheon by interrogator Cpl.
Leon Mazur. Both of the defendants submitted
a court doctor's statement about injuries
sustained.

During the night of November 15, 1982, Leszek
Kuzaj, deputy chairman of the Regional
Solidarnosc, was beaten at the Cracow Voivodship
Command on Mogilska Street in Cracow.
He had refused to testify, which is the right
of the suspect. Furthermore, the interrogator
is obliged to inform the defendant about his
right not to testify. However, one cannot
count on this, since the interrogator informs
the suspect of this right only in exceptional
cases.

During the trial of 13 workers of the Elana
plant in Torun (sentenced on June 22, 1982, by
the voivodship court) the defendants testified
about the methods used during investigations
to extract testimonies, both self-incriminating and against co-defendants, during
investigations. As a matter of fact, these
testimonies were the only evidence for the
charge. Mieczyslaw Patryka told the court
that the interrogator banged his head against
the desk and the wall. Aleksander Jamroziak
was beaten on the hands with a truncheon.

These and similar practices by the militia and the SB

sometimes lead to tragedies:

On August 4, 1982, Jaroslaw Brejza, a
17-year-old high-school student, of 41a
Jagiellonska in Inowroclaw, committeed
suicide. He had been beaten and harassed
during interrogation at the Bydgoszcz
Voivodship Command. Among other things, he was
forced to stand with his hands raised for six
hours. In a farewell letter to his parents
and friends, he wrote that he did not fight
for such a Poland, and did not want to live
for such a Poland. The funeral was held on

August 7, 1982, at the St. Mikolaj's Parish
Cemetary in Inowroclaw.

The Warsaw Militia, under the supervision of
the militiary garrison prosecutor, conducted
an investigation of Tomasz Sokolewicz, Marek
Marciniak, and Emil Barchanski, suspected of
setting fire to the F. Dzierzynski monument in
Warsaw and of "spreading false information".
All three were students at Warsaw high
schools. They were beaten during
interrogation; Emil Barchanski, who has
asthma, was especially brutually treated. He
was also shown forged statements supposedly
made by Sokolowicz. On June 30, he appeared
before the juvenile court and was put on
probation. He told the court that he intended
to retract his statement implicating
Sokolowicz, a statement made under duress. On
July 6, 1982, the body of Emil Barchanski was
fished out of the Vistule River.

In order to get the desired statements or testimonies,

interrogators also utilize various forms of psychologial

duress: threats, humiliations, exhausting interrogations

lasting many hours, deprivation of food and sleep, blackmail,

false evidence during interrogation, records of supposedly

incriminating testimonies of co-defendants or witnesses,

denial of correspondence, packages, and family visits, the

introduction of tougher regimen during imprisonment, the

manipulation of various permits for minor but critical

comforts during investigative arrest (for instance, the

refusal of permission to have eyeglasses), depending on the

contents of the testimony. These are only a few of the

methods used to break suspects and witnesses and destroy

resistance.   Also noted were instances of threats to use

weapons and spraying of the eyes with hand-held gas dispensors.

In the case of the workers from the Elana plant in Torun, Mieczyslaw Partyka was interrogated for 20 hours without a break, Kazimierz Noga for 23 hours, with threats of beatings; Jan Drazek - for 26 hours, Marek Koper - for 36 hours. He was yelled at, threatened with beating. None of them received anything to eat or drink during th entire time of interrogation. The interrogators rotated every few hours. Lech Rafinski was kept in isolation for ten days "for the purpose of preparing him for interrogation," as was explained to him. Tadeusz Piekarz, a worker of the WSK in Cracow, was subjected to exhausting interrogations at various times, including at night, at the Cracow Voivodship Command on Mogilska Street. Besides this, he was subjected to different types of harassment and humiliation. He was stripped naked for interrogation, was given laxatives and when he vomited, was not even given a pail and had to use the cell floor. He was denied a doctor's care.

Ewa Paulszek, a worker at the Pollena plant in Bydgoszcz, detained on March 18, 1982 at the plant, was interrogated for over ten hours straight on many occasions. Krystyna Gojawiak, a former employee of Bydgoszcz Solidarnosc, a co-defendant in the same case, was interrogated in a similar fasion for up to eleven hours. While detained at the militia jail in Bydgoszcz from February 25-March 17, 1982, she was refused essential medication for her chronic intestinal illness. For six weeks she was denied visitors.

Another defendant, Irena Wisniewska, a worker at the Organika-Zachem Chemical Works in Bydgoszcz, while imprisoned from February 15-March 22, 1982, did not receive any information about her 13-year-old child, who had been left at home with no one to care for him (the father of the child was also arrested). She was prevented from receiving any letters from the child. Finally, on March 8, 1982, three weeks after she was detained, investigative officer Capt. Pawlowska permitted a telephone conversation with the child, followed by a five-hour interrogation, immediately after the conversation. Irena Wisniewska sufers from a neurological condition which became more serious during her arrest. The prison doctor refused to provide medication.

Regina Jung, co-defendant in the trial of Jan Waszkiewidz and others at the Gdansk Voivodship Court, suffering from ulcers, was interrogated about 20 hours. Only after a hysterical shouting match (as she herself stated) she was permitted to take medicine needed when an ulcer sufferer does not receive food or drink for a long time. She was not allowed to wash the medicine down with anything - another shouting match was needed. She refused to answer any questions. Despite this, the questioning continued about 20 hours. As she testified in court: "One does not necessarily have to beat the defendant in order to torture him. It is entirely sufficient, for example, to harass sick people by denying food and drink for many hours from sick people, it is sufficient not to allow critical medication and thus exacerbate a chronic illness."

Stanislaw Demediuk, a worker at PAFAWAG factory, testified at the trial of Wladyslaw Frasyniuk at the Wroclaw Voivodship Court that during interrogation at the militia he was threatened with trial or internment. During the same trial, Zbigniew Kruszynski testified that he was threatened with a beating when he tried to exercise his right to refuse to answer questions which could be self-incriminating. He was frightened, since he had already been beaten during his detention on October 5, 1982.

Adam Borowski of 14 Odolanska Street, Apt. 5, Warsaw, suspected of pouring stinking fluid in the Komedia theatre in Warsaw on July 7, 1982, was threatened during interrogation with beatings and even with being killed during a faked escape attempt. For many months, he was denied visits and letters from his immediate family.

On December 20, 1981, Krzysztof Jankowski, a student at Gdansk University, was detained in Gdynia and later sentenced to five years of prison for preparing and disseminating illegal publications. He was transported in a militia vehicle from Gdynia to Gdansk and was beaten by his guards. One of them, Sgt. Jan Krzywoszejew, placed the barrel of a pistol into Jankowski's mouth, threatening to kill him.

Janusz Domagala, chairman of Solidarnosc at the INSTAL plant (Katowice Steel Works), was beaten on several consecutive days, at the Katowice Voivodship Militia Command on Lompy Street. He was detained on January 7, 1982. As a result of beatings he repeatedly lost consciousness, suffered a spinal injury, a concussion, and a broken hand, and other less serious injuries. On January 16, he suffered a heart attack but was not taken taken to the prison hospital until January 21.

During the detention of Piotr Bednarz, who succeeded Wladyslaw Frasyniuk as chairman of the Regional Strike Committee in Lower Silesia, militiamen from the Wroclaw Voivodship Command held a pistol to his temple and stomach. He was also hit in the stomach and neck. When he refused to appear before a camera especially mounted in the precinct building, he was stripped and held for a half hour in a cold cell with the window open. This was in November 1982.

In February 1982, Malgorzata Chmielecka, born 1952, residing in Gdynia-Orlowo at 48 Bohaterow Stalingradu Street, a student at Gdansk University arrested on January 23, 1982, was interrogated at the Okopowa Street Prison in Gdansk. Her interrogations were generally conducted at night, her arms and fingers were twisted, and a blinding light was directed at her eyes. Chmielecka was put into a cell together with a so-called "criminal". After being moved to

investigative arrest on Kurkowa Street on
February 13, 1982, she was threatened during
interrogations with being moved back to the
same cell on Okopowa Street.

During the investigation conducted by
Bydgoszcz Regional Prosecutor Winiarska at the
trial of Marek Majka and others (no. IIIk
175/82 at the Bydgoszcz Voivodship Court), all
the workers fired after a strike at the
Organika-Zachem Chemical Plant in Bydgoszcz
were interrogated. During the interrogations
they were threatened with jail and also
promised their jobs back in return for
incriminating the suspects. The majority of
the witnesses, under the duress of threats,
submitted the desired incriminating statements
and, as a result were reinstated at their
jobs. In court, they retracted them and
described the circumstances of their
interrogation.

Various types of force were used, not only in political

cases.

On June 9, 1982, in Legionowo near Warsaw,
militiamen rounded up four grammar-school boys
at the Commissariat, suspected of stealing
money. During the interrogation the boys were
beaten with truncheons, fists, and knees. One
of them lost consciousness as a result of the
blow.

The record of an interrogation is the
protocol, which of courser, does not reflect
the actual proceedings when any force was
used. The protocol is signed by the suspect
or witness. When the person being
interrogated refuses to sign the protocol
written down by the interrogator -often very
different from the actual statements
-pressures are applied as described above.
These induce the person being interrogated
both to say the desired statements and to sign
these statements that "I have read this
protocol and its contents accurately reflects
my statements. Signature." In many cases,
the person being interrogated is not given a
chance to read the protocol before signing it.

He signs without knowing the content of what
is being signed. This happens primarily in
interrogations conducted by the militia. In
the prosecutor's office, these types of abuses
occur much more rarely, but the bulk of interrogations are conducted by the miltiia.

People who have been subjected to force during
interrogation usually speak about this only before the court.
To a lesser degree, such complaints are submitted to the
prosecutor supervising the investigation. This is because
many people equate the prosecutor's office with the militia.
Moreover, many do not believe in the ability of the
prosecutor to take action against the militia or SB. This
view is quite justified. In addition, many of those
interrogated remain for weeks under arrest, for all practical
purposes at the mercy of the militia or SB. The filing of a
complaint can, and in fact does, involve dire consequences.
The militia and SB act in such a way that the very thought of
submitting a complaint no longer enters the suspect's mind.
It is also futile to withdraw a statement made at the militia
or SB post, when appearing before the prosecutor. It is no
accident that many prosecutor interrogations are often
conducted with militia assistance.

Thus, the basic evidence for the trial is collected in
this way, despite Art. 157, par. 2 of the Criminal Code
Procedures, which states that "statements and testimonies
submitted under conditions that do not allow for free
expression cannot be used as evidence."

Of course, the interrogations described here do not always occur. But they happen often enough that it is necessary to speak up and condemn them.

From documents in our possession, it is clear that when there is no evidence and the methods described above prove unsuccessful, the investigators rely on witnesses - militiamen and the SB - especially those that pretend to be aggressive demonstrators in the crowd. They are frequently used in cases having to do with participation in demonstrations. In many of these cases, they are the only witnesses:

> Case No. IV K 640/82, tried at the Warsaw Voivodship Court, of Marian Penicki, charged with violating Art. 275, par. 1 (demonstratng on November 10, 1982, in Warsaw near Dzierzynski Square): Zenon Waczocha, a militiamen, was the only witness to testify. On the basis of his statements charges were summarily filed and Marian Penicki was arrested. The case of Zbigniew Gola (Lublin Voivodship Court), charged with active participation in a protest demonstration in Lublin Square, was handled in a similar way.

> The case of Rev. Jan Borkowski, Rev. Tadeusz Kurachow and Henryk Jurachow, charged with leading 300 persons in a demonstration, and other crimes on August 31, 1982, in Gdynia: the only witnesses in the investigationon were ZOMO. Formal charges were filed on their testimony.

They incriminated the suspects (later the accused), so that the detainees, rightly or wrongly, could be arrested by the prosecutor and convicted by the court. During

demonstrations, passers-by were detained (as discussed
elsewhere). The militia "dispersing" the demonstrations were
given instructions to detain primarily young people (as was
the case on August 31), or people wearing tennis shoes.

> On November 10, 1982, at the Gruba Kaska
> Restaurant on Dzierzynski Square in Warsaw,
> all those who had not yet ordered their food,
> or who were eating from the same plate, were
> detained.
>
> On May 3, 1982, in Lublin, two students at the
> local Academy for Physical Education, Jerzy
> Plozewski and Eugeniusz Wrona, were arrested
> at the time of a demonstration. They were
> dressed in sportsclothes and were on their way
> to classes at the Academy. They were not
> taking part in any street incidents.

The criteria for detention, if they existed, did not
have much to do with the involvement of a given person in a
demonstration. To make the detention credible, in some towns
the militia would have specially prepared forms, the
so-called "report of detention," which had blank lines for
identification of the detainee, plus a choice of places and
reasons for detention, along with a list of objects found in
the detainee's possession. All the militiaman had to do was
"cross out what does not apply."

When testifying as witnesses, the militia would give an
account of the events and the detainees' role in them, in
accordance with the "report of detention," which then became
decisive evidence in the case.

It should be kept in mind that for the militiaman who first detained a person on the street, and later testified against him, the testimony becomes a personal justification of his action. The militiaman has a vested interest in the outcome of the trial and knows that his testimony has a large bearing on that outcome.

While we are on the subject of investigative activities, a few words should be said about searches. According to the law, searches require a warrant from the prosecutor or court, and only in exceptional cases, a warrant from the militia unit commander or simply a militiaman's ID may be sufficient. In practice the exception became the rule - the militia warrant replaced the prosecutor's warrant. Thefts frequently occurred during searches, especially when the militiaman was a collector of books, antiques, or other interesting objects (these types can be found mainly in the SB). The people conducting the searches were particularly zealous in stealing independent, uncensored publications. The entries in the search protocol would only contain publications that were of no interest to the searcher. There have been instances where the militia would sell independent publications that they had stolen during searches at prices far exceeding their real value.

Solidarnosc publications, issued during the period when the trade union was legal, are also seized when discovered at

searches. There are no grounds for this seizure, since
there has never been a provision in the martial law decree
forbidding their possession. As a rule, efforts made to
regain these items are not successful. It
appears that there are instructions to destroy these
publications.

Thefts of money, appliances, and even food also
occurred:

> On September 21, 1982, at 5:00 p.m., nine SB
> agents entered the locked apartment of the
> Stefaniak family while they were not at home,
> in order to conduct a search. When Mr.
> Stefaniak returned he saw that 5,000 zlotys
> and some dried sausage were missing. In
> addition, the method that the SB men used to
> enter the apartment was very characteristic.
> The main door had been shattered by three
> shots from an automatic weapon.

Of course this destruction of property and theft results in a
great deal of financial loss. The perpetrators are not
worried about paying for damages. Some apartments are
literally demolished after a search, such as the case of the
brothers Mark and Wieslaw Szubrychow in Torun on July 5,
1982, and in the case of Zbigniew Tomysa of 29 Pomorska
Street, apt. 4, in Gdynia, on April 19, 1982. In both cases,
the searches were conducted for suspected continuance of
union activity.

Use of force against the owners or other persons present
in the apartment during a search also occurred, for example
in Szczecin in November 1982, when SB agents severely beat

the mother of Jerzy Borowik, a 65-year-old retiree living at
21 Czorsztynska Street, apt. 3. The mother asked to see a
search warrant, which provoked the beating.

Sometimes the searchers go even farther:

> In May 1982, SB agents in Krakow searched the
> apartment of Dr. Sobolewicz from the Higher
> Pedagogical School. The agents wanted to
> force his 16-year-old daughter to identify
> certain people in photographs. When she
> refused, they beat her and placed a hot iron
> against her thigh.

The methods of SB agents in Krasnik were equally
despicable:

> Unable to find the head of the Solidarnosc
> factory committee at the Krasnik Ball Bearing
> Factory (Janusz Szlafka), and wanting to
> provoke him to come out of hiding, the SB
> entered his apartment, where they found his
> wife and three-year-old child. Three men
> remained in the apartment while three
> covered the staircase. She was informed
> that she was detained and that the child would
> be put into an orphanage. Mrs. Szlafka
> replied that she could only be detained with
> her child. At that point, they attempted to
> wrest the child from her, but she kept trying
> to hold it in her arms. The child fell to the
> floor, and with a superhuman effort, she
> pushed the two agents out of the apartment and
> grabbed a knife. Seeing this, the third agent
> fled.

Informal interrogations, not linked to any ongoing
investigation, became a method widely used to frighten the
population. According to official sources (a statement by
the deputy minister for Internal Affairs before the Sejm
Internal Affairs and Judiciary Committee on December 9,
1982), SB agents conducted about 150,000 conversations of a

so-called "warning nature" (these are the pseudo-interrogations) with persons suspected of intention to engage in anti-
state activities.

D. Investigations and Trials Inspired by the SB

Some trials are held at the suggestion of, or are

conducted outright, by the SB. Among the cases known to us,

two are undoubtedly of this type:

> Marek Kaworucki, a surgeon at the Voivodship
> Hospital in Gorzow Wielkopolski, was arrested
> during the night of August 31 and charged with
> assaulting ZOMO men with rocks during the August 31
> demonstration. He was then sentenced on September
> 23, 1982, by the Gorzow Voivodship Court (at a
> summary trial) to three years' imprisonment and two
> years' loss of civil rights (Case II K 115/82 DOR).
> There is sufficient reason to state that the
> evidence for the charges was prepared by the SB,
> and that in fact, Kaworucki was convicted because
> on December 15, 1981, he had provided medical
> assistance to striking workers at the Ursus
> Mechanical Works in Gorzow, and then had refused to
> provide the SB with a list of the persons wounded
> during the breaking-up of the strike.
>
> Two priests, Jan Borkowski and Tadeusz
> Kurach,from the Sacred Heart of Jesus Parish
> in Gdynia, and the lay worker Henryk Kardosa,
> were detained on the street in front of the
> parish building when they went outside to see
> what was happening in that part of town.
> (This was, after all, the 31st of August.)
> They were charged with taking an active part
> in the demonstrations, leading a large group
> of demonstrators, building barricades,
> insulting ZOMO men, and throwing rocks at
> them. During the trial, massive discrepancies
> were noted in the statements of the ZOMOs and
> the statements in the investigation and later
> at the trial. The discrepancies concerned
> such basic issues as the place where the
> accused were seen; acts that the accused
> committed; the time of arrest; and the
> presence of other people at the time of

arrest. From testimony by an orthopedic
surgeon summoned by the defense, it was
evident that the Rev. Kurach, as a result of
limited use of his right arm, could not have
thrown rocks or do any of the other things
with which he was charged. The Gdansk
Voivodship Court, however, gave credence to
the ZOMO men and, in a summary trial,
convicted both priests on November 6, 1982 to
three years' imprisonment, and Henryk Kardosa
to three and one-half years.

Marian Przykucki, Bishop of Chelm, stated in an

October 2, 1982 letter to the people of Gdynia:

From the material gathered by the Commission
at the Episcopal Court in Pelplin, convened
by me, it is evident that the priests and
sexton were arrested without cause, on fabricated, spiteful, and untruthful charges by the
ZOMO. The actions with which they are charged
absolutely did not take place.

Someone at that time really needed "proof" that priests

took part in street battles.

Examples of a different type of manipulation by the SB:

Anna Walentynowicz, one of the heroes of the
August 1980 strikes, and Barbara Hejcz, a
pedagogy student at Gdansk University, were
both arrested on August 30, 1982, in Gdansk,
where, together with others, they were
continuing a hunger strike begun at the Jasna
Gora Monastery in Czestochowa. They were
charged with organizing the hunger strike.
During the investigation, the charges were
twice changed. "Organizing a hunger strike"
was at first changed to "continuing union
activity during the state of war," and then
Barbara Hejcz was charged with disseminating
illegal publications, and Anna Walentynowicz
with organizing a strike at the Lenin
Shipyards on December 14, 1981.

From the way that the investigation was conducted, it is
clear that it was first decided that they should be arrested
and eventually convicted. What was missing was a
well-conceived concept of the charges. In the case of Anna
Walentynowicz, they went back to a charge of striking eight
eight months after the incident, although nothing
prevented them from making these charges directly after the
strike, if there were any grounds for the charges. After all,
the investigation into the strike at the Lenin Shipyard was

begun the day following the strike. Anna Walentynowicz was
interned December 18, and there were no indications that
she would be charged. At that time, there was simply no
thought of arresting her; she was, after all, in custody.
The thought came later. This was probably done on
instructions from political authorities. The charges had no
purpose, except to give the impression of legality of the
arrest. But this was only an impression.

E. The Prosecutor in the Investigation Process

The prosecution, both civil and military, began carrying
out the orders of the WRON (Military Council for National
Salvation) from the first days of the state of war.
According to official data, between December 17-20, 1981,
prosecutors began summary investigations against a total of
177 persons for acts of a political nature: 33 persons for
continuation of union activities (Art. 46, par. 1 of the

decree); 87 persons for organizing or leading protest actions
of strikes (Art. 46, par. 2); and 57 persons for
disseminating false information that could weaken the defense
readiness of the PRL or incite public unrest or riots (Art.
48, pars. 2-4). All this took place within four days.

According to official data, the distribution of people
arrested between December 13,1981, and December 31, 1982, is
as follows:

```
12/13/81 - 02/15/82    964
02/16/82 - 10/11/82    1,396
10/12/82 - 12/08/82    1,256
12/09/82 - 12/81/82    about 50 persons
```

One more statistic should be highlighted: 367 persons
were arrested following the August 31, 1982, demonstrations.
It is especially interesting to note that according to these
statistics, between October 23 and December 8, 1982, in only
six weeks, the number of people arrested is almost the same
as for the eight-month period between February and October (a
period which includes the date of August 31). These
are observations based on officially released statistics. We
have doubts as to their validity; they appear to have been
deliberately lowered. This information is in the process of
being verified by independent documentation and analysis
committees, including our own Committee. The official
statistics eliminate certain crimes from the political
category, for instance assault of a militiaman (Art. 234,

par. 1 of the Criminal Code), opposing authority (Art. 235 ;
insulting public functionaries (Art. 236); that is, acts
committed during street demonstrations are categorized as
crimes, despite the fact that they result from a specific
negative view of authority and are committed while expressing
these views through demonstrations. This view holds only if
we assume that these acts were actually committed, and not
just ascribed by those conducting the investigations.
Sometimes in order to make the official version credible, it
is claimed that "unruly mobs" or a "band of punks" attacked
ZOMO, who, in "defense" were forced to use firearms, for
instance.

Thus the differences can result, on the one hand, from
using lower figures in official statistics, or on the other,
from a different method of classifying.

The data presented relate to cases conducted by summary
procedures. In practice, the prosecution continuously used
summary trials through the state of war, in almost all
political cases arising from the martial law decree.
Investigations at the normal pace were conducted in these
cases on an exceptional basis, almost always when the accused
were minors unde 17, pregnant women, or illiterates. In
these cases, summary trials were not permitted (Art. 3 of the
state of war decree). A charge of violating the decree was
usually accompanied by a ruling that the accused was a

serious danger to society, and thus summary proceedings and temporary arrest followed. It was slightly different in cases of participation in street demonstrations. Summary trials were used only for some of the detained; the rest were subjected to summary trials by courts or tribunals.

In many decree cases, prosecutors used temporary arrests because they did not have evidence of sufficient quantity and quality; the evidence was often based exclusively on operational decisions by the SB. Thus, investigations were discontinued and the arrested persons were released while the case was still being conducted. For example:

Jacek Marchewzyk, Jan Sredon, and Pawel Studnicki, academics from Cracow, were put under temporary arrest at the end of November 1982, charged with taking part in an underground cell of Solidarnosc. On December 29, five weeks from the date of their arrest, they were released and the investigation suppressed because of a lack of sufficient evidence. There was also no evidence at the time of arrest. The arrest was in fact based on material from the SB.

Under similar circumstances, Leszek Kuzaja, deputy chairman of the Malopolska regional directorate of Solidarnosc, was released from arrest in January 1983.

On March 17, 1982, on a decision by the Bydgodzcz Military Garrison Prosecutor, Krzysztof Maciejewski, an assitant professor at the Agricultural-Technical Academy, was arrested and charged with the publication and distribution of leaflets (Case No. PG Sl. II-80/82). He was arrested despite the fact that his wife was pregnant. On June 15, 1982, after three months of investigation, the prosecutor, Wieslaw Gielzecki, issued a decision

to discontinue the investigations due to the
lack of sufficient evidence.

Formal charges were filed against many of those arrested
despite the lack of evidence.

> In Case No. SmW 138/82 , K. Kos et. al., at
> the Naval Court, Tadeusz Klein was arrested on
> March 31, 1982, in spite of the lack of
> evidence that he had committed the acts with
> which he was charged. On August 19, 1982, the
> Court found him innocent. Without any grounds
> whatsoever, this innocent man spent over five
> months in jail.

> Czeslaw Rakowski, a worker at the Bydgoszcz
> Organika-Zachem Plant, was arrested on
> February 16, 1982, and charged with producing
> and distributing leaflets. The investigation
> was conducted by Czeslaw Gielzecki,
> Bydgoszcz Military Prosecutor. On July
> 7, 1982, the Coastal Region Military
> Court found him innocent. Four and
> one-half months had passed since his
> arrest.

However, there are those who are convicted and sentenced
to more than symbolic terms, despite the lack of evidence.
We write about them elsewhere.

But do those who are arrested without just cause have
the right to compensation? In theory, according to law, they
are entitled to compensation for the period spent under
wrongful arrest, if the arrest is clearly wrongful. In
practice, this prevents the awarding of damages. Thus, the
prosecution never suffers any consequences, even liability
for damages for their mistakes, or for intentional illegal
actions against citizens.

A person held under temporary arrest may, under Art. 212 of the Criminal Procedures Code, appeal to the court. In political cases, summary procedures, the proper court to appeal was the voivodship court or the military court. Complaints made by a suspect did not, however, come into the hands of just any judge in the court. The examination of these complaints was made only by judges who enjoyed the highest confidence of their superiors, who would not make surprise verdicts releasing the suspects.

We should add here that suspects are not always informed of their right to appeal the decision on temporary arrest. Such complaints are also often examined by the court weeks after they were submitted. This does not result in any procedural consequences. If those responsible for examining complaints were inactive, this did not invalidate the decision of arrest, about which the complaint was made in the first place.

In cases of great importance, the decision on the temporary arrest was made outside of the prosecution and judicial system.

Art. 218, par. 1 of the Criminal Procedures Code states

> if special reasons prohibit, temporary
> arrest should not be applied especially
> if depriving the suspect of freedom would
> pose a great danger to his life or
> health.

In practice, this law was frequently broken. Here are the most egregious examples:

Jan Jozef Lipski, KOR and Solidarnosc activist and eminent scholar, joined the striking workers at the Ursus Plant on December 14, 1981. He was detained and then arrested along with a few other persons and charged with organizing and leading the strike. There was no evidence to support this charge and there was also no fear that Mr. Lipski would go into hiding or destroy the evidence of his activity. His health was very poor. In 1978, he had undergone complicated heart surgery. On December 19, 1981 he was transferred from the Ochota Precinct to the Warsaw Medical Academy Clinic (cardiology department) with a suspected heart attack.

He was diagnosed as suffering from severe cardiac insufficiency. Nevertheless, the temporary arrest was not lifted. The doctors at the Medical Academy prescribed the same treatment as given after a massive heart attack. However, Lipski remained for many more days under investigative arrest on Rakowiecka Street; this was what the prison doctor, Dr. Wronski, had decided. During the trial before the Warsaw Voivodship Court, a witness called by the defense, a cardiologist, testified that Mr. Lipski should be excused from the trial because it posed a potentially fatal threat to him. The arrest, however, was not lifted. The court directed him to the Mokotow Investi-gative Arrest Hospital for observation despite the fact that the hospital was not equipped to provide the constant, specialized care that the specialists felt was required.

Temporary arrest was only lifted in May 1982, when Lipski was allowed to travel to England for medical treatment. When he returned in October 1982, he was once

again arrested in connection with the KOR
case. The state of his health had not
improved. The opinion of the specialists
is that he should remain in a special
clinic. On November 22, 1982, Lipski was
released pending trial.

Miroslaw Krupinski, deputy chairman of
Solidarnosc, on December 13, 1981, headed
the National Strike Committee in the
Lenin Shipyard in Gdansk. After the
pacification of the shipyard, he was
arrested and suffered a heart attack.
This did not prevent the prosecutor from
continuing the investigation and
upholding the temporary arrest. During
his recovery, he was tried and
sentenced.

Zdislaw Cieniewicz, Solidarnosc chairman
at the Bialystok Fruit and Vegetable
Plant, was placed under temporary arrest
by the Bialystok Regional Prosecutor and
later sentenced by the Voivodship Court
to one and a half years of imprisonment
for hiding the banner and documents of
the Solidarnosc plant committee.

He remained under temporary arrest for
many months, despite previous leg problems
and epilepsy. Finally, the Supreme Court
released him on health grounds.

Temporary arrest cannot be used if special circumstances

prohibit it, or if particularly heavy burdens are placed on

the accused or his immediate family. In many cases, the

prosecutors did not take such factors into consideration.

Mothers with several children and no means of support had to

rely on the church's charity; sometimes children were left

unattended if both parents were under arrest.

Albin and Irena Wisniewski, workers at
the Bydgoszcz Organika-Zachem Chemical
Plant, were arrested in February 1982 by
the Bydgoszcz Military Prosecutor. Their
13-year-old daughter was left without any
care for six weeks. On March 22, after an

-136-

intervention by her attorney, Irena was
released from arrest and put under
militia supervision.

During investigation, a suspect held under temporary

arrest rarely receives permission for family visits or even

visits by the attorney. As a rule, only after the

investigation is completed and charges are filed that a

defense attorney is given access to the case, permitted to

see his client and allowed the view the evidence and charges.

This is a clear violation of the right to defense. In

practice, the prosecutor decides how much involvement the

defense attorney can have in a case.

An example of not permitting family visits during

investigations is the case of Jacek Kuron:

> Kuron was placed under temporary arrest
> in the KOR case on September 9, 1982,
> eight days before his death. His father,
> Henryk Kuron, submitted a request to the
> Warsaw Military District Prosecutor for
> permission to visit his son:
>
>> "I request that a meeting with
>> my son, Jacek Kuron, be
>> arranged. I must see him, for
>> I need his spirit and his
>> optimism . . . I fought in the
>> war of 1920, in the Slask
>> uprising, in the defense of
>> Lwow in 1939. After 1941, I
>> fought as a soldier of the Home
>> Army. Despite wounds, I
>> survived all these wars. I
>> will die in the course of the
>> most nonsensical war in the
>> world and who needs such a
>> sacrifice. . .

The prosecutor responded: "The
circumstances described in your letter do
not indicate a need for a visit of a
father with his son." Henryk Kuron died
on September 17, 1982.

During the state of war, many functions of the ordinary

courts were taken over by the military courts . The

organizational structure of military courts is as follows:

garrison courts, corresponding to regional courts in the

civilian court system; military district courts as well as

the courts of the various armed services, corresponding to

the voivodship courts. The highest level in the military

court system is the military chamber of the Supreme Court.

During the state of war, in addition to garrison courts,

there were the Coastal Region Military Court in Bydgoszcz;

the Slask District Military Court in Wroclaw; the Warsaw

Military District Court; and also two armed services courts:

the Naval Court in Gdynia and the Air Force Court in Poznan.

The expansion of the jurisdiction of the military courts

during the state of war, especially for district courts using

summary proceedings, resulted in the practice of district

court trials in mobile sessions. For instance the Warsaw

Military District Court held trials in mobile sessions at the

headquarters of the Military Garrison Court in Cracow,

Rzeszow, Kielce, Lublin, Bialystok, Lodz, and Olsztyn.

Desite the formal retention of the status quo (five courts in

the district system), in practice the number of the courts

was multiplied several times in order to meet the needs of martial law. The judicial staff was reinforced by calling reserve officers in for active duty - judges from the civil courts who sat on cases as auxiliaries to the chief judge, appointed from among career military judges. Many civil prosecutors reinforced the staff of the military prosecutor in a similar fashion.

During the state of war, no substantive organizational changes took place in the civil courts in comparison to "peacetime" conditions. In order to have enough judges to examine cases in the voivodship court system, in summary proceedings, the system of transferring judges between lower and higher levels was expanded. Thus, many judges from the regional courts sat in summary proceedings on voivodship court panels. Judges from the Supreme Court were delegated to the voivodship court only in exceptional cases. A typical panel was made up of two judges from the voivodship court (one of them presiding judges) and one regional judge from a regional court. For example:

> In case II K 175/82 DOR in the Bydgoszcz
> Voivodship Court, involving Marek Majka
> and others charged under Art. 46, par. 1
> and 2 and Art. 48, pars. 2 and 4 of the
> martial law decree, the judicial panel
> was composed of Judge Henryk Mroz (chief)
> of the Voivodship Court; Judge J. Dachter
> of the Voivodship Court and Samenberg,
> president of the Swiec Regional Court.
> In the panel of the Olsztyn Voivodship
> Court, in the case of Tadeusz Pozniak et.

al. (No. II K 78/82 DOR), the presiding
judge was Supreme Court Judge T. Rink.

As we mentioned in Chapter III, judges worked in an
atmosphere of pressure, harrassment, threats, and a lack of
elementary decency and good form (informing overzealousness).
Under these circumstnaces, in order to assure the proper
(from the authorities' point of view) judicial repression, it
was most important that the appropriate panel of judges be
selected. In the most famous and serious cases, the judicial
panels were and are chosen with special care. Despite a
careful screening, there were instances when the fully
trusted judges, "disappointed" the authorities by acquitting
or by handing down too lenient sentences. However, such
decisions were effectively reversed by the Supreme Court.
Col. H. Kostrzewa, representative of the KOK, evaluated the
decision of the Supreme Court in glowing terms, in
contrast with those of voivodship courts and even military
courts. This fact speaks for itself. Finally, the
authorities made the exceptional reviews by the Supreme Court
their normal means of appeal - their third instance.

There were, however, judges who were utterly obedient,
or simply cowards. The names of some of them are known and
actually epitomize the military law courts - judges of the
Warsaw Voivodship Court - Helena Gawlicka, Maria
Pszczolkowska-Chlopecka, Helena Kopytowska; judges of the
Wroclaw Voivodship Court - Boguslav Wloczewski and Marian

Mizio; from the Warsaw Military District Court in Rzeszow -
Lt. Col. Mieczyslaw Przybos; from the Bydgoszcz Voivodship
Court - Judge Henryk Mroz; from the Naval Court in Gdynia -
2nd Lt. Andzej Grzybowski, Lt. Andrzej Fiuke, and Lt.
Aleksander Glowa. There were times when judges did not even
attempt to feign objectivity at trials. This was the reason
why Wladyslaw Frasyniuk formally requested that Judges
Wloczewski and Mizio be excluded from the panel trying his
case in the Wroclaw Voivodship Court (the request was denied
on November 13). Judge Wloczewski, in an opinion in an
earlier case (No. III K 27) against Wladyslaw Ozarowski, had
written of the "extremist views" of Wladyslaw Frasyniuk.

The following is an excerpt from the October 27, 1982
decision of the Supreme Court in Case UKR 134/82, against
Blicharz and Urban, convicted by the Cracow Voivodship Court
for organizing a strike at the Unitra Plant.

> The case is political and as such must be
> examined from a political perspective and
> only secondly from the legal perspective.
> The defendants should feel lucky that
> they are not tried before the South
> American Tribunal (?!) People like them
> have brought on the necessity of imposing
> the state of war! (Judge Rink)

We still do not have definite figures on the number of
people convicted during the state of war in political cases.
An estimate would be 3,500 people. According to information
from the Ministry of Justice for the first half of 1982,

voivodship courts held summary trials in 435 cases of people

charged with continuing union activities despite their

suspension, and of organizing or leading strikes or protest

actions (Art. 46 of the martial law decree). The courts

handed down verdicts in summary trials of 183 persons, of

whom 122 (66.7%) were sentenced for organizing or leading

strikes. One hundred fifty-nine (86.9%) were convicted; 22

found not guilty (12%); while 112 persons were convicted and

10 found not guilty for striking.

Of those convicted, 53 were given sentences of less than

3 years' imprisonment; 67 persons were sentenced of 3 years'

imprisonment; 27 received sentences of 3-5 years; and 12 were

sentenced to more than 5 years' imprisonment.

For organizing and leading strikes, sentences of up to 3

years were given to 27 persons; 3 years to 52 persons, more

than 3 years to 36 persons. Two hundred and fifty two

persons were tried by voivodship courts after summary

proceedings were changed to normal procedure; 226 were

convicted, 17 found not guilty. In voivodship courts

convicted 385 persons (88.5%) violations of Art. 46, and

found 39 not guilty. In 92 cases (23.9%), sentences of

imprisonment were conditionally suspended. The data

presented pertains only to civil courts which were

significantly more lenient than military courts. There were

regional differences but, on a national scale, this was the rule.

This data is limited. It does not include actions tried under Art. 48 of the decree if the charge did not also include continuing union activities. Figures for court cases linked to during street demonstrations are also missing. According to information from S. Zawadzki, Minister of Justice, as of December 8, 1982, the courts sentenced a total of 672 persons for assault of militia or security personnel and for participation in "public gatherings" in conjunction destroying property. One hundred seven were found not guilty of such charges and proceedings were suspended in 10 other cases. The data is for the period of December 13, 1981 to November 26, 1982, and concerns cases tried in summary, accelerated, and normal fashion.

The following is a brief analysis of the decisions handed down by courts in the Warsaw and Gdansk Regions:

Warsaw courts sentenced 115 people for political activity during the state of war; 52 of them were sentenced to jail terms, while the remaining 63 received conditionally suspended sentences. In addition, at the end of 1982, 108 persons were awaiting trial. Eighty-one of them were detained under investigative arrest; the others remained at liberty.

Six persons were given sentences of more than 5 years of imprisonment. These sentences were passed at two trials, of the Confederation of Independent Poland (KPN) (Leszek Moczulski - 7 years' imprisonment; Romuald Szeremietiew - 6 years; Tadeusz Stanski -5 years) and of the so-called "Grodzisk Affair" (Robert Chechlacz - 25 years; Tomasz Lupanow - 13 years; Stanislaw Matejczuk - 6 years; and Rev. Sylwester Zych - 6 years). All of them were sentenced by the Warsaw Military District Court. One person, Krzysztof Olka, was sentenced by the Warsaw Voivodship Court on January 25, 1982, to 4 years.

Ten persons were sentenced to 3 and 4 years; 13 persons from 2 to 3 years; 12 - from 1 to 2 years; and 9 - up to one year imprisonment.

The average length of sentences handed down by the Warsaw court is three years. If we exclude the KPN trial (charges filed for activities prior to the period of the state of war) and the "Grodzisk Affair," where the sentences were a result of the charges (for the murder of militiaman Zdzislaw Karas) a militia sergeant, with a firearm), the average sentence would be one year and 10 months' imprisonment.

Six among the 11 handled by summary trials, were convicted by the Warsaw Military District Court and the remaining 5 by the Warsaw Voivodship Court. The overwhelming majority of Warsaw cases involved the editing, copying, and distribution of Solidarnosc publications. Among the 115

convicted, 65 were found guilty of these "crimes" (57%).
There is a similar percentage among those awaiting trial.
The convicted of strike actions number about a dozen people,
who were brought before the courts for organizing and leading
strike actions at the ZM Ursus plant, the Warsaw Steel Works,
the Passenger Automobile Factory, the Institute of Nuclear
Research, and the Polkolorze Plant in Piaseczno.

The number of those convicted of various forms of
participation in street demonstrations reached a similar
total.

A number of very serious cases with many defendants have
not yet been completed. A trial of nine people accused of
organizing, directing, and broadcasting Radio Solidarnosc
continues at the Warsaw Military District Court.

Investigation continues of a group of people suspected
of participating in the Interfactory Working Committee of
Solidarnosc, and of a seven-member group of Solidarnosc
leaders. In the major cases in the Warsaw Region,
investigation continues in the case of seven Solidarnosc
leaders and a group of KOR members accused of attempting to
overthrow the government by force. There is reason to fear
that the results of these cases will fundamentally change the
statistics presented. In addition, there are also verdicts
that are not yet legally binding, since reviews and appeals
are still going on. The possible changes of the verdict may

somewhat change the numbers presented here but the basic trends will look the same.

Decisions handed down in by the Gdansk regional courts in look somewhat different. According to our records, out of 160 persons convicted by Gdansk courts, the overwhelming majority received sentences. Of the 94 sentenced at summary trials 29 were sentenced to more than 5 years, 75 were convicted by the Naval Court in Gdynia and only 19 by the Gdansk Voivodship Court. Among the most severe cases (five years or more), this disproportion is especially noticeable. All of these sentences were handed down by the Naval Military Court.

Sixty percent of the verdicts passed by Gdansk courts at summary trials concerned the December protest strikes at large factories in three coastal cities. The balance, in approximately equal proportions of 20% each, were cases concerning the preparation and distribution of leaflets or taking part in demonstrations, mostly those of August 31, 1982.

The sentences handed down by Gdansk courts, and especially the Naval Military Court, were much more severe than the verdicts of Warsaw courts which, as it becomes evident from various comparisons, were among the most lenient. The Gdansk courts are at the opposite extreme.

The number of sentences passed at summary trials, for instance in Gorzow Wielkopolski, were five times the number of these types of sentences in Warsaw. In Szczecin, 32 persons were sentenced at summary trials before August 31, 1982.

Very severe sentences were also passed in Katowice, Rzeszow, Wroclaw and Bielsko Biala. The Katowice courts passed sentences of 5 or more years' imprisonment of freedom on 19 occasions. Eleven of these were to "get even" for the December strikes staged after the state of war decree; seven for publishing and distributing illegal publications.

During the entire period of the state of war, stress was on the so-called preventative and protective functions of penal law, and on the public effects of sentences. Sentences at political trials were meant to frighten people, to make quite unattractive the prospect of engaging in activities disliked by the authorities, to enforce absolute obedience, to break society's resistance. It was no accident that the most severe sentences were passed in the first two months of the state of war, especially after protest strikes and, a few months later, in cases dealing with August 31 demonstrations. This has nothing to do with the commonly accepted idea of justice. The role of the courts was here limited to being the authorities' instrument of terror against society.

In the opinion of the authorities, the courts, however, both civil and military, did not fully perform their assigned functions. The situation in the judiciary, as described earlier, had a certain effect as did the state of mind of the society, of which these judges are also, of course, a part. Gen. Jozef Szewezyk, the chief military prosecutor, illustrated this in one of his statements on the activities of the prosecutor's office, in which he also commented on the work of the courts. He concluded that starting in March 1982, the effectiveness of the prosecutors had decreased. A lack of cohesiveness between the policy of the prosecutor and the courts emerged. In order to reduce these discrepancies, many talks were conducted at the voivodship level with the participation of party functionaries as well as consultations with the court administration. The Supreme Military Prosecutor informed the Military Council for National Salvation (WRON) of this situation. These initiatives proved to be ineffective, and the prosecution policies began to be adjusted to the lenient policies of the courts.

Signs of dissatisfaction appeared very soon. Already in March 1982, during a conference of the presidents of voivodship courts, Deputy Minister T. Skora and a delegate of KOK, Col. Henryk Kostrzew, expressed umbrage at the "scandalously" short sentences in cases concerning the state of war decree. They stated that over 80% of the sentences are appealed by the Prosecutor General and around 94% of these appeals are upheld by the Supreme Court. On October 6, attention was called to the fact that the courts were inadequately taking into consideration the degree of danger to society of certain acts, especially those involving participation in demonstrations. There were speeches on the necessity of increasing the repression since too many prison sentences were in the lower range of the possible term. As Col. Kostrzewa stated: "a severe political battle is being fought. The courts are an organ of the authorities and state. Three years should be the exception not the rule."

Not all courts were subjected to official criticism. There were many that fully implemented the established penal policies. Among these were the Naval Military Court in Gdynia; the Warsaw Military District Court at sessions in Rzeszow; the Slask District Military Court at session in Katowice. We spoke of the Gdynia Court earlier; the Rzeszow Court as a rule sentenced in summary proceedings, and even minor infractions from the decree, irrespective of the circumstances, lead to a severe sentence.

> On March 4, 1982, Irena Kula, a librarian at the Rzeszow offices of Solidarnosc appeared before the court. She was charged with collecting, hiding, and transporting in the regions of Rudna, Rzeszow and Krakow during the period from December 14, 1981 to January 29, 1982, five (!!!)copies of publications containing supposedly false information and of producing three copies of these

writings and passing them on to other persons. For this "crime," she was sentenced to three years imprisonment and two years' loss of civil rights.

The president of this court, Lt. Col. Mieczyslaw Przybos, handed down even more severe sentences than those demanded by the prosecutors. Such was the case, for instance, in the trial against Franciszek Mazur from Mielec, who on March 15, 1982, was sentenced to six and one-half years' imprisonment for "creating new union structures" and producing and distributing "illegal" publications. The prosecutor had demanded four and one-half years of imprisonment.

This was the case in the trial of Mieczyslaw Copa, Janusz Dziewa, and Andrzej Maslach accused of organizing and leading a five-minute strike in the Stalowa Wola steel mine. The Rzeszow court distinguished itself also in the large number of cases dealing with abandoning work in a militarized enterprise. The average sentence in these cases was three years' imprisonment.

Because of the serious differences in sentencing, signs of new practices have appeared in cases of importance. Whole panels are delegated to judge special cases in different courts, for instance, in the Radio Solidarity case in the Warsaw Military District Court, the judicial panel was made up of judges from Szczecin.

Attempts to correct the sentencing process are made through the use of extraordinary appeals in cases where the sentence was passed in summary proceedings or through regular

appeals followed at times by extraordinary reviews in the
remaining cases.

Ministry of Justice data shows that until June 30, 1982,
the Supreme Court decided appeals concerning 111 persons
sentenced under Art. 46 of the decree, there were only 19
prosecutor's appeals, 18 by the defense, and 74 persons had
both the prosecutor and the defense appeal the case. The
Supreme Court sustained the sentences of 38 persons, and in
29 cases increased the sentence. Twenty-nine cases were sent
back for retrial.

During this period, the Supreme Court also deliberated
a number of extraordianry appeals, to the detriment of persos
convicted for political crimes. Until March 5, 1982, the
General Prosecutor had submitted to the Supreme Court
extraordinary appeals of 28 sentences in summary trials
against persons convicted of decree violations. The Supreme
Court reviewed the appeals of 11 persons during this time,
each tiem agreeing with the prosecutor. Until June 30, 1982
the General Prosecutor submitted 34 more such appeals. The
Supreme Court increased the sentence in 26 instances. The
Minister of Justice submitted cases of 13 persons, of which
10 were increased. Extraordinary appeals generally dealt
with the most serious cases from the initial phases of the
state of war. For example, in April of 1982, the Supreme
Court upheld the extraordinary appeal of the Prosecutor

General and changed the December 30, 1981 sentence of the

voivodship court in Lodz by increasing the time of

imprisonment for Solidarnosc leaders in Lodz. Andrzej Slowik

and Jerzy Kropiwniecki were intially sentenced to four and

one-half years for organizing protest actions in the regional

offices of Solidarnosc in Lodz on December 13, 1981. The

Supreme Court agreed with the General Prosecutor that these

sentences were insufficient and increased them to six years

of imprisonment.

Prosecutors' appeals concered mainly sentences which

were too lax for them, especially cases when major

differences between the sentence requested by the prosecutor

and the verdict of the court occurred. According to the

instructions of the Prosecutor General, an appeal should be

mandatory when the difference between the sentence asked for

and that given is greater than two years. It seems that the

sentences asked by the prosecutor defined the optimal length

of sentences for the state of war authorities. A good

illustration of the prosecutor's view on the question of the

length of the sentence for a violation of the decree:

> Nine persons were charged with organizing
> and leading the strike at the KWK Wujek
> coal mine in Katowice. The trial from
> February 3-9, 1982, at the Slask Region
> Military Court in Wroclaw, in session in
> Katowice. The prosecutor's sentencing
> demands in theis case were particularly
> interesting. In the case of 1) Jan
> Hasnik, the prosecutor demanded 12 years'
> imprisonment and 6 years' loss of civil

rights - the court found him innocent; 2)
Marian Glucha, 13 years' imprisonment and
10 years' loss of civil rights
- sentenced to 3 years of prison and 2
years' loss of civil rights; 3) Jan
Wiegus, 9 years imprisonment and 5 years'
loss of civil rights - the court
suspended proceedings; 4) Adam Skwira, 12
years' imprisonment and 8 years' loss of
civil rights - the court gave 3 years'
imprisonment and 2 years' loss of civil
rights; 5) Stanlislaw Plotka, 15 years'
imprisonment, 10 years' loss of civil
rights - sentenced 4 years imprisonment
and 3 years' loss of civil rights; 6)
Stanislaw Saternus, 12 years'
imprisonment and 5 years' loss of civil
rights - found innocent; 7) Jerzy Wartok,
13 years' imprisonment and 10 years' loss
of civil rights - sentenced to 3-1/2
years' imprisonment and 4 years' loss of
civil rights; 8) Alina Mucha, 8 years
imprisonment and 4 years' loss of civil
rights - acquitted; 9) Zdzislaw Kabat, y
years' imprisonment and 5 years' loss of
civil rights - acquitted. The plaintiffs
in these cases were prosecutors from the
Katowice military prosecutor's office,
Maj. Klaczkowski and Lt. Brol.

To answer the question how such differences could come
about, we will cite a statement by one of the judges in a
conference held in October 1982 in Warsaw:

...A punishment of three years is a harsh
sentence. Judgments are not being made
by some revolutionary tribunals but by
normal judges for whom three years is a
sentence for a crime and every judge
reflects when he hands it down.

The Katowice case is not exceptional; rather it can be
seen as typical.

Prosecutors consistently appealed, demanding longer
sentences. As an example, we cite two other cases handled in

December by the Supreme Court, which was entirely obedient to the authorities during the first few months of the state of war.

On December 8, 1982, the Supreme Court upheld the Provincial Court's in Slupsk sentenced (Ryszard Kulesza to three years' imprisonment for "leading the August 31 demonstrations." The prosecutor asked in the appeal that the sentence be raised to five years.

On December 29, the Supreme Court upheld the sentence against Stanislaw Fudakowski, a member of the Gdansk Council Solidarnosc, sentenced to three years' imprisonment for organizing and leading a strike at the Lenin Shipyard in Gdansk. The prosecutor, as in the previous case, asked that the sentence be raised to five years' imprisonment.

Despite the obligation to implement the directives of WRON, the courts and the prosecutor differed in the administration of justice. This brought about a certain disappointment and the reproaches mentioned earlier, as well as the statement by the Supreme military prosecutor. As we have emphasized, this only pertains to some of the courts. During the state of war, there were also severe sentences which cannot be explained either by the articles of an especially harsh law or even the directive to increase judicial repression for political reasons. Instead of verdicts and sentences, in these cases we can speak of

something that could be called the "terror of the courts,"
with verdicts as an instrument of terror and nothing else.
We have mentioned such sentences previously.

Let us now mention something else that aroused general
indignation and opposition -- the case of Ewa Kubasiewicz and
others.

The scene is the Naval Court in Gdynia (Case No. SmW
13/82) on February 3, 1982. On this day, the judicial panel
was made up of Second Lt. Andrzej Grzybowski, Lt. Amdrze
Fiuke and Lt. Aleksander Glawa who handed down a sentence
that was a reincarnation of the grim Stalin era. Ewa
Kubasiewicz was sentenced to 10 years and Jerzy Kowalczyk to
9 years' imprisonment for organizing and leading a strike the
Higher Navy Academy in Gdynia and for publishing, copying,
and distributing in the Tri-city area a strike communique
containing, in the opinion of the court, false information
which could weaken the defense readiness of the PRL. The
third among the accused, Wladyslaw Trzcinski, was sentenced
to 9 years'imprisonment because he transported a copying
machine, on which leaflets were printed, in his own car, on
many occasions. Wieslawa Kwiatkowska was sentenced to five
years' prison because, during the period of December 13-20,
she collected documentary data on the December 1970 events
and because she took part in a meeting in the Lenin
Shipyard.

Cezary Grodziuk was sentenced to 6 years' imprisonment for possessing leaflets and a copying machine. Three more accused, Jaroslaw Skowronch, Slawomir Sadowski and Krzysztof Jankowski, were sentenced to 5 years, imprisonment for publishing, storing and distributing leaflets. The son of Ewa Kubasiewicz, Marek Czachar, was sentenced to 3 years' imprisonment for providing his friends with an apartment in which to print leaflets.

From the trial materials, it is evident that the strike in the Naval Academy lasted for only a short time - about twenty hours. It began on December 14 and ended the next day with voluntary call off the strike following discussions with the administration of the school. The decision to end the strike came after the rector of the Academy in the presence of a member of the WRON, Rear Adm. W. Glinski, declared that there would not be reprisals against the strikers. He did not keep his word.

According to the the state of war decree (Art. 46, sect. 7) the voluntary termination of a strike allows the court to refrain from passing a sentence. The judges did not take this into consideration, nor other important circumstances. They passed over the fact that classes at the Academy were suspended from December 13 and that the strike, so short in duration, was even interrupted for discussions with the rector. In itself, the strike was only symbolic and did not hinder the functioning of the Academy. These considerations alone were enough to desist at least from conducting summary proceedings. Despite the obligation to do so, the court did not explain the reasoning that led it to conduct summary proceedings.

Ewa Kubasiewicz and Jerzy Kowalczyk were also charged with editing, copying and distributing a communique containing false information damaging the defense readiness of the PRL. Both only to preparing the communique. There was insufficient evident regarding copying and distribution. The communique contained information about the strike at the Academy and about the removal of the rector of this school, and was consistent with the actual occurrences. The court, however, without any grounds whatsoever, accepted that the communique contained falsed information. And that is not all. It also accepted that the text of the communique affected the defense readiness of the PRL - also without any basis. The Court did not take any into consideration any mitigating circumstances. This was also the case with the rest of the accused. Testimony about the irreproachable character of the accused,about their professional competence, testimony by the Bishop of Gdansk, Kaczmarek, were of no interest to the court. Instead of refraining from sentencing for the strike and passing a not-guilty verdict for the communique, the harshest sentence in Poland under the state of war decree was handed down.

Wladyslaw Trzcinski was treated in a similarly harsh manner, despite the fact that he was charged and sentenced only for transporting the copying machine. His action was described as "abetting a crime," according to Art. 48, sec. 1-3 of the decree.

A number of the accused were convicted for copying and distributing leaflets. Neither the copying machine nor the leaflets were found. Without knowning the contents of the leaflets, the court decided that the information that the accused allegedly distributed was false. The decision to convict was based on the testimony of a few witnesses who withdrew their testimony at the trial and stated that they had been subjected to force during interrogation. (They were interrogated while lying down with a pistol held to their heads.) Nevertheless, the court decided that even these testimonies were sufficient for conviction.

On December 15, 1981, Wieslawa Kwiatkowska was in the striking shipyard; she did not, however, take part in any meetings - there was no proof of this. For a long time, then she had been gathering material for a book about December 1970. She continued to do this after the imposition of the state of war. Despite the lack of evidence, it was decided that she continued union activities, and that documentation

of the events of 1970 was therefore a crime. She was
sentenced to five years' imprisonment.

Finally, the last of the accused, Marek Czachar,
admitted that he gave the keys of his acquaintances'
apartments to other friends, who were staying there to avoid
internment. He know nothing about the fact that in this
apartment leaflets were copied. None of the accused, nor any
the witnesses, incriminated him in their testimony. He was
however, sentenced to three years' imprisonment. The thought
comes to mind: did this not happen because he is the son of
Ewa Kubasiewicz?

The court declared that the activities of the accused
were especially dangerous because of the social tension in
the Gdansk area and because of the incidents which took
place there on January 30, 1982. But the activities with
which the accused were charged ended on December 16 - six
weeks earlier.

In this case one can find examples of almost all the
abuses of the law which characterized judicial proceedings
during the state of war.

Accepting the illegality of that "legal" act leads to
conclude that all sentences under the state of war decree are
not valid in a legal sense -- they are illgegal sentences.
Many defense attorneys advanced this view during the trials,
but to no avail.

In order to judge the legal validity of convictions for activities in the first days of the state of war, it is important to determine the date of its imposition, i.e., the date from which the state of war decree began to be binding. A law providing grounds for sanctions must be in force at the time when the punishable act was committed. There exists a general legal norm that a law, decree, or other legal act of a similar nature goes into effect on the date of its announcement. Decrees must be announced in the Legislative Journal. The decree of the state of war was not announced until December 18, 1981. The majority of December strikes occurred before this date, before the announcement of the decree. Despite this, those accused of organizing and leading strikes were sentenced under this decree. In this way, one of the fundamental norms of civilized law was violated. Attorney Wladyslaw Sila-Nowicki made a statement on this subject during the trial of strike leaders at the ZM URSUS enterprise, in defending one of the accused, Jerzy Kaniewski: "...acts performed on December 14, cannot be judged under a law which in fact was announced on the 18th of that month. We have not had these types of cases in the entire modern history of our state, nor can we find them in the legal history...we face today an unusual phenomenon. This decree was announced, the penal provisions were announced -- these announcements were made four days after the events for which the accused are charged."

There is also a question of knowledge that an act is illegal. The decree was read over the radio and television on December 13, but even a few days after the introduction of the state of war, the decree was not even accessible to lawyers. Immediately after its announcement, it was in the possession of only the chief prosecutors and the heads of courts. The fact that a defendant was not aware of the illegality of strikes or distribution of leaflets immediately following December 13 should have deserved full consideration by the courts. This was not done at any trial. The point was the subject of many defense arguments. An example:

> Miroslaw Budrewicz, a law student at Warsaw University was charged with distributing on December 14, 1981 leaflets calling for a strike. The defense argued that the accused, being a future lawyer, was aware of the fact that he could not be punished under a legal act which was not yet announced in the proper manner. Despite this, he was sentenced. On January 23, 1982, the Warsaw Voivodship Court sentenced him to two years' imprisonment. After a few months, the Supreme Court decided (VKR 144/82) to conditionally suspend the sentence without ruling, however, on the matter of unawareness of the act.

In strike cases, the courts did not often take into account the important circumstances that strikes in most work places broke out spontaneously in December at the news of the imposition of the state of war. The Solidarnosc activists present at the work place used their personal authority to ensure that these spontaneous outbursts were kept under some discipline, to secure the safety of the plant, to ensure that when the security police arrived, unnecessary bloodshed would be prevented. The workers did not want to speak with the managers or commisars. The only ones who could speak and properly direct them were the Solidarnosc activists. This was their moral obligation and in most plants that obligation was fulfilled at the cost of several years' imprisonment. This was also the case at the URSUS plant. The defense attorney Sila-Nowicki said at this trial:

> At URSUS, blood was not spilled. The defendants prevented this. Thanks to them, there were no acts of desperation, thanks to them the property was not destroyed, which could have been a harmful form of protest. There were no battles with the forces of order...The circumstances dictated the absolute necessity and the moral imperative, directive from internal honesty and a directive from social norms - to stand among the workers, at their helm and to direct this absolutely spontaneous action.

As in other cases, the court did not take these circumstances into consideration. At any rate, they did not affect the sentences handed down. The Solidarnosc activists from Ursus were sentenced on January 15, 1982, by the Warsaw Voivodship Court as follows: Jerzy Kaszuba, three years' imprisonment; Arkadiusz Czerwinski, three years' and Bendykt

Filage, two years, for three years sentenced suspended.

The courts and prosecutors used the concept of

"organizing" strikes loosely and inconsistently.

> Leonard Krasulski, the head of
> Solidarnosc in the Beer Plant in Elblag
> was sentenced by the Naval Court in
> Gdynia to five years' imprisonment and
> three years' loss of civil rights only
> for conducting a vote on the subject of a
> strike among the workers. (The vote was
> negative; there was no strike.

> S. Jedrzejczak, a worker at the POLMO
> plant in Tczew, was temporarily detained
> on the charge of organizing and leading a
> strike from December 16-18, 1981. The
> charge was based on the fact that he read
> a leaflet aloud to other workers. That
> was enough. The Gdansk Voivodship Court
> sentenced him only for participation in a
> strike to a one-month term, recognizing
> that the act constituted only an
> infraction. This court's decision
> provoked an appeal from the prosecutor,
> who demanded a conviction for organizing
> a strike and a sentence of five years'
> imprisonment. On May 20, the Supeme
> Court upheld the sentence of the
> Voivodship Court.

Assessing the degree of social danger, which justified

the use of summary proceedings, was also randomly

interpreted. It happened that a completely trivial act of no

consequence became, in the opinion of the prosecutor or the

courts, a crime meriting summary proceedings.

> Formal charges were filed by the military
> prosecutor in Bialystok on November 26,
> 1982, (No. Pg. Sl. I-56/82) against
> Maciej Belina, Ryszard Kuczerh, Zdzislaw

Belczeski, and Jerzy Las under Art. 305
of the Criminal Code, as follows:

On November 10, 1982, in Czerwony Bor,
Lomza Voivodship, while on active
military duty, stationed at JW 3466, they
did not fulfill obligations of that duty
and refused to eat."

All of them were arrested on November 12,
and the formal charges were filed at the
Warsaw military district court in summary
proceedings. The court in this case
showed common sense - the accused were
found innocent. The prosecutor had
demanded a sentence of three years'
imprisonment and four years' loss of
civil rights.

Czeslaw Lachowicz was a lance corporal
serving his military duty in one of the
coastal units. During the last days of
December 1981, he brought two leaflets to
the unit and read them to a few friends.
He was charged with spreading false
information, and with activity aimed at
weakening the defense readiness of the
PRL. He was arrested by the Naval
Prosecutor in Gdynia, and summarily
tried. On January 12, 1982, the Naval
Court in Gdynia sentenced him to one
year. The act committed by Czeslaw
Lachowicz was ruled to be such a danger
to society that temporary arrest was
applied despite serious hardship for his
family. At the time of his arrest, he
was caring for his very ill wife and six
month old child.

In order to apply temporary arrest and
make a ruling on serious danger to
society, one leaflet given to a military
patrol was sometimes enough:

Janusz Kurmat, a Silesia Solidarity
office employee was arrested at the end
of December 1981 by the military
prosecutor in Wroclaw. Boguslaw Rajner
was arrested and later sentenced by the
Slask Military District Court in Wroclaw

to six years for producing a few small
leaflets in the Zielona Gora jail. It
was decided entirely arbitrarily that he
incited to unrest at this institution.

On May 3, 1982, Jerzy Jaworski, a construction
worker, was arrested in Gdynia. He was
charged with shouting slogans during a
demon-stration [that day]: "Solidarnosc" and
"Free-dom", in the view of the prosecutor,
endangered the socialist cohesion of the
nation; "Come with us," supposedly called on
ZOMO men to break the law; and the slogans
"Free Lech" and "Call off the state of war"
were in turn directed against martial law.
The case was tried summarily by the Gdansk
Voivodship Court and Jaworski was convicted
under Art. 282 of the Criminal Code (public
incitement to disobedience or counteracting
the martial law decree) to one year. The
verdict was appealed by the prosecutor. On
November 17, the Supreme Court (Case V KR
145/82) overruled the sentence and sent the
case for retrial.

One of the charges most often used in cases during the
state of war is that of "spreading false information which
could incite public unrest and disturbances." We know of
only one case where the court adhered to the obligatory rules
of procedure and honestly attempted to determine if the
information contained in an "underground newspaper is true or
false." This is a basic judicial condition that the
information disseminated must be false, for filing a charge
and beginning criminal proceedings. At the beginning of
December 1982, the Warsaw Military District Court suspended
proceedings under Art. 48 of the decree, against Stanislaw
Kozera, a Solidarnosc activist from the FSO Plant in Warsaw,
due to lack of evidence of a crime. It could not determined

if the information disseminated by Kozera was true or false.

This was, however, an exception. In any event, the ruling

was later dismissed and the accused convicted. The common

practice was that the place of publication determined the

falsity of the information. Information from publications

identified with underground Solidarnosc was false information

to the prosecutor and courts, with no exceptions. Sometimes

information that was difficult to verify was treated as false

information:

> In Case No. SW 140/82 against Krzysztof Kopica
> and others, heard by the Naval Court, the
> conviction read: "There was also [in leaflets
> distributed by the accused] information that
> incited the readers, whose veracity is largely
> or entirely impossible to establish. . .
> contained much information and opinions at
> least difficult to verify or unverifiable."

> The Warsaw Military District Court, in the
> justification of a one-year sentence in the
> case of Leszek Chajewski and others charged
> with putting up leaflets on December 14,
> 1981,in Warsaw, stated that the information
> was false since the leaflets stated
> "Solidarnosc will win," whereas Solidarnosc
> will almost certainly not win. The court in
> this instance did not provide any other
> rulings.

In a similar manner the courts determined that the

distribution was undertaken with the aim of spreading and

introducing hostile slogans, that of the information could

incite unrest or riots, and so on. The interpretations were,

as a rule, the least advantageous for the accused and doubts

were resolved most often to their disadvantage. From an

analysis of some cases it is clear that the courts would

convict the accused even without conducting hearings, since

the results of these hearings did not have any effect on the

verdicts.   Two cases are illustrative:

> On April 9, 1982, the Naval Court in Gdynia
> sentenced Wojciech Kazimor to three years'
> prison for collecting and transporting
> leaflets with the aim of distribution.
> He was convicted despite the fact that he did
> not admit guilt and there was no other
> evidence against him. All instances of doubt
> were resolved by the court against him. This
> conviction was so shocking that the president
> of the military branch of the Supreme Court
> submitted an extraordinary appeal in favor of
> the accused, demanding a verdict of innocence
> due to lack of evidence. The Supreme Court
> found him innocent, in accordance with the
> terms of the appeal.

> On November 13, 1982, a case was heard before
> the Warsaw Regional Court in summary
> proceedings against Malgorzata Kopyscinska, a
> third-year student at the Lyceum Ksiegarski,
> charged with insulting a militiaman on
> November 11. The chief witness, the allegedly
> insulted and injured militiaman was not sure
> if it was actually she who had insulted him.
> There was no other evidence. The prosecutor
> and the defense asked for a verdict of not
> guilty - which rarely occurs. The judge, Piotr
> Aleksandrow, found, however, that she was
> guilty and sentenced her to imprisonment - for
> an infraction.

Even with these methods, the courts, as we mentioned

earlier, did not earn the full approbation of the political

authorities of the PRL.

In none of the cases were the proceedings closed, but

the public did not actually have access in all cases. In the

first few months of the state of war, entry to court
buildings was limited. For instance, in Warsaw, the right to
enter was given only to persons on official business at the
court or those subpoenaed to appear before the court. In
this way, open access to trials was significantly limited.
This was also true of virtually all provincial courts, at
least when political cases were being tried. In order to
enter the courthouse and then the courtroom at the time when
the most important, publicized cases were being tried, one
had to have a special pass. The passes were issued in limited
numbers by the president or deputy president of the court.
In order to get a pass, for instance, to the trial of Jan
Waszkiewicz and others at the Gdansk Voivodship Court one had
to submit a written request with a justification. As a rule,
passes were issued to the immediate family and journalists.
The SB entered the courtrooms without passes. It happened
that limits were set even on the number of immediate family
members, for example, in the case of Zbigniew Romaszewski
and others (Radio Solidarnosc), entry to the courtroom was
limited to two members of the family of each of the
defendants. Decisions about the issuance of passes were
made, for all practical purposes, by the SB; in this case it
was Maj. Okon from the Warsaw Militia Command.

During some of the trials, the courthouses were
surrounded by the militia or the army. Handbags were often

searched. Such was the case, for example, during the trials
of Wladyslaw Frasyniuk in Wroclaw and Mieczyslav Gil and
Edward Novak of the Lenin Steelworks in Cracow. But
formally, the trials were open to the public.

F. Misdemeanor Courts

Misdemeanor courts are administrative penal tribunals at
local government administration offices at the level of the
commune, district, town, or voivodship. A change occurred on
December 1982; regional and voivodship courts have acted
since then. The courts deal with offenses, i.e. punishable
acts that do not constitute crimes. According to the law on
the structure and procedures of misdemeanor courts, these
tribunals are civic, rather than professional, bodies.
Appointment procedures for tribunal members resemble the way
in which court assessors are chosen. They are appointed by
the National Councils [governmental bodies for local
administration] from among persons who live or work in their
area, and who have been nominated by social organizations and
local institutions and enterprises. Court chairpersons are
required to have college degrees in law or administration.
According to the law, the courts are supervised by the
Minister of Interior. Art. 3 of the Code of Misdemeanor
Procedure states that persons acting as tribunal judges are
independent. Militia officers serve as public prosecutors
before these courts. The courts can impose three principal

penalties: fines of up to 20,000 zlotys; the penalty of limitation of freedom; jail terms of up to three months. The court may, upon detention of the accused, try a case using accelerated procedures. Verdicts issued at such proceedings are carried out immediately. Only if the sentence calls for a jail term can the convicted person appeal to a [regular, criminal] court; otherwise the appeal may be made [only] to a higher misdemeanor court.

Art. 21 of the decree concerning special procedures for crimes and misdemeanors during the state of war, issued on December 12, 1981, mandated accelerated procedures before misdemeanor courts throughout the country, in cases of various offenses enumerateed in the decree, above all, offenses against public order as well as offenses listed in Art. 50 of the state of war decree. Among misdemeanors mentioned there, the most important are: 1) change of temporary or permanent residence without required permission, or violating the conditions thereof; 2) violation of the restrictions imposed on freedom of movement; 3) violations of the obligation to carry an identity card in a public place.

Art. 50 of the decree also makes it a misdemeanor to participate in a strike or protest action. Since June 7, 1982, this has been punishable by up to three months in jail and a fine of up to 20,000 zlotys.

The manner in which proceedings before the misdemeanor
courts have been conducted, and the verdicts themselves,
violated fundamental principles of such proceedings and rules
for determining guilt and punishment. Proceedings usually
took no more than a few minutes. Examination of the evidence
was limited to the reading of the affidavit of detention, and
hearing the testimony of the accused. Verdicts were based
almost exclusively on the affidavits. Detailed descriptions
of such procedures, together with appropriate examples, can
be found in Chapter IX.

During the state of war, about 100,000 people were
subjected to the proceedings before misdemeanor courts for
violations of the decree. A majority of cases concerned
[acts committed during] the first few months of the state of
war, when violatiosn of the rules or order were still
classified as misdemeanors. In the first two months of the
state of war, the courts convicted 85,000 people for
violating the decree; 70,000 of these were charged with
violating the curfew. As can be seen in individual case
files, especially in December 1981 and January 1982, the
courts were often improperly constituted, failing to fulfill
the requirements of the law, and were thus issuing judgements
illegitimately. This came about because there were
difficulties in getting the needed number of tribunals. In
such cases, the courts were filled with the employees of the
local state administration. There were cases where whole

tribunals were composed of such persons. On a given day, with a large number of cases, it sometimes happened that even such employees were not enough.

A few words about another type of misdemeanor: Many people were given large fines, or even sentenced to jail, for wearing a button, or an article of clothing with the Solidarity logo, in a public place. Such behavior was usually regarded as a misdemeanor under Art. 61, par. 2 of the Code of MIsdemeanors, which prohibits wearing insignia or uniforms which have not received official authorization. These were the formal grounds for the punishment. The courts, as well as those who issued instructions, ignored the fact that Solidarnosc did not have an [official] organizational logo, much less a uniform, and a button or article of clothing with the word "Solidarity" expressed only certain sentiments of an individual.

> On December 21, 1982, Edward Malocki, the
> former chairman of Rural Solidarnosc branch
> in the Marianska Forests in Skierniewice, was
> sentenced by a misdemeanor court to a fine of
> 20,000 zlotys or, in case of non-payment, to
> three months in jail, for wearing a Solidarity
> cap while driving a tractor through the
> village.

This short analysis, the remarks in Chapter IX on public demonstrations, as well as dozens of documented cases, are sufficient, in our opinion, to form proper judgement concerning the role of the misdemeanor courts in the system of repression in the PRL. After August [1980], there were demands to deprive the misdemeanor courts of the right to pass sentences. These demands were an attempt to make [Polish] legislation conform to the Internaitonal Covenant on Civil and Political Rights, which states that one can be deprived of freedom only by a court proper. However, the misdemeanor courts are too important an element in the system of repression, since they are empowered to deprive one of freedom, for the political authorities to give them up. The authorities need tribunals that are illegitimate and violate the law, that can proclaim verdicts without evidence or in spite of it, that initiate repressive moves at every nod, in the name of a peculariarly understood "peace and order."

The facts presented here did not prevent the highest representatives of the authorities from expressing complete self-satisfaction, to be downright ecstatic with the alleged legality of their acts - a legality of words only:

> From the beginning of the state of war, we have acted legally, we have adhered to the principles that the verdicts of the courts conform with the law and the autonomy of the judiciary... The party does not demand harsh verdicts, it wants them to be just, to defend the interests of socialist social justice. (Miroslaw Milewski - during the IX Plenum of the Central Committee of the Communist Party, June 14-16, 1982).

> The laws under the state of war were not abused by the authorities. We strive and will continue to strive that they be applied in the most extensive manner possible, in conformance with the Polish mentality, with the socialistic political culture. (Wojciech Jaruzelski, June 21, 1982 session of the Sejm.)

-169D-

The documents and evaluations presented here do not allow, in our opinion, agreement with this type of assessment. The Polish reality of investigations and trials was different from that which appears in the above citations. It seems there were two realities.

On October 8, 1982, a verdict was reached in the case of members of the Confederation of an Independent Poland.

Arrested on September 23, 1980, they were gradually released after a few months under the pressure of public opinion. On July 9, 1981 they were arrested again. Their imprisonment (during the time of Solidarnosc they were the only political prisoners) caused numerous protests, including mass demonstrations and hunger strikes. Throughout the country, numerous Committees for the Defense of Prisoners of Conscience were formed.

Just as today, protests against the jailing of people for their convictions did not take into account the nature of these convictions, according to the principles that it is wrong to jail a person for his convictions and that one does not conduct discussions with the person in jail.

Immediately after the arrest of KPN members in 1980, the KSS-KOR group issued a protest. While Solidarnosc was active and the Committees for the Defense of Prisoners of Conscience were under its protection, the authorities had not dared to conduct a trial. They did so now.

Sentenced were:

Leszek Robert Moczulski, seven years in prison.
Romuald Szeremietiew, six years in prison.
Tadeusz Stanski, five years in prison.
Tadeusz Jadziszak, two years and a suspended five
years.

In September, seven KSS-KOR activists were charged unde

Art. 128, which relates to Art. 123, par. 1 of the Criminal

Code.

For four of them - Jacek Kuron, Adam Michnik, Jan

Litynski and Henryk Wujek - the arrest warrant meant simply

moving from the internment center in Bialoleka to prison at

Rakowiecka Street in Warsaw. The fifth, Zbigniew

Romaszewski, who had been in hiding from the first day of the

state of war, was arrested on August 30. The sixth, Jan

Jozef Lipski, arrested during the pacification of the strike

at the URSUS plant in December 1981, was released from prison

due to poor health and went abroad for treatment. He returned

to Poland, knowing that he would face trial for "attempting

to overthrow the system by force and weakening the defense

readiness of the PRL". He was arrested on the day after his

return. After a while he was released again. The seventh,

Miroslaw Chojecki, is abroad and will possibly be tried in

absentia.

The arrest of the KOR activists shook public opinion

mainly because of the absurdity of the charges.

KOR was formed in 1976. It purpose was to defend

workers who had been beaten, jailed, and thrown out of work

for the June protests against the raising of food prices.
The Committee members always acted openly, signed their
statements with their full names, and included their addresses
and phone numbers. The Committee had members with very
different convictions, from socialists to priests. The
Committee did not have a political program.

The Committee cannot thus be associated with an
anti-government conspiracy but with the struggle for
democracy in Poland. Initiatives independent of the
the authorities were formed around KOR - journals, publishing
houses, and education.

The work of the Committee contributed to giving the
workers' protest in August 1980 the character of a social
movement, rather than of street scuffles. Between the
eruption of 1976 and August 1980, KOR influenced the
positions of Polish workers, teaching peaceful and legal
methods of struggle for one's rights, developing civic and
democratic attitudes.

In 1981, KOR dissolved itself, recognizing that
Solidarnosc had taken over its tasks.

Of the arrested, three were members of the Solidarnosc
leadership: Romaszewski and Wujec of the National Commission
and the Regional Directorate of Mazowsze and J.J. Lipski of
the Regional Directorate of Mazowsze. Kuron, Michnik, and
Litynski were advisors for the union.

On December 23, while releasing the remaining internees from jail, the authorities charged seven of them (under Art. 123 of the Criminal Code) and moved them to investigative arrest.

Elected union activists were arrested who, to the day of the proclamation of the state of war, fulfilled their union functions according to instructions under the control of the electorate.

Arrested were: Andrzej Gwiazda and Marian Jurczyk - deputy chairmen of Solidarnosc; Seweryn Jaworksi, Grzegorz Palka, Karol Modzelewski, Andrzej Rozplochowski, and Jan Rulewski.

Art. 123 of the Criminal Code:

> He who, having the goal of depriving of
> independence, annexation of a part of
> territory, overthrowing by force the political
> system, or weakening the defense force of the
> Polish People's Republic, conducts in
> conspiracy with other persons activities
> leading to the realization of this goal, is
> liable to punishment of imprisonment for not
> less than 5 years or the death sentence.

Article 128 of the Criminal Code:

> He who conducts activity to plan the crimes
> defined in Arts. 122, 123, 124, par. 1, or
> Art. 127 is subject to a punishment of
> imprisonment from one to 10 years.

CHAPTER VII

PRISON CONDITIONS AND THE STATUS OF POLITICAL PRISONERS

There are no political prisoners under the state of war in Poland. This statement seems inherently contradictory and may seem paradoxical but, strictly speaking, that is exactly the case.

The actions referred to in the decree of December 12, 1981, especially in Articles 46 and 48, are political in nature. These articles are considered to be political by those sentenced under them -primarily Solidarnosc members and activists, and members of other independent groups who describe themselves as social, democratic, or oppositional. These people acted or simply expressed their beliefs out of a sense that their system of values was entirely at variance with the prescribed one. The actions they took, and for which they were condemned, were motivated by their convictions. These people are political prisoners in the eyes of most and probably virtually all of Polish society. They are considered to be such by the legal profession, whether legal theorists, teachers or practicing attorneys.

The actions addressed in Arts. 46 and 48 of the decreee are described as "matters of a political nature" in the Ministry of Justice's 1982 semi-annual report on the courts.

Yet, in fact, these people are not political prisoners. In prison, they are treated like ordinary criminals because the concept of "political prisoner status" does not exist in the Polish People's Republic. Why? Simply because the lack of such a status makes it possible to subject imprisoned members and activists of Solidarnosc to retribution,with all the features of a political vendetta. It is not an easy task to marshal evidence for this statement since the authorities are clearly not anxious to reveal their methods.

Non-official, reliable sources are unable to supply exhaustive information. It is impossible to conduct a thorough investigation. In spite of this, we will describe conditions for political prisoners in the Polish People's Republic, beginning with some background on the conditions and operations of the penal institutions which affected those whom the ruling powers deemed to be dangerous adversaries.

We estimate the number of political prisoners to be about 1,500 persons. To put it more precisely, this is the minimum and even somewhat less than minimum number of those sentenced and imprisoned under only two articles of the decree - Arts. 46 and 48. Those prisoners are held in the following prisons, called penal institutions in official terminology: Czarne, Bartoszyce, Kalisz, Klodzko, Leczyca, Mielecin, Opole, Potulice, Raciborz, Stargard Szczecinski, Strzelce Opolskie, Wroclaw, Wronki, Hrubieszow and Jastrzebie-Zdroj. Women are kept in the following prisons: Fordon, Grudziadz, Krzywaniec, Myslenice, and Ostroda. (These listings of prisons are not complete).

The life of prisoners sentenced under provisions of the decree of December 12, 1981, is governed by a regulation - defined as temporary (introduced under Order No. 11 of the Minister of Justice, dated January 25, 1974) -on punishment by deprivation of liberty. Originally, this ruling provoked objections from penology experts, and the fact that it was never published in the official newspaper (Monitor Polski) indicates that the authors wanted it contents to remain unknown.

The basic tenet of this regulation - apart from reform through work - is to apply severe measures in cases of insubordination or petty infractions by the prisoners. Thus, it imposes the obligation to work under supervision, e.g., in quarries or mines, primarily but not exclusively upon recidivists who are paid an amount equal to 1/5 of the normal wages. The implementation of this work principle has met with severe criticism, based on information leaked from so-called "Centers of Social Adjustment" and also from prisoners working in prison workshops. This information attests to the fact that work was not treated as a means of re-socialization but of repression.

The regulation limits the prisoners' contact with their families to a maximum of one outgoing letter every two months, one incoming letter every two months, and one visit from a relative every two months under conditions that make conversations on private matters impossible.

All prisoners (irrespective of whether they are serving their sentences under severe, strict or regular regimes) can be punished by reducing their food rations, which is contrary to the international conventions signed by the PLR. This punishment consists of "reduction of food rations by not more than one-half for the duration of 14 days." Other punishments include deprivation of all visits and correspondence, hard beds (often cement slabs with one or no blanket), and solitary confinement for up to six months. The regulation does not exclude the application of two kinds of punishment for one transgression.

These regulations were applied to the letter. Moreover, the prison staff intensified the prescribed regimen and there were frequent cases of brutal repression and even torture Such treatment was also meted out in correctional institutions for juvenile offenders. According to official figures, 15 inmates committed suicide in 1980. It cannot be ruled out that treatment by the prison staff induced these prisoners to kill themselves.

The authorities' treatment of prisoners can be summarized as follows:

1) ruthless enforcement of prison regulations

2) application of "unwritten" procedures, amounting to increased repression.

3) divergence between the content of the

regulations and their implementation.

The material presented above deals with the first two

types of treatment of prisoners. The third type of treatment

is illustrated by the problem over religious services, so

fundamental to the prisoners. This matter is regulated by an

order of the Minister of Justice, issued in 1956. It

introduced religious services in all 36 prisons which existed

at the time. Gradually, the number of old prisons was

reduced, and monthly masses and Easter confessions were not

allowed in new prisons, even though such religious services

were provided for in the 1956 order. On April 24, 1981,

General S. Jablonowski, a departmental director in the

Ministry of Justice, declared that, currently, radio

broadcasts of Sunday mass could be heard in all penal insti-

tutions and jails. Actually, this was not the case in at

least some of the prisons, since the prisoners' insistence on

religious services was one of the demands in their protest

actions undertaken after April 24, 1981.

Other information given to journalists by General S.

Jablonowski on April 24, 1981, is noteworthy in view of the

fact that it is very much at odds with the subsequent protest

actions of the prisoners. The announcement of changes in the

prison situation at first inspired optimism but apparently

turned out to be meaningless was only partially

implemented. This can be seen in the prisoners' demands,
which upon introduction of reforms their conditions,
supposedly already changed, according to the General's
announcement. Thus, the changes which were to be introduced
into the regulation governing the serving of prison sentences
included: abolition of the strict regimen, an increase in
the quantity of correspondence, an extension of time allowed
for exercise, and an increase in the number of food parcels
allowed.

The situation in the prisons was, or rather was to be,
one of the subjects of negotiation between the National
Coordinating Commission (KKP) of Solidarnosc and the
government of the Polish People's Republic. In the notes for
these negotiations, prepared by the KKP, it is stated that:
"The penalty of imprisonment raises the greatest number of
objections. Food rations, excessive overcrowding in cells,
and lack of individualized treatment of inmates, not only
make the penal institution a place of further demoralization,
but also lead to the violations of the basic rights of the
inmates."

The situation in the prisons, as generally described
here, led to a series of mass protest by the prisoners.
The protests began in the spring in the Bialoleka Prison and
on April 6, 1981, at Wronki, and lasted until the middle of
that year. According to official information from Colonel

Julian Petrykowski, deputy director of the Central
Administration of Penal Institutions, protest actions took
place in 37 prisons, or approximately one-third of the
prisons in Poland, including Ilawa, Zaleze, Strelce Opolskie,
Wroclaw, Zabrze Wronki Zaborze, Bydgoszcz, Chelm, Wadowice,
Tarnow, Kaminsk, Czarne, Wolow, Szczecinek, Nowy Sacz,
Brzesk, Debica, Piotrkow Trybunalski, Grudziada, Medyka,
Siedlce, and also in the Konrad Copper Mine where prisoners
worked.

The protests took the form of hunger and sit-down
strikes. The prison staff responded with force. There was
also punitive beating of non-resisters, which was clear abuse
of authority.

The demands drawn up in all of the prisons had the same
or similar contents; the demands of the prisoners in Wronki
are typical.

The scale and the nature of the protests attests to the
fact that they were not directed against the pathological
behavior of individual prison officials, nor were they
critical of the conditions in particular prisons; this was a
fundamental protest of the imprisoned against the prevailing
penal system.

There is a protocol of the settlement between the
striking prisoners and representatives of the Ministry of
Justice, Solidarnosc, the penal court, and the administration
of penal institutions which was prepared on June 5, 1981,

following a protest action of prisoners in Wroclaw. We do
not know to what degree the agreement initialled by the
parties concerned was implemented in that Wroclaw prison, nor
whether the demands submitted by prisoners in other penal
institutions were met. It can be stated, with little
likelihood of error, that the incorporation of those demands
into the routine of prison life - even if it was begun - was
halted or entirely abandoned with the introduction of the
state of war. The situation of the prisoners could not have
improved since those who were the mediators in the conflict
between the prisoners and the authorities, themselves became
prisoners of those authorities.

We have presented some background on the system,
conditions and treatment which prevailed in the prisons of
the PLR before the introduction of the state of war. The
prisoners sentenced under Arts. 46 and 48 of the decree were
engulfed by the system because, as we said, there is no
political prisoner status in the Polish People's Republic.
We will now endeavor to show the consequences of the lack of
such status based on the scant information which has reached
us from the prisons. We will not categorize this information
by subject, i.e., living conditions, repression, health
service, etc., since only all of these elements together can
illustrate the prison situation.

One of the first accounts was a report from the prison
in Jastrzebie-Zdroj, dated March 2, 1982. Here are a few
highlights:

> -crowding: an average of eight persons in a
> cell not exceeding 20 square meters;
> -cold water available for only one
> hour a day;
> -damaged sanitation facilities;
> -damaged buildings due to the fact that the
> prison is located in an area of intensive
> mining;
> -lack of adequate medical care.

Message from the prison in Leczyca:

> until May 6, 1982 the prisoners did not have
> the right to receive parcels from their
> families.

The prison in Raciborz during early May, 1982:

> the prisoners (numbering approximately 120
> people from southern Poland and the Katowice
> area) are entitled to a 30-minute walk per
> day, one food parcel weighing 3 kg. every two
> months, and one family visit every two months.
> Often, disciplinary punishment is meted out
> for singing religious songs. Church
> representatives are prevented by the prison
> administration from seeing the prisoners. In
> spite of inadequate medical care, receiving
> medical supplies from outside is denied. Not
> even the smallest parcels with hygienic
> supplies are allowed. Books also are not
> permitted.

The prison in Gdansk at Kurkowa Street:

> Tadeusz Klein an employee of the Gdansk Repair
> Shipyard, who suffers from psychological
> disorders (among others, a fear of the dark),
> was placed naked in a cold, sound-proof cell
> on the night of May 29-30, 1982, and he was
> beaten with clubs on May 30. G. Makiela from
> Starogard Gdanski was also beaten.

> On July 23, 1982, at 5:30 a.m. a brutal
> action was begun in order to prevent a hunger

strike anticipated by the authorities (but which had not started). The prison wardens, armed with clubs and guns, led prisoners stripped naked out of their cells into the corridors, beat them, and set dogs on them. Some were beaten for refusing meals, and 20 juvenile prisoners, weakened after 40 minutes of hot showers, were dragged out by their hair and also beaten. Neither prisoners awaiting placement in a psychiatric hospital nor the sick were spared. It is certain that at least 15 people fell victim to this brutality.

The prison in Strzelce Opolskie:

26 members and activists of Solidarnosc (previously incarcerated in Raciborz) were brought here on June 4, 1982. Among them were Patrycjusz Kosmowski, Chairman of the Sub-Beskid Region Board; Mieczyslaw Gil, Chairman of Solidarnosc at the Lenin Steelworks, Edward Nowak from the same steelworks, and also Krzysztof Bzdyl, a member of the Confederation for an Independent Poland (KPN). They were placed under a strict regimen: very poor nutrition, overcrowded cells, an exercise area measuring only 10x5 meters, and blacked out windows. Their books were confiscated and the visits promised them in Raciborz were denied.

The prison in Hrubieszow:

P. Kochmaniewicz from Warsaw was beaten on August 3, 1982; Leszek Chajewski from Warsaw was beaten in a soundproof cell.

The food is of poor quality (rotten and wormy), rations are often reduced, there is a lack of adequate medical assitance and the medicine sent to prisoners often disappears. A fuller report on the situation in this prison was transmited in September 1982.

Forced feeding of prisoners on hunger strike began on September 20, 1982. Anyone resisting was beaten and kicked. On September 22, Tomasz Dzieran from Lodz was beaten. Sergent Pachle was exceptionally brutal: he hit people about the head and face. Lt. Zarajew watched calmly. On September 23, Jon Klasa

-183-

from Bochnia, Yacele Bartosiewicz from Warsaw
and Krystof Binkowski from Radam were beaten.
Despite the fact that he had a permit in his
possession, Rev. Miecznikowski was not allowed
access to the prisoners on hunger strike.

We will cite parts of a report written by a prisoner on

October 17, 1982. It illustrates the many factors, all

negative in this prison, which determined the fate of the

prisoner.

Conditions - During visits you cannot accept
food, even fruit. The food we receive here is
pilfered, so that it would be embarrasing to
call it a subsistence ration, which is
supposed to contain 2,800 calories. All this
is done to force us to work. Last night was a
nightmare: a colleague had a kidney stone
attack and they would not call an ambulance,
explaining that he would not drop dead till
morning, even though the boy was really writhing in
pain...

Penalties - In retaliation for singing in the
evening and fasting on the monthly anniversary [of
martial law imposition] writing materials, visits
and correspondence are withheld, and instead, a
hard bed is given. The last penalty is the worst,
since you are alone in a dark and damp compartment
four meters square, sleeping on cement slabs under
one blanket, undressed to your shorts (they take
away your clothes). There are rats in these
cells.

Repressions - We have been locked up for 10 months
already in four-man cells. We are constantly
subjected to personal and cell searches during
which things always disappear. They behave with
impunity, this whole apparatus is one big gang.
They brew moonshine in all the prisons and always
walk around drunk...whoever complains a lot gets
beaten or is penalized for insulting officials.

Feelings of Impendency - It is clear why I joined
the hunger strike. After all, some things may
happen to me soon

Psychological Terror -Among us there are also
people who are here accidentally, who want to
regain their freedom at all costs. X,Y, and Z
entered into bargains with the security
police. The sentences of the first two were
suspended. This was arranged for them by the
warden, because they were informing on us so
well.

The prison in Klodzko, information from November 8,

1982:

The prisoners are harassed - going for walks,
mass, and to the community room, always
entails searches of the prisoners, who have to
stand naked with their hands up, in the
corridors. This procedure is repeated upon
returning to the cells. Such methods are not
used in dealing with criminal prisoners.

The prison in Wroclaw:

Eight prisoners were beaten during evening
prayers on November 11, 1982. Drunken
officers from the prison administration
participated in the beatings. For three
prisoners, the regimen under which they are
serving their sentences was made more severe.

The prison in Potulice:

Four people were beaten with clubs on June 11,
1982, during a search in Barracks No. 7.
Mariusz Ugriczicz was beaten with clubs and
fists; a cross was torn off his neck. Andrzej
Milczanowski, W. Korolewski, and S.
Niewiadomski were also beaten. After six days
of fasting, Andrzej Milczanowski was put into
solitary confinement, where he is suffering
from gastritis and kidney pains. There is no
continuous medical care.

Information from August 1982:

The food is atrocious; showers once a week for
10 minutes. The prison doctor allows sick
individuals to be put into solitary
confinement (on cement beds without
mattresses, and only one blanket) as
punishment.

Information from November 12th, 1982:

Two gravely ill persons are serving their
sentences in prison: Waclaw Kicinski, who has
acute attacks of asthma and heart pains, and
Antoni Grabarczyk, who was cruelly beaten in
July, which caused spinal pain and partial
dislocation of a disc -he is not able to move
(he is being treated solely with pain
killers).

Prisons for women:

In Fordon, prison guard Antoni Paszkowski
beat Krystyna Gajowiak on April 29k 1982.

The following information is based on a letter to the

Minister of Health and Social Services from Irena Malenczyk,

sentenced under the state of war decree:

In the Grudziadz penal institution, which
serves as a prison hospital, all of the
surgical and gynecological procedures are
performed in the same operating room.
Pregnant women are detained in cells without
sanitary facilities -unaided, they themselves
have to carry waste in containers the size of
three pails, to a drain which is several dozen
meters (over one hundred feet) away. The
sick, who are waiting to be operated on, lie
in five-person cells and have to bring water
for washing and for cleaning the toilet-bucket
three times a day in the same pail.
Prescriptions can only be filled outside the
prison, and so the sick are often deprived of
medicine.

One prisoner at Fordon, seventeen-year-old
Anna Stawicka, was sentenced to 3 years of
incarceration. On August 4th, 1982, her
classification was changed from a regular to a
strict regimen by a commission not having
appropriate authorization. A description of
this case, and of the conditions in which this
seventeen-year old is serving her sentence, is
contained in a letter of complaint to the
penal court of the Pomeranian Military
District in Bydogszcz.

The material presented in this chapter supports the
statement that, in being deprived of political prison status,
those sentenced under the decree of December 12, 1981, are
serving their sentences under very difficult conditions.
They are subjected to persecution, repression and violence.
This situation has provoked widespread, large-scale protests
by prisoners. Hunger strikes were conducted in Strzelece
Oposkie (begun on August 15, by 70 prisoners and lasting
several days), Potulice (in mid-August), Hrubieszow (begun on
September 12 by about 130 prisoners), Klodzko (November 8)
Krzywaniec (where 21 women prisoners go on a hunger strike on
the 21st and 22nd days of every month), and elsewhere.

The main purpose of the protests was to gain political
prisoners status, and also - even before this is attained -
immediate improvement of prison conditions. The prisoners
even drew up their own drafts of such a status. The
protests and petitions were not answered. The only response
that came, a negative reply, was a letter from the Director
of the Regional Administration of Penal Institutions in
Bydgoszcz, Lieut. Col. Boleslaw Sylla, M.A., to Wojciech
Slodkowski, who had petioned for political prisoner status.
Wojciech Slodkowski's petition was directed to the Minister
of Justice, Prof. Sylwester Zawadzki. Through the prison
warden, Lieut. Col. Sylla informed W. Slodkowski that his
petition was not sent on "through channels".

On September 14, 1982, 40 law professors and attorneys

issued an appeal asking that political prisoner status be granted to political prisoners. This appeal was directed to the Minister of Justice of the PRL, the Parliamentary Commissions for Legislative Affairs, Internal Affairs and Judicial Proceedings, and Implementation of Social Agreements. The following persons were informed of the appeal: Primate Jozef Glemp; Aleksander Gieysztor, President of the Polish Academy of Science; Jan Szczepanski, Chairman of the Socio-Economic Council; and Mieczyslaw Rakowski, Chairman of the Socio-Political Committee of the Council of Ministers of the PRL

Up until December 1982, there were no indications that the situation of political prisoners in the PRL will undergo any change. The authorities remain silent. In this situation, an appeal from the prisoners in Potulice for political prisoner status to the United Nations Commission on Human Rights in Geneva, assumes particular importance.

CHAPTER VIII

INTERNMENT CAMPS

The decree on the state of war announced on the radio at

6:00 a.m. on December 13, 1981, and officially published in

the Legislative Journal a few days later, contained the

following provisions:

> Art. 42.1 Polish citizens who have completed
> 17 years of age and concerning whom, because
> of their past behavior, there is justifiable
> suspicion that, in remaining at liberty, they
> will not observe the legal order or will
> conduct activity threatening the security or
> defense interests of the State, may be
> interned in isolation centers for the duration
> of the state of war. These terms do not
> violate any immunity stemming from any
> specific regulation.
>
> Art. 43.1 The voivodship militia commander in
> whose jurisdiction the person subject to the
> proceedings resides or resided before going
> into hiding, makes the decision about the
> internment and directs ex officio the
> proceedings in matters concerning internment.
>
> Art. 43.2 In matters of internment, proceed-
> ings may be conducted without the
> participation of the person concerned.
> Art. 43.3 The decision to intern is to be served
> in person to the internee at the moment of
> detention by the militia The decision to intern is
> subject to immediate implementation.

Under these articles, internment commenced at midnight

on December 13, 1981, and in certain cases, even a bit

earlier. Patrols of the militia and SB spread out into

residential buildings, equipped with crowbars. In many

cases, they broke down doors and dragged people out of beds.

Frequently, people were not allowed to take anything with them, and sometimes were not even allowed to dress but were dragged out in their underclothes despite the freezing cold.

Frequently, the internees were handcuffed. Sometimes, particularly in the smaller villages, they were beaten. Sometimes both parents were interned and small children were left at home (e.g., internees Sergiusz and Kinga Kowalski from Warsaw were informed that their one-year old infant would be taken to a children's home run by the militia.)

We do not know of a single case where Art. 43.3 of the state of war decree war was observed. The decisions to intern were most often served after weeks or months and not, as required by the decree, at the time of detention. Reasons for detention were either not given at all or false reasons were given. We know of cases where people protected by court immunity were interned. (See Chapter IV).

Thus, already in the very first hours, the authorities grossly violated their own state of war "laws".

The detainees were transported to militia's precincts and headquarters from where they were taken to camps after a certain period of time (ranging from a few hours to a few weeks). As a rule, conditions (including treatment of the internees, food and sanitation) in the militia's jails were actually worse than in the camps. There were frequent cases

of beatings. Later, the length of stay in the militia
precincts before transfer to the camps was prolonged. There
is a documented case of a 10-week wait to be transported to a
camp.

A. Categories of Internees

Internment affected many groups of people:

- activists, employees and advisers of Solidarinosc;

-activists and employees of Rural Solidarnosc;

- activists and employees of the Independent Students'
  Association (NSZ);

- activists of the Clubs of Catholic Intelligentsia;

- activists of Patronat, the society for the protection
  of prisoners;

- activists of independent social organizations, such
  as: the KOR Social Self-Defense Committee (KSS-KOR),
  the Confederation for an Independent Poland (KPN),
  the Movement for the Defense of Human and Civil
  Rights (ROPCIO), the Young Poland Movement (RMP), the
  Committee for the Defense of Prisoners of Conscience
  (KOWP), the Independent Scout Movement (NHR);

- intellectuals, known for courage in voicing
  their opinions, among them some of the participants in
  the Congress of Polish Culture, which was being held
  in Warsaw on December 12, 1981, including the Chairman
  of the Liaison Committee of Scientific and Artistic

Organizations (KRST), Prof. Klements Szaniawski;

- employees of independent printing establishments;
- activists in the so-called "horizontal structures" in the Polish United Workers' Party (e.g., Z. Iwanow).

Therefore, this repression affected workers, farmers and intellectuals; it affected representatives of groups associated with left, Christian, and national political views - in other words everyone who expressed their aversion to the totalitarian rule and insisted on democratic freedom.

A fairly small group of criminals was also interned. Most probably this was done in order to discredit the status of internment in the eyes of international public opinion.

There are strong indications that the lists of people selected for internment were prepared several months in advance (probably in the Spring of 1981). The names of people who had been abroad for a long time were found on these lists. Some orders gave as the place of isolation a penal institution which had burned down in September 1981 and was not yet functioning by December 1981. An analysis of the lists indicates that they included people who had been particularly active at the end of 1980 and the beginning of 1981, and so did not take into account personnel changes that had taken place during the latter year. Special internment forms had been prepared long before December 1981. The internment orders, handed to the internees after some

delay, contain laconic, absurd justifications such as:
"overly attached to Solidarnosc," "intended to overthrow
the regime," and "conducts activity in conflict with the
law," etc. An example is Lech Walesa's internment order.

B. Regulations for the Camps

On December 13, 1981, the Minister of Justice issued
Order No. 165, directing that treatment of the internees be
in accordance with regulations applicable to persons detained
temporarily. They were to be treated as criminals against
whom the strictest preventative measures would be applied.

On December 30, 1981, the Minister of Justice issued a
subsequent order, No. 189, regarding regulations governing
the stay of interned persons in isolation centers. These
regulations gave very wide lattitude to the commanders of
those centers. They defined the numerous obligations and the
few rights of the internees. The provisions of the
regulations were violated by the prison staff, and the
regulations themselves were not made available in most camps,
despite the requirement that they be made known to the
internees (Chapter I, par. 2.1).

Regardless of the fact that the provisions of the
regulations were not observed, it is necessary to point out
the fundamental conflict between them and the international
obligations of the PRL.

In particular, the Geneva Convention of August 12, 1949, concerning the protection of the civilian population in time of war, is at issue here. The Polish authorities maintain that regulations on the state of war, and particularly on internment, do not have to be in accordance with the Geneva Convention, since there was no war (January 21, 1982, letter of the Minister of Justice to the Episcopate). This is an astounding position, since it means that during peace time Polish citizens can be treated worse than citizens of an enemy country would be in wartime. The decree of December 12, 1981, "On the State of War," already partially violates the Geneva Convention. Art. 49 of the decree warns of criminal penalties in the case of escape from an internment center, which is at odds with Art. 120 of the Convention. The terms of the Convention are most clearly violated by the December 30, 1981 order of the Minister of Justice, mentioned above. A few examples will illustrate this:

(1) Art. 82 of the Convention provides for keeping families of internees together, while in Poland they remain separated.

(2) Art. 86 of the Convention provides for a separate facility for the practice of religion, while only in some centers did the persistent demands of the internees lead to the provision of such accommodations.

(3) Art. 94 of the Convention provides for educational facilities and programs, recreation and sports, etc., while

even interned students were not given any opportunities to study, despite such proposals from educational institutions - high school seniors were not given the opportunity to take exams to graduate, despite their requests to be allowed to do so.

(4) Art. 98 of the Convention provides for special financial assistance to enable internees to make certain purchases (presently the internees can make purchases with their own money, but only up to a certain monthly limit).

(5) Art. 102 of the Convention allows the internees to elect their own committees (in Poland, the formation of such committees is not only disallowed, but contacts among internees from different cells or wards of the same prison is impossible).

(6) Art. 135 of the Convention provides for the return of the internee, after release, to his/her place of permanent residence, at the expense of the state (in Poland, travel expenses after release are paid for by the internee, unless he/she lacks sufficient funds - only then will the authorities cover such costs).

By order No. 50/81 of the Minister of Justice, dated December 13, 1981, 49 internment centers were created. With the passage of time, some of them were closed, while new ones were opened. They can be divided into roughly four groups:

- Militia headquarters (e.g. Mogilska Street in Cracow; Lompy Street in Katowice;

- Penal and Investigative Prisons (eg. Warsaw-Bialoleka, Strzelce Opolskie, Wronki);

- Detention centers within the compounds of military units (eg. Polubice);

- Detention centers in rest homes which were created somewhat later (Goldap, Jaworze, Darlowko).

C. Living Conditions

The conditions in detention centers varied greatly. They were most severe in the militia headquarters, with respect to both hygienic conditions and treatment of internees. In this regard, the Militia Headquarters on Lompy Street in Katowice had an extremely bad reputation. Over a dozen internees were placed in cells designed for four, while walks and visits were limited to 10 minutes. The internees were beaten by the militiamen.

A great majority of the internees was held in centers set up on the grounds of investigative jails and penitentiaries. Extreme congestion (a little over one square meter per person) prevailed during the first few months in these camps. The internees spent whole days in cells and only a half-hour walk was allowed. Sanitary conditions in a typical camp were as follows: the cells contained one toilet or else a hole in the floor, which was not screened. In some centers, the cells had a sink with running water, while in other, less luxurious ones, water had to be brought in pails. The regulations provided for weekly access to bathing facilites; as a rule, these actually consisted of a tepid shower, with three to four people together, hastily washing themselves under a single showerhead. The bedding (two sheets and a pillow case) was changed not more than once every two weeks. In many camps, there were no supplies of toiletries, soap, detergent, or toilet paper.

For the most part, the food was monotonous, greasy, devoid of vitamins, and tasteless. Although its quality varied in different camps, it was satisfactory in camps located in rest homes and exceptionally bad at militia headquarters.

Access to information was blocked for the internees. Possession of radios was not allowed. Access to the television in the prison recreation room was difficult or even impossible. It was possible to subscribe to newspapers, although in some centers the selection of permissible titles was strictly limited (e.g. in Bialoleka, subscriptions to Zolnierz Wolnosci were not permitted, only Trybuna Ludu, Zycie Warszawy, and Rzeczpospolita were allowed.) Radio receivers smuggled into the centers by various means were confiscated during searches.

Par. 28 of the regulations states that:

1. An internee may, once a month, be visited by rela-
   tives - and with permission of the commander -
   by others;

2. Visits take place under supervision and last not
   longer than 60 minutes. The conversation during the
   visit must be conducted in a language understood by
   the guard;

3. In justifiable cases, the commander may allow longer
   and more frequent visits.

These regulations enabled the commanders to blackmail
internees. This led to individual and group protests. More
frequent or longer visits than those stipulated in the
regulations was also a means of exerting pressure on the
internees. It was not unusual for sick and elderly parents,
who had travelled hundreds of miles to visit their son or
daughter, to be sent away from the gate without having seen
them.

Correspondence did not facilitate contact with family
and friends, since it had to pass through triple censorship:
the prison, militia, and postal censorship introduced
throughout the country. Letters were delivered weeks after
they had been mailed, and many never reached their
destinations.

Groups of internees were frequently transported from one
center to another; some went through about a dozen camps.
These transfers, which were perceived as a form of

harassment were undoubtedly intended to break any evolving bonds among internees. As a rule, the transports took place under very arduous circumstances, in crowded, unventilated prison vans. They lasted many hours, the vans often stopped along the way in great heat or freezing cold.

A doctor was present in every camp; however, as a rule, he was overworked (by also having to take care of criminal prisoners). Prison pharmacies were very poorly supplied; there was a lack of basic drugs, antibiotics, and vitamins. Great difficulties were experienced whenever there was a need for a medical specialist; this required transporting the internee outside the camp. The sick were often transported in handcuffs. In some centers (e.g., Bialoleka), there were similar problems with dental care. One had to wait several weeks for a visit to the dentist and, in certain cases, internees had to be moved outside the center. The security police and the prison authorities had access to medical records. They frequently used the medical information, against the internee.

The hospitalization of the more seriously ill was a real problem. The SB, if it agreed to hospitalization at all, would propose moving the sick to prison hospitals or to hospitals at the Ministry of Internal Affairs; as a rule, the patients did not agree. This led to dramatic situations. Against the doctors' advice, the SB sometimes took patients

undergoing treatment out of the hospital and transported them
to prison (e.g., Zaleze).

There was a relatively large group of chronically ill
and elderly people among the internees. The internees
repeatedly launched protest actions demanding that the
seriously ill be released.

A complete list of the gravely ill who were held in
camps is in the possession of the International Red Cross,
which had its doctors examine the majority of the internees
in question. For ethical reasons, the authors of this report
decided not to include that list.

Interned women were at first placed separately
throughout the country (eg., in Warsaw's Olszynka Grochowski
Prison) and later transported to a camp in a rest home in
Goldap, and also to a camp in Darlowko (a camp in a rest home
set aside primarily for the chronically ill and the elderly).
Another camp, set aside mainly for intellectuals, was located
on resort grounds in Jaworze. The standard of living was
substantially higher in the camps set up on the grounds of
rest homes than in the others. Such camps were used by the
military authorities as showplaces, and access to them was
facilitated for journalists and reporters.

D. Repression of Internees

Repression of internees can be divided into
four types:

- individual punishments provided for in the regulations,
- individual punishments outside of the regulations,
- collective penalties as provided for in the regulations,
- collective penalties outside of the regulations.

The regulations (par. 33.2) provide for the following disciplinary penalties:

1. reprimand in private or in the presence of other internees.
2. withdrawal of the right to possess certain items (books, letters, personal photographs, writing materials, etc.), to receive additional parcels or be allowed extended walks.
3. limitation of the right to correspondence (up to one month).
4. withdrawal of the right to receive parcels (up to one month).
5. withdrawal of the right to buy food and tobacco (up to one month).
6. placement in solitary confinement up to seven days.

In practice, only the penalties listed in points 4,5,
and 6 were meted out. The internees treated the penalty
cited in point 1 as a distinction, and the one cited in point
2 was impractical due to the number of people in the cells
and the solidarity of the internees.

In the majority of the camps, during the second
half-year of the state of war, more frequent visits by family
and friends began to be allowed, rather than the one time
per month permitted by the regulations. In this situation
the threat of denying additional visits constituted a
frequently-used form of blackmail.

The principle of collective responsibility was
instituted in the camps. It was possible to conduct punitive
searches of cells and individuals without breaking the
regulations. Personal belongings of internees were destroyed
in the course of these searches, particularly mementos (such
as letters from families and drawings sent by children to
to their parents) objects needed in the camp, religious
artiefacts; even better food and other personal property
disappeared from the cells during searches. Increasing the
severity of the imposed regimen was another form of
collective repression allowed by the regulations. In the
spring, the duration of the daily walk was extended in a
majority of the camps and, in varying degrees, contacts among
internees confined in different cells were allowed, and the
duration and frequency of visits were also increased.

Imposition of a more severe regimen became a possible form of repression.

Severe mass beatings were the most drastic repression encountered by the internees in camps. Known incidents of this type occurred on February 13, 1982, in Wierzchow, on March 25 in Ilawa, and on August 14 in Kwidzyn. Eighty-one persons were beaten in Kwidzyn, 50 of them severely. Twenty persons had to be hospitalized. Several persons suffered damaged kidneys, many sustained brain concussions, and one individual required psychiatric treatment.

There were frequent incidents of beatings of individuals. Such incidents recur in many of the accounts. We have not ascertained any cases of fatal beatings in the internment camps; however, we know of several cases where death occurred shortly after release from camp, possibly as a direct consequence of ordeals experienced while in confinement.

It may be assumed that regulations governing treatment for people in temporary detention were applied in practice during the first months of the state of war. Walks lasted from one-half to one hour, and the rest of the time was spent in the cells. In time, the regimen became more lenient: the duration of walks and the frequency of access to bathing facilities were increased, and contact among internees in various cells was allowed. There were also cases of return to more strict regimen, e.g. in the Kielce-Piaski camp, the harshness of the treatment of internees was suddenly intensified in October 1982, in comparison with the practices of December 1981.

It should be understood that the decisions concerning changes in the actual implementation of the regulations were not made so much by the commanders of the camps, as by the SB who were "taking care" of those camps. They were constantly supervising the internees. On several occasions, listening devices were found in the cells (as in Zaleze). There were cases where SB agents were planted for short periods of time as internees in the camps. The SB made attempts to informally interrogate the internees throughout the entire time that the camps existed, although the pressure to submit to such interrogation diminished with time. During these informal hearings (unrelated to any pending investigation and ambiguous in character), propositions were made and pressure was exerted to sign the so-called "loyalty oath" and to cooperate with the SB by becoming an informer. There are reasons to suspect that signing the oath influenced the authorities' decision to release an internee.

E.   Quantitative Data

We are relied on official data in assessing the number of people interned during the state of war. On December 8, 1982, General Stachura, the deputy minister of Internal

Affairs, informed the Sejm Commission on the Administration of Justice that, up to that day, a total of 10,131 persons had been held in camps for varying periods of time. This number can be accepted as the final figure since there were no new internments after that date. It is consistent with the data that we have collected.

Internments on the night of December 12, 1981, were the most extensive. They included about 5,000 persons. According to information from General Kiszczak, 6,647 persons were confined in camps by February 26, 1982. At the end of December and in January 1982, mostly participants and leaders of strikes were interned, who for some reason, could not be prosecuted.

A large number of internees was released at the end of April 1982. The wave of internments in May largely involved participants of demonstrations.

Women internees were released on July 22, 1982. However, instances of renewed internment of women did occur subsequently.

The relatively extensive internments at the end of August 1982 were to intimidate people prior to the anniversary of the signing of the Gdansk Agreements and the demonstrations planned in conjunction with that anniversary. An analysis of the duration of internments in camps indicates that individuals detained on the night of December

12 were interned the longest. Many of them left the camps only after a year of confinement.

F.   Internees After Suspension of the State of War

The internment camps were closed in Poland on December 23, 1982. They were replaced by military camps into which authorities began to draft persons -including many former internees suspected of opposition activities. Men were drafted to perform "military service" in these camps regardless of their age and state of health -sometimes they were invalids. The isolation in these camps is much greater than it was in the internment camps during the state of war, and living conditions are worse.

CHAPTER IX

BEHAVIOR OF POLICE AND MILITARY FORCES

DURING STRIKES AND STREET DEMONSTRATIONS

A. Strikes

After the imposition of martial law, a wave of strikes swept throughout Poland. At some workplaces, the strikes were ended forcibly by brutal police intervention. Below are descriptions of the most serious cases.

Martial law was declared on the night of December 12-13, 1981 (Saturday and Sunday). On Monday the Lenin Shipyard in Gdansk was surrounded by the armed forces. They refused to evict the strikers by force. An eyewitness gave this account:

> Although the shipyard is surrounded by armored carriers, tanks, on the vehicles and in the tank gun barrels there are flowers, and on the tanks there are SOLIDARNOSC signs in large letters; soldiers are drinking tea; they are being invited by the strikers to join them for meals.

Much of the information coming from all over the country indicates that the forces deployed to break the strikes were the ZOMO [motorized units of the militia], entirely obedient and especially trained for street combat. Regular army units were only used in the initial phase of the action (for example, for breaking down entrance gates) and for securing the rear.

During the night of December 14, the ZOMO broke into the Lenin and Paris Commune Shipyards, and most of the workers of the Paris Commune Shipyard left. The attack on the Lenin Shipyard was unsuccessful and it was repeated on Wednesday, December 16, early in the morning. Tanks rammed Gate No. 2, causing the guard's booth to collapse. People who were perched on the roof fell to the ground; there were some wounded. The army units pulled back and ZOMO entered the shipyard. Using truncheons and threatening to shoot, the ZOMO forced the workers outside the perimeter of the shipyard. About 60 persons were arrested.

On Saturday, December 19, the strike in the Gdansk port complex collapsed. That evening, the strike in the refinery was crushed. The strikers were forced to lie on the ground, face down in the snow; they were then beaten with truncheons and their hands were crushed. Some of the workers were handcuffed and taken away.

During the night of December 15-16, an attack was made on the Swidnik WSK Factory near Lublin. The workers offered passive resistance. After breaking down the fences with tanks, ZOMO forced out the workers using teargas, grenades, explosives and 75-cm long truncheons. They beat people with such force that fur-lined leather jackets were splitting, as were collar-bones and other bones. Eyewitnesses reported:

> During the second attack we could not maintain
> our formation. Resistance was broken first
> into a few, and then into many small groups,
> weakened, the more so since ZOMO left only the
> areas toward the main gain relatively free,
> pushing us in that direction, all the while
> beating us mercilessly, even the women. Those
> who put up the strongest resistance were

to the ground in the snow, and kicked in the
head, stomach, and ribs by several ZOMOs at
once, until the ZOMO officers intervened,
sending their men forward to finish up their
main job, which was to break up our group
- piecemeal.

In the Polkowice mine, the strike lasted until December
17. ZOMO units attacked using teargas and water cannons.
The miners who came out of the mine tried to make their way
into the town in a closed group and were doused with water
from the water cannons, in sub-freezing temperatures. Two
miners were wounded by explosives. Explosives and teargas
canisters were also hurled at a group of women (as in
Swidnik) who were trying to get close to the mine.

In Lodz, female workers at the Marchlewski Textile Works
abandoned their strike after several hours when they were
threatened with the arrest of their children.

On December 14, after an initial unsuccessful attack on
the Katowice Steelworks, ZOMO organized a display of beatings
of the people who stood outside the factory gates, including
wives and mothers who were bringing food to the strikers.
Then they kept the factory under siege, surrounding it with
tanks and armored vehicles. After ten days (December 23),
the strike collapsed and ZOMO entered the steelmill compound.
An eyewitness reported:

> Armored vehicles drove through the steelmill
> in a show of force. Then ZOMO gorillas came
> out of the carriers in droves, armed with riot
> shields and truncheons and also with tear gas
> and gas masks... not everybody managed to run
> away. I was told that the ZOMO chased people

towards the recreation building and there,
against the wall, they beat people while
forcing them to kneel in the snow, with their
arms raised. I also was told that people were
chased out of the factory showers, naked,
barefoot, onto the snow, and dispersed in
every direction with truncheons.

Of the 2,000 people who held out in the Steelworks to

the end, one third was placed under arrest for 48 hours.

The most drastic action of all occurred during the

pacification of miners at the Wujek Coalmine in Katowice.

The location of the mine contributed to the drama of the

developments which took place there between December 13 and

17. The mine is situated very close to the center of the

city and is surrounded on all sides by buildings. A busy

street runs along one of the walls surrounding the mine

compound, with heavy bus and car traffic; around the mine

there are many houses, which are part of the mine's housing

development. The population here is a close-knit,

established community. The entire mine compound is clearly

visible from the windows of the surrounding buildings. Thus

a "quiet" pacification of the establishment was not possible

and the military cordon set up around the mine presented no

obstacle to the observers and supporters of the miners who

were on the outside.

On Wednesday, December 16, tanks surrounded the mine.

One eyewitness account puts their number at 54. The local

population gathered at the gate (around 500 persons, among them many women and children) and attempted to block the access, but they were was dispersed with water cannons (temperatures were below freezing and there was a severe wind). Several women threw themselves on the ground in the path of oncoming tanks, but they were literally washed out of the way with strong jets of water from the water cannon.

The tanks proceeded to break down the walls around the mining compound in several places. ZOMO units armed with riot shields, helmets, truncheons and tear gas followed. The tanks began shelling the mine with blank cartridges. The whole area was enveloped and hidden from view by clouds of gas.

The ZOMO were attacked from the rear by a desperate, if small, group of people from the housing development, who threw back at them containers with teargas as well as stones and bottles. The miners defended themselves successfully with hammers, picks, chains and hot iron rods. They managed to grab three ZOMO men as hostages. The first attack was repulsed. It was then that the attackers and opened fire on the miners killing six of them on the spot. Those killed were:

> Zbigniew Wilk
> Ryszard Izik
> Jozef Czekarski
> Krzysztof Gize
> Roman Zajac
> ? Kopacz
> Andrzej Palka died on the way to the hospital.
> One person (name unknown) died as a result of
> injuries

Another person (name unknown) also died as a result
of his injuries

The three ZOMOs held hostage were released in exchange
for a promise given to the strikers that they could return
safely to their homes. Only later were 300 people arrested.

Another matter is the way in which ZOMO dealt with the
ambulances, nurses and doctors arriving at the mine. At the
first sound of shots, several civilian ambulances rushed to
the mine site. A struggle broke out between the medical
personnel and ZOMO over the wounded miners whom the ZOMO were
trying to finish off. Equally violent was the confrontation
over the bodies of those killed. Seven bodies were taken
away by ambulance, and for this reason the official news
agency reported that seven miners were killed in the Wujek
mine. These seven bodies were placed in the hospital morgue
and two hours later the hospital refused to turn them over to
the militia. During the autopsy it was determined that two of
the miners who died of shots in the abdomen could have been
saved if they had been treated sooner.

The following report on what happened to the medical
staff at Wujek came from the emergency care unit of a
hospital in Katowice, published by Fakty, (monthly
information bulletin of Solidarnosc, Mazowsze region, issue
No. 2, January 1982):

> Forces of order intervened while the medical
> staff was trying to administer aid to the
> wounded at the Wujek mine. Nine ambulance
> workers were beaten, and an ambulance driver,

Kopera, was detained and taken to an unknown destination. Another driver, Alfred Gowor, is in the neurosurgical unit, while the other wounded were treated in the surgical out-patient unit. The medical staff were forcibly dragged out of their ambulances, still in their hospital uniforms.

Wounded emergency and ambulance staff were: ambulance attendant Ilone Lykbo - general beating; attendant Olga Kabat - general beating; Janusz Soja - general beating; attendant Adam Zdyb - general beating; driver Janusz Majewski - general beating, head wound; driver Zdislaw Krawczyk - general beating; driver Andrej Kopera - detained; driver Edward Morawiecki - general beating; driver Andrej Gabor - in serious condition in the neuro-surgical unit. All of them were unable to continue their shift. In many cases, medical teams were prevented from helping the wounded. This happened, for example, with the resusci-tation unit.

A doctor from the first ambulance to arrive attempted to take the most severely wounded miners to the hospital: a ZOMO officer demanded that only injured ZOMO men be taken. When the doctor refused, the ambulance crew was beaten and a ZOMO driver took the injured militiamen in the ambulance.

Reports from several hospitals indicated that injured ZOMOs who were brought in for treatment were under the influence of narcotics. ZOMO losses: 4 killed, 41 injured.

On December 15 at the July Manifestso Coalmine, ZOMO units broke into the assembly hall where the coalminers had gathered. The ZOMO formed a tight ring around the miners, turned their backs to the group and started hurling explosives and gas-filled canisters over their shoulders into the midst of the miners. Panic ensued, and people started to break out of the ZOMO ring and to run for cover. The militiamen were beating all those they could catch. People scattered all over the place, some jumping out of the windows, slashing themselves on broken glass and falling straight on to the truncheons of ZOMOs lined up below the windows.

On Tuesday, December 15, ZOMO units beat up miners from the Staszic coal mine who had gathered at the miners' hostel. There were so many injured and wounded miners that they had to be taken to several hospitals all over the voivodship. At least 40 were brought handcuffed on stretchers to Rapty Slaskie. The ZOMO demanded that some of the wounded be handed back to them after receiving first aid. They threatened to take away all the injured. A firm stand by the doctors at the hospital forced the ZOMOs to back off. They left the hospital premises but stationed a tank at its door.

On December 15, after midnight, ZOMO units entered the Wroclaw Institute of Technology. About 100 militiamen rushed into the university classrooms where people were sleeping. They beat the strikers with clubs, and forced them to go from the second floor down to the ground floor. During this ZOMO assault, an engineer, Mr. Kostecki, died of a heart attack. ZOMO proceeded to chase everyone outside, in freezing temperatures. The people, some barefooted, some in pajamas, accompanied by the President and the Vice President of the University, and carrying the wounded, headed for the student dormitory building. On December 15, at 2:00 a.m.,

ZOMO, in full combat uniform, broke into the garages of the Municipal Transit Company in Nowa Huta. They terrorized the employees with machine guns, forcing them to sign military draft papers and go back to driving. Three persons were arrested.

According to all accounts, ZOMO units indulged in totally unscrupulous destruction of property and furniture in the establishments that they entered. In many instances, interiors were completely demolished. Witnesses of these scenes often described them as a "release of aggression." Suspicion has been voiced repeatedly, based on the observation of the unusual behavior of ZOMO men, that they had taken narcotics or other mind-altering drugs before going into action. Similar statements came from a number of doctors who had attended injured ZOMOS.

The last strike to collapse was at the Piast coal mine – without any intervention from the police. But as a result of exhaustion, lack of food, and a sense of hopelessness in further resistance, it was called off on December 26.

It is impossible to compile a complete list of those wounded and injured or to estimate the total, because many people were afraid to admit that they were injured, and medical personnel (with very rare exceptions) stood firmly on the side of the population, giving first aid and assistance without maintaining any records, and helping in every conceivable way. This state of affairs lasted throughout the duration of martial law. The list of those killed is, of, course, also incomplete.

B. Street Demonstrations

Solidarnosc was most reluctant to organize street demonstrations, because the strikes seemed to be a safer way of protest for the participants. During the period of martial law, after the pacification of workplaces and the evictions from factories, political protest was taken into the streets. Nationwide demonstrations took place during the first weeks of the state of war; on May 1, 3, 13; on August 31, and on November 10, 1982. There were also many local demonstrations. In each instance, the militia tried to disperse the demonstrators. The May marches were an exception. These proceeded without obstruction, probably because all the ZOMO were guarding the official state parade.

In other cases, the ZOMO intervened in a very brutal fashion. The demonstrators usually responded by throwing rocks and the demonstration would turn into a regular street battle.

Objections to the behavior of the militia are as follows:

1. ZOMO attacked everyone who happened to be within its reach, making no distinctions between active participants in a demonstration and ordinary pedestrians or bystanders, presumably acting on the premise that "anyone in the way is an enemy." Tear gas was hurled indiscriminately, not

necessarily at demonstrators, but at any group of people, for example, those waiting at a bus stop. The amount of teargas used was so great that in areas of particularly intensive ZOMO action (as for example, in the area of the Old City in Warsaw on May 3 and August 31), pedestrians' eyes were still watering on the second and third day after the attack. Homes of people living in the area were filled with tear gas.

The high concentration of tear gas even elicited protests by some official institutions.

> The chairmen of the the Polish Ecological Club, Prof. T. Szafer and A. Kalamus, addressed a lettter to the president of the city of Cracow informing him of the pollution of the environment and of serious danger to the health of the population posed by the use of tear gas on May 13. (Tygodnik Mazowsze, No. 20, 1982).

2. ZOMO units behaved as though all people were dangerous or could become dangerous. This point is well illustrated by an eyewitness account of disturbances in Gdansk on December 17, 1981:

> ...I could not leave the railroad station because an armored vehicle was driven onto the platform, hurling petards, spraying with some liquid and blowing tear gas around...I could not understand what was happening and why people were not being allowed to leave the station, and why the entrance had been blocked. There was nowhere to go —no trains were leaving for Gdynia although there were trains standing at both platforms, but the people from those trains were held up on the platforms...It turned out that a crowd of demonstrators in town was marching towards the shipyard, and the police were afraid that the passengers from the trains might join them.

The interesting point here is not that the train passengers were stopped inside the station, but that the station had been filled with tear gas.

The active demonstrators were, on the whole, young people who were physically fit. The ZOMO often turned on casual pedestrians when they could not get to the demonstrators.

> In Elblag, on May 3, the militia also attacked the public waiting at bus stops or going to mass at nearby churches. Tear gas was hurled at windows and balconies. In Szczecin, the militia attacked not only the demonstrators, but also people returning from work, waiting at bus stops, as well as students in dormitories. (Tygodnik Mazowsze, No. 13)

> On August 31, 1982, in Wroclaw, the militia dragged passengers out of a streetcar going towards Biskupin, confiscated their identification papers,then transported them to the part of town where street fighting was going on. There, the streetcar passengers were lined up in front of a ZOMO unit which was going to attack the demonstrators, and were used as a "live shield". All these passengers were later fined by the military tribunal for taking part in street demonstrations. (Tygodnik Mazowsze, No. 20)

> The most shocking scene: A slender, young girl came out of a building together with a boy, into a street which had just been "mopped up" - and the butchers [the ZOMO militiamen] were bored. After checking the young people's identity papers, the ZOMO man, in order to "chase" the couple, simply whacked them on the legs with his club and screamed, "Run, you bastards, or I'll kill you." The young couple started walking fast. This was not enough. "What did I tell you. Run, you whore." The young people started running. The ZOMO, however, decided that he should punish them and chased them. The boy ran faster and escaped, but the girl got caught. The ZOMO hit her over the head with his truncheon and

she fell. That appealed to a second ZOMO who
hit her in the back and then kicked her. Then
the first ZOMO picked the girl up from the
ground by her hair and hit her several times
with his club, in the face and over the head,
cursing all the while. The girl, crying with
pain and holding her hands to her bleeding
head, ran for down the street a way, chased
from side to side. The band of ZOMOs enjoyed
itself fully. Finally, they let her through.
(Cracow, May 13 - eyewitness account).

People not involved in demonstrations received injuries

and even died as a result of ZOMO activity.

The hospital branch of Solidarnosc in Wroclaw
reported several cases of hospitalization of
children on June 13 in very serious condition
as a result of gas poisoning. Tear gas had
been used that day against demonstrators in
the vicinity of Grabiszynska street. The
children suffered severe poisoning, some
required cardio-pulmonary resuscitation and
placement in oxygen tents.

On November 11, 1982, Tadeusz Czajkowski was
returning home with his mother. He was hit in
the back by an explosive, and went into shock.
He was diagnosed as having extensive
contusions and inflamation of the back
muscles. He was treated at the Bielany
Hospital in Warsaw.

Around 10:30 p.m., Krystyna Narona, 21, was
severely beaten as she was leaving work at the
bank on Main Square in Cracow. She suffered
facial and cranial injuries, including
lacerated skin over the eybrow requiring
stiches, and serious damage to her right eye,
caused by bleeding.

Wladyslaw Durda, an ironworker at the Szczecin
port authority died on the night of May 3-4
from tear gas poinsoning. During the street
demonstrations earlier that day, he had not
left his home. The apartment, however, became
filled with teargas from the street to the
point where around midnight Mr. Durda began to
choke. ZOMO militia stationed nearby in a
radio-equipped car refused to allow Mrs. Durda
to call an an ambulance. Mr. Durda died one

one hour later as a result of collapse of the respiratory system.

ZOMO attacked children, older people, the sick and even disabled persons, as indicated in the following eyewitness accounts:

> I was on a trolley, some time between 7-8 p.m. At the intersection of Krakowskie Przedmiescie and Staszic streets, I and the other passengers on the trolley saw two ZOMO men hitting an older woman on crutches with their clubs. Another ZOMO was beating an elderly man with his truncheon (Lublin, May 5, 1982, Bulletin No. 23).

> A 70-year-old woman was brought into the Eye Clinic in Witkowice. Her eye had been knocked out by a water cannon (Cracow, May 13, Tygodnik Mazowsze, No. 16).

> During the pacification of Nowa Huta on September 13, 1982, ZOMO sprayed a group of children coming out of a catechism class with a jet of red-dyed liquid. Twelve children were then detained for 48 hours - without notification of their parents - and were questioned and threatened (Actualities, No.35).

> In Wroclaw on August 31, 1982, ZOMO hurled explosives into a passing ambulance. The driver of the ambulance managed to jump out before the explosives went off. A woman was pulled out of the flames, which engulfed the vehicle.

> Two explosives were thrown at the Skarbowe Street Hospital in Cracow. One landed in the nurses' room in the Internal Medicine Ward; the second in the patients' room in the Neurosurgical Ward (Cracow, May 13, Tygonik Mazowsze No. 16).

Arrests were also made in an indiscriminate and haphazard way: people were taken from foodlines, bus stops - whoever happened to be around could be taken. Usually this was accompanied by brutal manhandling.

-220-

3. The militia used firearms to break up demonstrations. This happened at least three times in Gdansk, during the December 16-17, 1981 incidents; in wroclaw and in Lublin on august 31, 1982; and in Nowa Huta on October 13, 1982. ; The exact number of persons wounded by machine gun fire is not known, because of caution on the part of the victims and of discretion on the part of the doctors who attended them. the following, however, are known:

> In Gdansk, on December 17, 1981, the following were shot with machine guns by the militia: Antoni Browarczyk (23); Wieslaw Adamczyk (22) and Grzegorz Zakrzewski. Slawomir Dobrzynski (15) was wounded by an explosive. Antoni Browrczyk was fatally wounded and died of his injuries.

> In Lublin, on August 31, 1982, 18 people were shot with firearms, and 15 of them were wounded: R. Stefanowicz, J. Lac, A. Dudziak, Z. Hetka, M. Kwiatkowski, B. Wieczorek, K. Musin, H. Hudlewicz, L. Stefaniak, E. Wertka, N.H. Huzarowicz, S. Szewdzyk, J. Klopacz, M. Jablonski, Bortka). Three were killed: Andrzej Trajkowski, 32; Mieczyslaw Poznaniak, 25; and Michal Adamowicz, 26. Andrzej Trajkowski died before reaching the hospital, of a head wound from a bullet. Mieczyslaw Poznaniak was admitted to the intensive care unit already near death. The doctor who examined the body stated that a bullet wound in the back of the head was the cause of death.

From the accounts of other victims:

> Ireneusz Lac (shot wound in right knee): At 4:30 p.m. I suffered a shot wound while walking in the vicinity of the parish building. The shot came from a group of militiamen who were trying to disperse a crowd, from a distance of about 200 meters. It would be hard to hit anyone with a stone from that distance."

Edward Wertka (puncture wound at the back of
the right shoulder, a large wound in the front
of the right shoulder, the size of a ten-zloty
coin, bleeding profusely -which indicated that
the shot came from behind): "They shot at me
twice, once near the meadow, from a moving
police van, the second time close to the
parish building, as I was running. I felt my
shoulder give a violent jerk."

Andrzej Dudziak (shot in the back of the left
thigh): "I was sitting on a low garden wall
on Mieszko Street. I first felt -it was in an
instant -that I had a hole in my trousers, and
only then did I feel the pain."

Kazimierz Rusin (shot in the proximity of left
hip joint): "I was walking home with my wife
down Rzeznicka Street. This is at least 700
meters away from Market Square. The street
was empty. Suddenly I felt a pain in my left
thigh. My wife returned to the bus garage and
informed the manager, who then assigned a bus
to take me to the hospital. I didn't see
anyone and I don't know where the shot came
from."

As is apparent, at least some of the shots were directed
at casual pedestrians, far from the area of the
demonstrations (Market Square).

On August 31, 1982, Tadeusz Wozniak, 49, was
shot to death during a demonstration in
Wroclaw.

On the same day in Gdansk, Piotr Sadowski, 22,
employee of the Lenin Shipyard, died of head
wounds caused by an explosive.

On October 13, 1982, in Nowa Huta, Bogdan
Wlosik, 22, was shot to death.

Two other men were wounded: Y.T., 22,
employed at the Lenin Steelmill (facial bullet
wound with perforation towards the base of the
skull), and C.A., 29 (wounded in the palm of
the hand.

The circumstances leading to the death of Bogdan Wlosik
are as follows:

On the evening of October 13, 1982, the plaza
in front of the church in Nowa Huta was quiet
except for when a group of civilians attempted
to start a fight. It was obviously a
provocation intended to create a pretext for
the ZOMO to intervene. One of the priests
succeeded in restoring calm. However, a short
while later, during mass, a fight broke out
again. A civilian started to struggle with a
14-or 15-year-old boy. Someone in the crowd
shouted: "He is an ubek" [SB man]. The
civilian began to run away. Bogdan Wlosik (an
electrician at the Lenin Steelmill and 3rd
year student at the technical school for
workers) followed the man and almost caught
him, when the man turned around and shot
Wlosik point blank. He then escaped. The
time was between 7:10-7:15 p.m. The wounded
boy was placed on a church pew. The bullet
shell was found. After fifteen minutes an
ambulance arrived. Wlosik was taken to the
Zeromski Hospital, where he was not admitted
because the authorities had passed an order
that all those wounded during demonstrations
could be admitted only to the Military
Hospital or the militia hospital on Gallo
Street. He was already dying when was brought
to the Military Hospital, and probably died
during the initial phase of the operation.

Subsequently, on the spot where Wlosik was
shot, people began to place flowers and burn
candles. On October 15, ZOMO pacified the
houses nearest the spot. An eyewitness
reported:

"At 7:00 p.m., a great number of ZOMOs arrived
and tightly cordoned off the housing development - two large apartment blocks. Sixty
ZOMOs entered each staircase, i.e., six ZOMOs
per apartment. They moved all at once on
command. In groups of six, they entered each
apartment and demanded to know whether there
any non-residents on the premises. Regardless
of the answer, they searched the apartments
and the balconies. The residents were
forbidden to turn on the lights or stand by
the window. In the event of disobedience,
explosives were thrown inside the apartment.
If a non-resident was present, without even
being asked to show identity papers, he was

beaten up, kicked, and dragged off to a police
van. In such cases, apartment owners were
advised that they would be fined 50,000 zloty
for harboring strangers in their apartments.
Apartments were searched throughout the
entire night and the same apartments were
searched several times."

During the next days, ZOMO tried to block the
access to the place where Wlosik was
tragically murdered.

4. Interventions by ZOMO were, at times, very brutal - to
the point of causing the death of the persons manhandled.

During the demonstrations of February 13,
1982, in Poznan, Wojciech Cieslewicz, 28, was
beaten with a club or some other heavy
instrument. Medical examination indicated
brain and skull damage. During surgery,
trepanation of the skull, a blood clot had to
be removed with part of the damaged brain
tissue. The patient died on February 27
without regaining consciousness.

Adam Szulecki, 32, beaten on May 3, 1982, in
Warsaw, died on May 9 at the hospital in
Praga.

Malgorzata Lenartowicz, 20, resident of
Warsaw, Prozna Street No. 14, apt. 28, beaten
on May 3, 1982, in Warsaw; died in a hospital
on May 5, 1982.

Mieczyslaw Radomski, 56, on May 3, 1982, was
taken by ambulance from a place where ZOMO had
attacked a group of people (at the
intersection of Marszalkowska and
Swietokrzyska Streets), died on the way to the
hospital.

Wlodzimierz Lisowski, 67, died on July 13,
1982, of injuries received as a result of
being beaten on Market Square in Cracow on May
13. The immediate cause of death was a
perforation of the liver; the diagnosis on the
death certificate was cancer of the liver.

Stanislaw Krolik, of Bogulslawski Street, No.
22, apt. 66, Warsaw, was beaten on November

10, 1982, in Warsaw, near the Church of the
Holy Cross. ("A police van, accompanied by a
ZOMO patrol on foot, drove through the first
gate of the apartment building on Krakowskie
Przedmiescie Street, herding pedestrians into
the inner courtyard of the apartment complex.
ZOMO men then proceeded to beat the
pedestrians with clubs while those from the
van shelled the people with tear gas
grenades.") Mr. Krolik died in a hospital on
Bielany.

The brutality of the police forces caused minor and
major injuries to many people (both participants of
demonstrations and passersby. The medical services personnel
in Cracow compiled the so-called "Cracow Doctors' Report" of
cases treated by them, adding the following commentary to the
description of incidents taking place on May 13, 1982: "The
medical personnel is shocked and outraged by the exceptional
bestiality and cruelty of the militia and SB, to which the
defenseless population of Cracow has been subjected. An
extensive report on the terrorist activity in our city will
be submitted, together with a written protest to the
International Red Cross."

The number of people who, in Nowa Huta alone, received
serious injuries on August 31, 1982, was estimated by doctors
to be from 100-150. After the October 1982 demonstrations,
38 people were hospitalized as the results of injuries
requiring surgical intervention, in the hospital at which
Wlosik died

The murders committed by the ZOMO in addition to
the pacification actions must be enumerated separately:

On the night of January 31, past the curfew
hour, a ZOMO patrol stopped Tadeusz
Matuszynski, 25, and his brother-in-law.
After a blow on the head with a truncheon,
Matuszynski fainted and was thrown into a
police van. The blow on the head caused
hemorrage and death. His brother-in-law
suffered lesser injuries.

On the evening of May 13, 1982, on the steps
of a church on Fredro Street in Poznan, Piotr
Majchrzak, 19, a student at the gardening
school, was beaten up by ZOMO during an
identity check. He died a few days later in a
hospital. The SB came to the house
of a photographer who had been taking
photographs of Majchrzak's funeral and
confiscated the pictures and the film.

Stanlislaw Kot, an engineer at the Meat
Processing Plant in Rzeszow, died on April 3,
1982 as a result of brutal beating by the ZOMO
on March 31. He had been stopped at the city
tollgate in Rzeszow. After a few hours the
militia took him to the "sobering up" station
for alcoholics, which refused to admit the
battered and unconscious man. He died without
regaining consciousness at the voivodship
hospital where he was taken. The autopsy
listed several fractures of the extremities,
injuries of the spine, a broken jaw, brain
concussion and internal hemorrage.

C. The Fate of the Arrested Following Street Demonstrations

1. Circumstances of Arrest

Analysis of descriptions and accounts shows that in most cases arrests occurred beyond the immediate area where militia forces were deployed, i.e., beyond the vicinity of the demonstrations. Arrests often were made in places far from the hub of the demonstrations and were unrelated to it. There were also instances of arrests in trams and buses. This was the case on November 10, 1982,in Cracow. Here is an excerpt from the account of one of the arrested:

> ...the bus was stopped on Czarnowiejska Street several meters from the intersection with Mickiewicza Street by a ZOMO unit of at least a dozen or so men, armed with combat sticks and automatic guns. The ZOMO checked passengers' identity papers and then took away all the students.

Our materials indicate that brutal force against detainees was constantly used. It took various forms, depending on the instructions of the moment received from superiors on how to detain during and after the demonstrations, as well as on the attitudes of various militia and military men who were to carry out the instructions. Beating was an essential part of the arrest. People were beaten at the moment of arrest, they were beaten while inside militia vehicles, in jails, and in interrogation cells of militia headquarters - often very severely. The so-called "health paths" were the rule. They are best described by the following account of someone arrested in Gdansk on

December 30, 1981:

> It was in Pruszcz Gdanski. There we were
> shown what 'health paths' look like in
> practice. We were told to get off the car
> on the run and then came the shock. We had to
> run between two lines of ZOMOs who were armed
> with sticks, with police dogs trained to
> attack. The lane was wide enough to enable
> the ZOMOs to take hefty swings to hit people.
> So we had to run along that lane getting blows
> in our backs, heads and limbs. We had to run
> to the doors of the militia station, then up
> to the stairs, along the corridor to the hall
> where we joined about 150 others. Some of us,
> especially those weaker physically, fell down
> -and then others behind them tripped, and all
> of them were beaten, kicked and treated with
> most brutality...

There are similar reports from Warsaw:

> When we were at Wilcza Street the militia was
> pretty busy. We heard the sounds of blows,
> the cursing militiamen, and the cries of those
> beaten. After curfew, they brought a man for
> whom they prepared a run under sticks and then
> beat him until he lost consciousness. Even
> when he stopped moaning, we still heard the
> sounds of blows.

> ...then the arrested were taken to the
> Mostowski Palace [police headquarters].
> Inside, in the courtyard, the ZOMO formed two
> lines at the end of which stood two
> militiamen. The arrested were ordered to get
> off and were beaten with sticks as they ran
> between the lines. The two militiamen at the
> end of the "health path" were beating the
> runners at random with their fists. The
> people protected their heads and faces but
> some were not able to avoid the blows of the
> militiamen, who smelled of alcohol. One of
> the arrested got a blow in the jaw and fell
> down flat on the ground."(A report from KSMO
> Warsaw, November 10, 1982.)

Similar practices were used on May 3 and 4, 1982, at the
militia station in Elblag, Gdynska Street. The following

reports were given during a trial (June 21-July 5, 1982 at

the district court in Elblag) by the defendants in a summary

trial of participating in demonstrations: A. Kurek, L.

Skowron, R. Juzwuk, K. Kedzierski, D. Kucharski.

> "Health paths" for the arrested were used
> at the Gdansk militia station in Stogi on May
> 4 and on the same day at the militia station
> at Polnocna Street in Lublin; then on August
> 31 in the Wroclaw Voivodship Militia Command;
> at a Lubin District militia station in; in the
> Cracow Voivodship Militia Command on Mogilska;
> at the Katowice Voivodship Militia Command on
> Lompy Street, and at the Warsaw station
> on Wilcza Street, already mentioned, as well
> as the local militia stations on Walicow and
> Zytnia Streets and also at Cyryl and Metode
> Street in Warsaw. On November 10, "health
> paths" were set up in the courtyard of the
> KSMO in Warsaw and then at Wilcza Street.
> These are only some examples of places where
> "health paths" were used

Here are additional examples of beatings related to

demonstrations.

> On September 2, 1982, militia arrested
> seventeen-year-old Dariusz Rybka in Lubin. He
> was beaten on his way to the local militia
> station, and suffered a brain concussion. On
> November 10 in Warsaw, in the vicinity of the
> Church at Swierczewskiego Street, the ZOMO
> arrested Roman Koch, a worker at MZK. They
> took him to the local militia station at
> Zeromskiego Street. There he was beaten and
> as a result, suffered brain concussion, a
> ruptured spleen, and a broken leg. He lost
> consciousness during the beating. He was
> hospitalized at Kasprzaka Street.

> Due to the intensification of these kind of
> police practices in Gdynia on April 26, 1982,
> the Rev. Jastak, a priest at the Holy Virgin
> Mary Church, filed a complaint with the Naval
> Prosecutor's Office. The complaint had no
> effect.

> On May 4, in the Gdansk-Stogi militia station,
> people were beaten in the face and abdomen,
> kicked in the groin, and their heads were
> shaved. Both men and women were treated in
> this way. On that day about 70 arrested
> persons passed through that station.

Such militia actions resulted in very serious injuries,
sometimes in death. An example:

> On May 3, 1982, the ZOMO arrested 32-year-old
> Adam Szulecki in Warsaw. During
> transportation in the militia vehicle to the
> district militia station in Cyryl and Metode
> Street, the militia beat him on the head with
> sticks. He arrived at the station
> unconscious, and was not admitted to Praski
> Hospital until the next day. He died on May
> 9, 1982, without regaining consciousness.

Physical pressure used against the arrested is a violent
attempt to break any kind of resistance. It is also a way of
releasing the accumulated aggression that is stimulated in
many ways. It significantly affects the investigation, for
which it constitutes a peculiar psychological preparation.

D. Subsequent Fate of the Arrested

People arrested in connection with demonstrations
were:

a) released without any legal consequences.

b) directed within 48 hours from the time of the
arrest to misdemeanor courts and summarily tried.

c) released after 48 hours and tried routinely.

d) directed to regional courts within 48 hours
and tried summarily.

e) temporarily arrested, and after examination brought
to voivodship courts for summary trials (in

-230-

departures from summary justice in the course of examination - which happened very seldom - to regional courts, and tried routinely.)

What criteria decided the procedure according to which the arrested were tried? It is assumed that some people who were released without any further consequences consented to cooperate with the SB. The collected evidence also decided the fate of the arrested. Lack of any evidence against the arrested meant that the proceeding was usually brought to the misdemeanor court. If there was evidence, even doubtful or incomplete, the cases ended up in courts. Often, an accident or SB whim decided a person's fate.

1. Summary Proceedings in Misdemeanor Courts

Thousands of people were brought to the misdemeanor courts during martial law in connection with street demonstrations. We lack accurate data, but attempts are still being made to acquire it. The only indications come from official figures on those arrested and tried after demonstrations. On May 3, 1982, 1,372 persons were arrested in Poland ,of which 890 were brought before misdemeanor courts. On May 13, there were 636 arrested; charges were brought against 569 people. On August 31, 5,131 people were arrested, some faced trial; 3,328 were brought before misdemeanor courts. The following are statistics on the number of people facing misdemeanor courts in selected voivodships (after the August 31 demonstrations):

Katowice - 425; Warsaw - 402; Gdansk - 189; Szececin - 201; Przemysl - 34; Rzeszow - 130; Czestochowa - 184; Cracow - 59.

Below is an analysis of the verdicts of the misdemeanor courts related to the demonstrations of May 3, August 31 and November 11, 1982, in Warsaw. The analysis covers only a small part of the proceedings, and deals only with those cases where the misdemeanor courts determined arrest as a penalty and where as a result of the defendant's appeal, the case reached a higher court. This analysis, however, presents a sufficiently accurate description of the most important features of the proceedings.

E. Jurisdiction of the Misdemeanor Courts Dealing With
    Demonstrations of May 3, August 31, and November 11,
    1982, in Warsaw

The analysis which follows covers a small part of the proceedings conducted by misdemeanor courts for offenses in 1982. It deals only with those proceedings in which the courts used the penalty of arrest. We are unable at this time to give the total number of those who were sentenced according to penal-administrative proceedings. Certainly, however, that figure numbers several thousand people.

However, a detailed analysis of several dozen of these cases, with information from people who were in direct contact with the proceedings allows us to draw some general conclusions.

Anyone who has observed street demonstrations in 1982 knows how people were arrested. By and large, after the commotion was over, often a few hours later, young men were rounded up and put into nearby police vans. The large-scale nature of the arrests, and the prevailing confusion made it difficult to secure any evidence of "participation in the protests," not to mention the fact that in most cases, there could be no such evidence because pedestrians were arrested at random.

The defendants did not plead guilty in any of the cases we investigated. As a rule, local courts did not examine any witnesses, and did not have any specific "evidence," not even properly written citations by a militiaman on duty, which would contain specific descriptions of the behavior of the arrested.

An example:

> Miroslaw Niedbalka, 20 years old, a lathe operator and watchmaker, was accused of participation in the protest action on November 10 in Warsaw. He was tried by the misdemeanor court on November 12 by Halina Slabik, Krystyna Mileuszek, and Julian Michalski. He explained that he came to Warsaw to do some shopping. He was on his way back home, and was sitting with his friends on a bench at the entrance to the Central Station, waiting for his train, when he was arrested. The local court did not conduct any legal proceedings and sentenced him to two months of arrest, effective immediately. In the records of the proceedings, there is a scrap of paper without any stamp, with an illegible scribble, stating "reason for arrest: aggressive behavior in a crowd."

Here is the justification of the verdict: the
defendant participated in the demonstration in
Warsaw on November 10, 1982... He deliberately
came to Warsaw from Jozefow in the afternoon,
knowing that there would be riots. The court
did not accept the defendant's story that he
had come with his friend in order to buy
clothes, and that the place where he was
arrested was not crowded. The defendant
admitted that he went back home from work. Why
did he come back to Warsaw? Because he wanted
to see and participate in street
demonstrations; this is what the document
enclosed in the records says. There, the cause
of arrest is clearly stated: aggressive
behavior in the crowd; he did not leave the
place when called by the militiaman. When the
misdemeanor court handed down the verdict, it
did not find any extenuating circumstances.

Miroslaw Niedbalka appealed to the higher
court. During the trial, the court listened
to the militiaman who had detained him. He
confirmed all the circumstances described by
the defendant - that he was sitting on a bench
near the Central Station; that it was peaceful
in that vicinity; and that he could not say
anything more about Niedbalka's behavior. He
detained him because he suspected that he had
participated in the demosntrations. After the
militiaman was shown the above "document," he
admitted that he had not written it. The
court found him not guilty.

On the same day (November 12), the same group
of judges sentenced two of Niedbalka's
friends, who were sitting with him on the same
bench. They were Krzysztof Gec and Andrzej
Pokszysz. They received the same sentences.
The evidence against them was the same. About
Krzysztof Gec (22 years old, topographer, good
recommendations), the court stated: "The
guilt of the accused is unquestionable ... the
accused knew very well that there would be
demonstrations; that they would be taking
place late in the afternoon, and therefore, he
came to Warsaw."

The last of the three, Andrzej Pokszysz (26
years old, milling machine operator, never

prosecuted before) was given more attention. The entire statement as recorded read as follows: "The defendant's explanation that he did not intend to participate in the protests, and that his presence was totally accidental, cannot be given credence, because it does not correspond to other documents we have on file; therefore, we condclude that the accused came to Warsaw deliberately. The sentence given should be a warning for the accused against similar excesses."

The "documents" mentioned by the court are nothing but a piece of paper, the size of one-fourth of a copy-book page, without any stamp or legigible signature, and another piece of paper, slightly larger, also without a stamp or legible signature, a copy about the arrest without specified time or details about the behavior of the accused.

Krzysztof Gec and Andrzej Pokszysz also appealed to a higher court. During the trial, all three defendants described the so-called "health path" to which they were subjected at the militia station after the arrest. They had to run upstairs to the first floor while the militiamen kicked them and hit them with sticks. Then they were ordered to stand facing the wall with their hands up, and were further beaten and pushed around. The higher court questioned the militiamen whose names appeared on the "documents". The militiaman who arrested them stated that there were no gatherings in the place where the three were arrested. After he was shown the "documents" he said that he hadn't written them. Another militiaman whose name also appeared on the document testified that he saw the accused only after they were brought to the militia station.

A particularly dramatic situation is illustrated in the following case of a person accused and brought before the court for an event on November 10:

Stanislaw Zemierowski, 25, was a worker at the WSK in Warsaw. Since childhood, he had been under neurological and psychiatric treatment

because of a central nervous system disorder
that had resulted in mental retardation. The
court, made up of Jolanta Zawadzka, Henryk
Szumigaj, and Zdislaw Cibicki, sentenced him
to three months in jail, effective
immediately. A militiaman, Leszek Wawrocki,
was called in as a witness. He testified that
the accused was part of a group which did not
leave a gathering and which was shouting in a
hostile manner. The reasoning of the
court is as follows:

"The court did not give credence to the
explanations of the accused, that he had found
himself by accident in the protest group.
The accused had known of the actions being
planned in Warsaw and despite that,
had come into town, saying that he was obliged
to accompany his grandmother home. The
witness testified that the accused took an
active part in the actions."

Stanislaw Zemierowski explained before the
court that he had been walking toward the bus
stop when he was hit on the back by a blank
round. At that point, two militiamen wearing
helmets and shields, approached and stopped
him. There was no gathering of other persons
around him, only militiamen who were shooting
blanks at windows. When questioned in detail,
the militiamen said that it was already dark
when the accused was detained. The militiamen
was wearing his helmet, glasses, and
shield, which limited his visibility to
only a few meters. He saw the accused for a
few minutes - perhaps for only a few seconds -
and was unable to say whether the accused was
behaving in a demonstrative manner,
particularly whether he was shouting anything.
This case also ended with a not-guilty
verdict.

Jacek Lubas, 17, a third-year student at a
technical school, was detained along with two
of his friends on November 10, 1982, at
Grzybowski Square. He and the others did not
plead any guilty when brought before the court
(D. Waleczynska, J. Pawlowski, and Piwowar).
The court questioned Z. Bebnista, a
militiaman, who testified that he had seen a

crowd on Grzybowski Square, which was shouting
"Gestapo". He rounded up 30 individuals. The
court gave him an unusually mild sentence: 2
months in jail, suspended for one year. As
the court stated: "It is a fact that despite
the peacekeeping authorities' prior warnings,
there was no need to go on the street, he
had wanted to go to the movies in another
neighborhood. With this action, he disturbed
the peace."

Jacek's two friends, Dariusz Dalmanski and
Dariusz Gawronski, detained with him, were
brought before the court on the same day
(November 12). However, the militiaman
who arrested them presented no motion for
punishment in their case. Later that same
day, all three were brought before the court
and accused of the same action, but with
another legal qualification, and summarily
tried. All three were declared not guilty. In
the appeal process regarding the court's
sentence, the boys described the "health
path"to which they had been subjected at the
militia headquarters. They described how they
had been beaten and forced to sign a statement
of cooperation with the SB, stating their
willingness to report all that is taking place
at school. Two of them had signed such an
agreement earlier and had been rewarded with a
removal of their records from the court's
files.

One of the first - and quite unusual- cases to come
before a misdemeanor court in the first days of martial law
was the case of four students from the Catholic Theological
Academy in Warsaw.

One of the students is the son of
Nalecz-Jawecki, president of the Consumers'
Federation. The students were accused of
having participated in a protest action on
December 14, 1981, at St. Barbara's Church.
The Academy's classrooms are located at this
church. The boys were apprehended in front of the
the Church. In court, they explained that on

that date, they had arrived for a previously
scheduled meeting to discuss an upcoming
Christmas communion. They were not aware of
any protest actions. The court, acting on
"evidence" similar to the militia notes
described above, sentenced Nalecz-Jawecki to
three months of prison. The other three
students were sentenced to two months in jail.
The militiaman who had arrested the boys was
not questioned until the appelate court
hearing. He testified that he learned about a
protest action from an individual who refused
to give his name for fear of reprisals. This
informant pointed out to the militiaman
individuals entering the church as those who
were participating in a protest action. The
militiaman had not taken any other steps to
verify this information and did not know
whether, indeed, there had been any protest
action at the church. On December 28, 1981,
the boys were declared not guilty.

Several months later, on August 31, 1982, in
front of the same church -St. Barbara's on
Wspolna Street -Antoni Ostaszewski was
detained. He is a man in his forties, father
of three children, employed as an engineer at
the Polish Academy of Sciences. The court
found him guilty of having participated in a
protest action and sentenced him to three
months in jail. At the appelate court
hearing, A. Ostaszewski explained that he was
on his way to St. Barbara's Church when he saw
a melee, police interventions, and people
running away. He was left alone on the street
holding an icon. He did not run away because
that was not his habit. Instead, he prayed
that hatred might disappear from people's
hearts. He didn't hear any calls for
dispersal. As in the cases mentioned
previously, witnesses were not questioned
until the second court hearing. A militiaman
testified that he had arrived before the
church in a radio-equipped militia car. After
a while, an unfamiliar officer of the militia
brought the accused over to him. He was
holding an icon of Our Lady of Czestochowa.
The militiaman did not know what the accused
was doing prior to this time. He saw no
gathering before the church. The regional court

sentenced A. Ostaszewski to a fine of 20,000 zlotys.

Several examples from the events of May 3, 1982:

Andrzej Kostrowicki, 30, bookbinder and father of one child, described how he was detained at Aleje Jerozolimskie on the corner of Pankiewicz Street. There was no demonstration at that place, and no protest action. The misdemeanor court (J. Soltysiak, I. Rozbicka, and W. Grochowski) sentenced him to three months in jail. The grounds for the sentence were as follows:

"According to the accused, who pleaded partially guilty, and according to the evidence, particularly to the report of detention, the court concludes that he participated in a protest action at 8:00 p.m. Considering both the public and material damage, the court sentenced him to a jail sentence."

"Evidence" in this case (witnesses were naturally not called) is exceptional, even compared with similar cases. In this case, the evidence presented were two notes written the day following Kostrowicki's arrest, by two individuals other than those who had, in fact, arrested him. Each of the notes shows a different hour and place of arrest, while the accused gives still a third version of the time and place. The reason given for detaining him is "provocative attitude toward the forces of order". Both militiamen, allegedly authors of the notes, said honestly that they had first seen the accused when he was brought into militia headquarters. He was acquitted.

Zbigniew Brelak, 30, a worker, was stopped on May 3, 1982, just after getting off a trolley near the Slasko-Dabrowski Bridge tunnel. The court (K. Kuster, B. Mosiej, and S. Krzeminski) sentenced him to three months in jail without any court proceedings. In the file of the case there is a note on his detention, prepared by a militiawoman. This time, the court did not even try to "fine-tune" its explanations. It stated: "The court did not give credence to

explanations of the accused because it decided
that these explanations had been skewed in
favor of the defendant's own defense. Rather,
it pronounced its verdict, considering it
sufficiently mild."

When cross-examined in appelate court, the
militiawoman testified that while her
signature appeared on the arrest warrant, she
did not write it. She did not know the
accused, nor his name. She was also unaware
of who brought in the accused. A not-guilty
verdict was passed on July 20, 1982. However,
this case is particularly poignant because
Zbigniew Brelak had, in fact, already served
over two months in jail before the court
acquitted him.

Marcin Lizewski and Krzysztof Pustal were
taken into custody on May 3, 1982. Both went
before the court (M. Szczepanski, H. Wronska,
and K. Brodzinski.) Each received a
three-month jail sentence. The motives put
forth for the sentencing are unusually terse:
"Guilt was established on the basis of
evidence included in the case file." This
"evidence" includes warrants for the arrest
which lack signatures, as well as information
on place and circumstances of arrest. The
militiaman honestly testified that he had
written his report at the militia station.
However, he had not been on the street that
day and was not familiar with either of the
accused. The militiaman agreed that this kind
of "arrest report" is a patent lie.

There were similar circumstances in the case
of Krzysztof Tolloczka, a student, who was
stopped on May 3 on the Castle Square at about
1:00 p.m. He did not plead guilty. The court
(St. Filipiak, H. Hrynkiewicz, and
Pierzynowski) sentenced him to three months in
jail. The evidence, as above, is a note on
the arrest. It is worth remembering that the
May 3 events in Warsaw began at
approximately 4:00 p.m., while the accused was
taken into custody at 1:00 p.m. The court
cross-examined the militiaman whose signature
was on the arrest warrant. He testified
before the court, as had others in previous

cases, that his signature only "fronted" for
the document. On June 9, 1982, a verdict of
not guilty was pronounced.

Similar situations could be described ad nauseum for
dozens of other cases; these examples were chosen at random.
It is no accident, however, that these repressive criminal
proceedings, conducted by the misdemeanor courts, end in a
finding of not guilty. At the present time, it is impossible
to give exact figures, but there is no doubt that in the
majority of cases appealed to the higher court in Warsaw, a
finding of not guilty resulted. We are aware, however, of
other courts' decisions where fines have been substitutted
for prison sentences, and where the court used evasive
maneuvers in the form of returning the case to the
misdemeanor court for "completion of the case".

This solution was recommended by the legal authorities
in the form of a telex sent by the Deputy Minister of
Justice, Tadeusz Skora, to all the courts on September 1,
1982. He recommended that in cases where evidence was
lacking, cases should be returned in accordance with Art.
344, par. 1 of the Criminal Code. This "proposal" by the
minister gave rise to both amazement and amusement. Art.
344, par. 1 talks about returning a case to the prosecutor
with a request to supplement shortcomings in
the interrogation or investigation. But everyone who has had
dealings with the court knows that it conducts no
investigations and the prosecutor only occasionally appears

before it only at the time of the actual hearing. The
minister does not, however, explain how, in his opinion, one
can supplement something which never took place. In fact, it
could not have taken place according to the relevant
regulations, since inquiries and investigations are required
for felonies, but not for misdemeanors.

Court decisions on appeals from the misdemeanor courts
are legally binding, yet in many instances the Minister of
Justice ordered an extraordinary review of the findings. When
the court imposed a fine, it could only be appealed to
another, higher, court, where as a rule, the original
decision is upheld. When the accused could not pay his fine
on the spot, he was jailed at once to serve an equivalent
prison sentence. As a result, it was often better to be
sentenced to a jail term, since in the final outcome, the
time spent in prison could be shortened.

The situation changed somewhat following the events of
August 10-11, 1982, because of mass participation by defense
attorneys at the hearings before the misdemeanor courts.
Acquittals were given, although only sporadicially, and some
cases were postponed so that witnesses could be questioned in
person.

One defense attorney who participated in such hearings
reported that after assessing the attitude of the judges and
their level of functioning, he often gave up any attempt to

gain an acquittal, and concentrated exclusively on persuading the court that it should not impose a jail sentence of a fine but only a suspended sentence. He believed that in this way he could properly defend his client on appeal to the court while minimizing the damage.

The conclusion to be drawn from the above analyses are self-evident. The evaluation of the misdemeanor courts conducted in 1980-81 by the legal profession and others regarding the functioning of these panels is vindicated. At the time, demands were made that the courts be deprived of the power to impose prison sentences. The events of the past year have clearly demonstrated to society how right these demands were. The misdemeanor courts in other towns functioned in a similar way. In many instances, regional courts reversed on appeal the guilty verdict of the misdemeanor courts.

These aquittals, however, came after several weeks. In most instances, the accused spent this time in jail. As an illustration, we will quote lengths of time spent in jail by those found guilty by the Central Crakow court following the events of May 13 and 31, and those of August 1982, and later acquitted by the Cracow Regional Court:

1) Docket #II KWS 10/82/S - Ryszard Trzoska - held under arrest from May 13 to June 28, 1982 (about six weeks)
2) Docket #II KWS 14/82/S - Jerzy Wasik - held under arrest from August 31 to November 2, 1982 (more than two months)

3) Docket #II KWS 16/82/S - Tadeusz Pilecki de Leliwa - held under arrest from August 31 to September 23, 1982
4) Docket #II KWS 23/82/S - Stanislaw Kroll - held under arrest from August 31 to September 20, 1982

All of the above were sentenced under Art. 50 of the Misdemeanor Code: "he who fails to leave a public gathering despite an order by the appropriate authority is subject to imprisonent or fine." As the above examples show, the accused served almost their entire sentences before the appeal was heard, because of the lapse of time.

Altogether, the Cracow District Court heard 11 appeals of prison sentences imposed following May 13 and August 31 by the misdemeanor court. The four persons named above were found not guilty. In four other cases, prison sentences were commuted to fines, and in two cases, prison sentences were suspended, effective immediately. In only one case, the misdemeanor court's sentence was upheld.

The misdemeanor courts gave prison sentences relatively infrequently. This was definitely influenced by the fact that prison sentences can be appealed to a higher court but a fine cannot. The same end can be achieved if the misdemeanor court imposes a fine payable immediately and convertible to time in prison, if the accused does not have the means to pay. He then spends time in jail with no right of appeal.

This type of sentence predominated in misdemeanor court proceedings. Below is some statistical data on court proceedings after the events of August 31, 1982. This information is based on official sources.

Through September 18, the misdemeanor courts in all of Poland handled 3,194 cases relating to events of August 31. Of these, 263 persons received prison sentences, 2,821 were fined and no punishment was imposed in 110 cases. At this time we have no data on how many fines were converted to prison terms. The findings of the misdemeanor courts in the Katowice region give us a basis for estimating the total. Here, following August 31, 425 cases were handled. Prison terms were imposed in 12 of these and fines were handed down 399 cases. In 200 instances, a provision was made to convert fines to prison terms if the fine was not paid. Other examples: in Wrocloaw on June 15 and 16, 500 persons were sentenced by the courts for participating in June 13 demonstrations. In all cases, the sentences involved fines convertible to prison terms. The law allows the misdemeanor courts to impose a fine payable within three days of sentencing. The courts used this procedure only sporadically. As a rule, the accused had to pay the fine immediately upon prounouncement of the sentence, or he ended up in jail.

This is difficult since the accused rarely has the necessary amount and his family is not notified of the time and place of the trial. In some cases, the family does not even know of the arrest. They have to conduct a search for their family member, wandering from one police station to the next. In the meantime, the trial has already taken place. It should be noted that until June 7, 1982, the maximum fine which a misdemeanor court could impose was 5,000 zlotys. Later, legislation was passed (on May 26, 1982) changing some provisions of the Penal Code and the Code of Execution of Sentences and giving misdemeanor courts the right to impose fines up to 20,000 zlotys.

The payment of fines was made even more difficult in another way. On August 1, 1982, in several precincts in Warsaw, including Zoliborz, the militia and the SB detained people for 48 hours who came to pay fines if they were not members of the immediate family of the accused.

1. Court Trials Under Accelerated Procedure

Some persons arrested in connection with street demonstrations were brought before a district court within 48 hours of their arrest under summary proceedings and charged with various crimes. The most frequent charges were: resisting the authorities (Art. 235); insulting a militiaman (Art. 236); insulting an organ of the state or a political organization (Art. 237); showing contemp for, damaging, or removing a publicly displayed emblem, pendant, flag, etc. (Art. 284, par. 1); and public agitation to disobey or oppose laws or legal orders of an organ of the state (Art. 282).

A press spokesman of the Ministry of Justice referring to the events of May 3, 1982, stated that 81 cases were handled under summary procedures against people charged with crimes committed, "during collective violations of public order." Following other demonstrations, in particular those of October 31 and November 10, more than 100 persons were processed under summary procedures. In some areas summary proceedings were used only after August 31. This was true, for example, in Cracow. Sentences imposed in these circumstances varied widely, but unconditional prison sentences predominated. There were regional differences, however.

2. Court Cases Under Summary Procedures

There is not enough data to estimate how many people charged with participation in street demonstrations came before the summary courts. The most frequent charges were: active assault of a militiaman (Art. 234, par. 1), which in general meant a charge of participating in a street gathering where stones were thrown at militiamen; public agitation to commit a crime (Art. 280, par. 2); and the organizing and leading a demonstration (Art. 46 of Decree 2). As a rule, the court imposed sentences close to the minimum under the summary procedures, that is, three years of imprisonment. A few examples:

> The district court in Katowice sentenced
> Andrzej Komaniewski and Jerzy Szymoniak (under
> the summary procedures) for participating in a

demonstration on October 13 at Dabrowa
Gornicza, urging the burning down of the
Communist Party Headquarters, and calling for
the murder of Party members. Under Art. 200,
par. 2, the sentence imposed was three years
of imprisonment and two years of deprivation
of civil rights.

The district court in Wroclaw sentenced
Zbigniew Piechota to three years of
imprisonment and two years' deprivation of
civil rights under summary proceedings for
actively assaulting a militiaman on June 13,
1982, near Perew and Grabowska Streets in
Wroclaw. The same court sentenced Joseph
Chwalisz to four years of imprisonment and two
years' deprivation of civil rights for
participating in a demonstration and
assaulting a militiaman on the night of
September 13-14. The district court in Gdansk
sentenced Jerzy Warowny to three years of
prison and two years' loss of civil rights for
participating in a street gathering and
throwing stones at a militiaman.

A more detailed description of the summary court

procedures can be found in Chapter VI.

CHAPTER X

REPRESSION OF WORKERS

Repression of workers consists of the following: dismissal on the basis of various laws; refusal to hire a worker for a position commensurate with his or her qualifications; or refusal to hire at all; discrimination in pay and other benefits at the workplace; denial of promotion; transfer to a position which offers worse working conditions and lower pay. These forms of repression play an important role in the system of repression practiced by the Polish People's Republic. They are not as drastic as murders committed by government functionaries, or beatings, arrests, or internment. But the widespread use of these methods and the painful consequences make them a dangerous tool in the hands of the authorities for suppressing and destroying instances of opposition.

The figures below testify how widely this tool can be used. According to the statistics, as of December 31, 1982, 12,219,400 persons were employed in the public sector. Only 225,300 were employed in the private sector. (These figures were taken from the official Statistical Yearbook for 1982). Even prior to August 1980, deprivation of employment was used on a limited basis as a means of repression of members of social and political organizations which had not been permitted by the authorities. Since the state of war decree, this tool has been used on a scale unprecedented since Stalin's day.

At this time, we are unable to present complete, verified statistics reflecting the scope of this form of repression on a national scale. In our estimation, it reaches tens of thousands.

A. The Right to Work Under the State of War and Its Implementation

The legal basis for employment in Poland is the Work Code, enacted on June 26, 1974 (Registry of Laws No. 24/74, sect. 141); executive directives of the Council of Ministers; legal directives of the Ministry of Work, Wages and Social Affairs; and labor contracts signed on behalf of the employer by the Minister, and on behalf of the employees by a trade union.

The state of war brought some substantial changes in the area of workers' rights. The most significant change concerned militarization of many enterprises and institutions. With militarization, the legal status of workers then employed by these enterprises changed. According to Art. 186 of the law on universal obligation to defend the PRL, enacted November 21, 1967 (Index of Laws No. 18/79, par. III), persons employed in units which have been designated for militizarization are, from that day, treated as persons drafted into a military unit. Any pre-existing employment agreement is suspended for the duration of this service according to Art. 187 of this law. At the same time, a military relationship is established governed by relevant

provisions of the law. What were the consequences? Art. 189
of the law states that: 1) persons serving in a militarized
enterprise may not dissolve their employment contract
unilaterally; 2) the employer may dismiss the employee only
under the following circumstances:

a. upon finding the worker incapable of performing
   work;
b. upon reaching retirement age (65 for men, 60
   for women);
c. for other causes, with the agreement of the
   administration

Implementation of these regulations led to disputes
based on the right to appeal a decision to dismiss from
service. Two basic positions were developped. One held that
dismissal from service required a simultaneous dissolution of
the employment contract giving the opportunity of appeal to
the Appeals Commission and subsequently to the Labor Court.
The other held that dismissal from service automatically
dissolved the employment contract, thus rendering an appeal
to the Appellate Commission or the Labor Court impossible.
Further, a challenge of the decision to dismiss could only be
made in the form of a complaint to the governing unit. The
procedure was not standardized until February 27, 1983. At
that time, the Supreme Court, composed of seven judges, ruled
that the decision of a manager of a militarized unit is not
subject to control by any organ of appeal, i.e., the
Appellate Commission or the Labor Court. The result was that
all external oversight of the contract obligations were
eliminated in these institutions. A worker could be fired

indiscrimately without recourse, since complaining to the
military unit was futile. Nor did he obtain any support from
the trade unions, since they were suspended and prohibited
from carrying out their statutory activities. Moreever, this
problem affected all social security enterprises, not only
those which had been militarized.

According to the labor law code, decisions terminating
employment, with or without fault on the part of the
employee, must be made in consultation with the trade union
local. The procedures and methods of such consultations are
specified in the code. Because trade unions were eliminated
under martial law, all decisions concerning termination of
employment were left to the discretion of the manager of the
enterprise. Although in principle there were regulations
which permitted an appeal to appellate commissions and
employment tribunals (except in militarized enterprises), in
practice these regulations were unclear and it took many
months for the decision to be handed down, making them often
meaningless. Not since Stalinism have employees been so
completely at the mercy of the managers.

Attempts were made to remove all limitations on the
managers' freedom to terminate employment by a very special
interpretation of already existing regulations. This was
aimed primarily at employees who were full-time trade union
activists. In reality, however, this affected only those
active in Solidarnosc. Art. 39, par. 1 of the labor law
provides that "management may not terminate the employment

contract with a member of the trade union board or a trade
union delegate." This clause was not repealed either in the
martial law decree or in any other regulations. Clearly, it
was in the interest of the authorities to violate this
clause, for their intention was to remove the employees
active in Solidarnosc, who were protected by Art. 39, par.
1. Often termination was accompanied by an order prohibiting
the employee from physically entering the workplace. For
example:

> On December 17, 1981, at the CERABUD
> enterprise in Sochaczewicz, two Solidarnosc
> shop stewards were fired for "failure to stop
> fund-raising activities among employees" (The
> proceeds were intended for the family of an
> interned employee.) Any pretext for the
> authorities was sufficient.

> On December 31, 1981, at the Cefarm
> pharmarceutical enterprise in Warsaw, five
> employees, members of the Solidarnosc
> enterprise board, were fired. The written
> notice of termination included the order:
> "forbidden to enter the premises of the
> workplace."

> In February 1982, at the ZUS Center in Warsaw,
> nine members of the Solidarnosc enterprise
> board were given notice of termination as well
> as orders prohibiting them from working during
> the period of termination.

> On February 26, 1982, at the Wire Factory in
> Gliwice, the Chairman and Vice Chairman of the
> Solidarity enterprise board were fired.

During the first few months of martial law, the
appellate committees and employment tribunals exerted some
degree of independence by reinstating some workers. In
certain cases, actual termination of employment took effect

only after extraordinary review and decision of the Supreme Court. An example of such a case follows. (We quote excerpts of the findings of the District Employment and Social Security Tribunal in Warsaw in the case of Danute Baldog and Jacek Luzwa. The Supreme Court upheld the termination by sustaining the Tribunal, which had stated:

> Due to the suspension of trade union activities, the Supreme Court has found that...all regulations protecting union activists...are no longer in effect. Decree No. 31 of the Chairman of the Ministers' Council concerning the suspension of trade union activities will govern all matters connected to the protection of such suspended organizations, as well as matters concerning the rights of the trade unions arising from the labor law code. It is evident that Art. 39 cannot be enforced since it states that, in order to terminate an employee, the enterprise must consult with the trade union.
>
> The trade unions, however, have been prohibited from functioning. Yet nothing permits the non-adherence to the portion of Art. 39 which provides for two years' protection for union activists after they have ceased such activity..."

We know of many instances where the management failed to abide by the rulings of the appellate committees or tribunals which had reinstated terminated employees who were elected union activists:

> During the first days of martial law in December 1981, Andrzej Gryga, the Chairman of the Solidarnosc enterprise board at MERA -PNEFAL, and Jan Sakiewicz, a board member, were terminated without notice on the basis of Art. 52 for refusing to obey the manager's order to paint over a Solidarnosc sign on one

of the buildings, painted by an unknown
individual. The District Employment and Social
Security in Warsaw reinstated them at their
jobs, but they were not allowed to enter the
premises until the work inspector fined the
manager.

Bogdan Bujak and Ewa Dabrowska, workers at ZM
Ursus, were reinstated at their jobs. The
manager nonetheless issued an order barring
them from the premises.

On August 6, 1982, the Warsaw District
Employment and Social Security Tribunal
reinstated Jan Zdanowski who had been
terminated after the May 13, 1982 strike at RW
SWPP and SM in Wlochy. The manager refused to
abide by the ruling.

On July 30, 1982 the District Employment and
Social Security Tribunal in Lodz reinstated
Miroslaw Cieslakowski, a member of the
Solidarnosc enterprise board at the Central
Textile Research and Development Institute in
Lodz. Again, the director did not allow him
to return to work.

Despite their annoyance with this law, the authorities
continued to avoid repealing the clause, and instead,
circumvented it. As with the previously mentioned ruling
affecting militarized enterprises, the Supreme Court was
again utilized. On May 5, 1982, the Court issued a verdict
which was added to the written set of legal statutes on July
27, 1982. It said that Art. 39, par. 1, does not apply
where trade union activity is suspended. Though
reinstatements became less frequent, some of those mentioned
above were decided upon following this ruling.

The rulings of the appellate committees and employment
tribunals were at variance with the position of the

authorities. There were too many reinstatements, and the
decisions of the managers were too frequently questioned. On
May 18, 1982, at the Warsaw Voivodship Court, a meeting took
place on "basic problems in resolving employment-related
grievances" in which military representatives from the
Ministry of Justice (Colonels Kostrzewa and Dubiel) took
part. Judges were instructed how o rule in cases involving
strikes and Solidarnosc activists. In cases where the judges
ruled in favor of employees, they would be subjected to
disciplinary proceedings. Moreover, on July 23, the Chairman
of the Council of Ministers distributed a memorandum to the
ministers and voivodship heads, in which he recommended that
enterprise managers be required to denounce "faulty" (i.e.,
in the employeess' favor--Ed.) rulings by appellate
committees and employment tribunals; to provide prompt
analysis of existing reinstatements subsequent to December
13, 1981; and to demand extraordinary reviews in cases where
such rulings should be reversed due to their political
nature.

Another problem for the authorities was the dissolution
of the employment contract with full-time employees of
national offices of Solidarnosc and Rural Solidarnosc. In the
first six months, the authorities terminated many employees
of both trade unions. The official explanation was the lack
of alternative employment and, in the case of Rural
Solidarnosc, lack of resources to pay salaries. According to

our information, dismissals began as early as February 1982, when the staffs of the Malopolska Regional Headquarters in Krakow and the West Central Regional Headquarters in Lublin were fired. The staff of the Opole Regional Headquarters were handed dismissal notices in March. The staff of the other regions received their dismissals in turn.

Most of the dismissed employees appealed to the appellate commission of labor affairs, questioning the right of the special commission administrating Solidarnosc funds to dissolve the work contract between employees and the trade unions, which at that time had only been suspended, not dissolved. For many months, the appellate commission delayed hearings evidently awaiting directives on how to handle the cases. On July 15, 1982, the Supreme Court once again helped the authorities to dispose of a problem, this time with a union staff. It ruled that Fund Administration Commissions were fully within their rights in protecting union funds from abuse and encroachment and in dissolving the work contract of trade union employees who, because of the suspension of trade unions had no work to perform.

Meanwhile, the legal situation has changed substantially. On October 8, 1982, the trade unions, at that time suspended, were dissolved.

The essential goal of the authorities was to dismiss people who were not sufficiently obedient and subjugate them by depriving them of employment and a means to make a living. Two methods were used. The first was to verify employees in government units which were seen by the authorities as particularly important: the executive branch, the courts and the prosecutor's offices, the mass media, the education system and some research facilities. The second method was to use various forms of repression in response to protest and strikes, as well as dismissals recommended by the secret police when they suspected that an individual continued to engage in union activities and other forms of opposition.

B. Verification

This process was implemented during the first few months of the state of war by a special commission which reviewed employees' qualifications for keeping their present jobs. It was a unilateral process. The authorities were most interested in the employees' political and ideological attitude to the new (post-December) reality. Their aim was to obtain a loyalty oath, particularly in writing.

As an illustration of the process of verification, we will provide examples of what took place in the national administration offices and mass media offices, particularly at the Polish Radio and Television.

1. Administration Offices

The grounds for verification were contained in a directive issued by General Michal Janiszewski, Chief of Staff of the Council of Ministers, on December 17, 1981. It was addressed to all Ministers, Directors of Central Departments, heads of voivodships and all town mayors. The document was numbered OS 1/52/81 and contained the following:

> ... we demand a special commitment, dedication, and an unequivocal declaration of loyalty to the service of the Polish People's Republic from government employees. However, membership by some employees in the Independent Self-governing Trade Union Solidarnosc denies us this guarantee...For this reason, with a view to the real and complete implementation of the duties of government offices, at the direction of the Council of Ministers, I request that special conversations be conducted in the next three days with all employees of Ministries, Central Offices, Voivodship Offices up to the lowest level, who belong to Solidarnosc. During the conversations, they should be fully enlightened that membership in the presently suspended union is incompatible with employment in a government office...

A condition for continued employment was the signing of a loyalty oath with a simultaneous declaration of resignation from Solidarnosc. As a rule, refusal to resign resulted in the dissolution of the employment contract.

Some figures for institutions subjected to such verification: The Ministry of Communication had 250 Solidarnosc members: 120 refused to resign from the union and were subsequently fired. In the Central Administration Bureau of Public Highways there were 50 Solidarity members; 30 refused to resign and were fired. In the National Bureau of Standards and Measures, 17 persons were fired after refusing to resign from Solidarnosc. These three examples

were chosen at random. The principles and methods of

implementing verification were condemned by the Polish Roman

Catholic Primate Jozef Glemp, who sent a letter to Gen.

Jaruzelski which stated in part:

> ...as a result of the above-mentioned
> directive, verifications were conducted in
> national administration offices, the Judiciary
> and Prosecutor's Offices. A large number of
> people were removed because they wished to
> preserve their dignity and beliefs and would
> not renounce their membership in a legal,
> albeit suspended trade union...The nature of
> the directive as well as its consequences
> filled many Poles with bitterness and
> resentment...I am asking you, General, to
> cancel the directive cited . . . and to
> abandon the practice of obtaining declarations
> of will under duress and to reverse the
> consequences of this directive...

On March 24, 1982, the Deputy Minister of the

Administration of Regional Economic Affairs and Environmental

Protection stated in an interview (Trybuna Ludu, No. 70/82)

that the method of verification had been somewhat modified,

at least officially. "Work evaluation" was substituted for

verification. It was governed by the following criteria:

1. Ideological/political attitude
2. Moral attitude
3. Professional competence
4. Organizational and administrative skills

Despite this "purging" of the ranks of administrative

employees, an incident occured in September 1982 which, in

our opinion, says a lot about the methods and quality of

verification. Fourteen employees of the Legnica Voivodship Office were fired, who had turned in their Communist Party cards after December 13, 1981.

2. Polish Radio and Television (PRTV)

On December 13, 1981, all employees of PRTV were furloughed with the exception of specially-selected editorial and production teams. The first stage of verification lasted several weeks in March 1982. As a result, the employment contracts of 513 persons were dissolved. Of these, 299 were employees of Warsaw Radio. Additionally, 109 persons were removed from administrative posts, while 134 persons were placed on "circumstantial furlough" even though they were found to be qualified for continued employment. They were banned from entering the premises of the Radio. This information comes from Wladyslaw Lorenc, then Chairman of the Committee for Radio and Television Affairs.

In September 1982, stage two of the verification process was conducted. Employment contracts were terminated for 200-250 persons. We do not have detailed information on the scope of the verification process in local radio and television stations outside of Warsaw. In January 1983, an additional 50 persons were fired from the Radio.

The verification was conducted by a commission composed of members of the Party, the Army, and Radio management. As a rule, an SB man was also involved. All employees were interrogated. The interrogation dealt almost exclusively with Solidarnosc activities and the political realities of the state of war. The interrogators would deliberately ask leading questions, such as: "What do you think of the fact that Solidarnosc wanted to murder Communists?" Many questions concerned the fiscal affairs of union locals, posed so as to insinuate fraud.

C. Repressions Against Workers Who Participated in Strikes and Protests

Art. 14, par. 2 of the martial law decree states that participation by a worker in a strike constitutes "a grave violation of the basic duties of a worker." A "grave violation of duties" is grounds for dissolving an employment contract without prior notice through the worker's fault as stated in Art. 52, par. 1 of the labor law. Par. 2 of the same article imposes the same consequences if, during the duration of the employment contract, the worker commits a crime that makes it impossible for him to continue employment, if the crime is self-evident, or if it has been declared to be such by a court sentence.

The Labor Law, together with the Penal Code and the regulations concerning internment, were the basic tools of oppression used following the strikes, demonstrations and other protests. The threat of employment sanctions was one of the elements used to dissuade people from organizing or participating in any form of protest.

The state of war decree identified strikes as "a grave violation of the basic duties of a worker," but did not identify protest actions in this way. Nonetheless, in a glaring violation of this law, participation in a protest was treated as being equivalent to participation in a strike. Participants in such protest were fired for "just cause" being found (despite the law) guilty of "grave violation of basic workers' duties."

Employment penalties constituted a punishment for exhibiting opposition or participating in a protest prohibited by martial law. These penalties began being imposed immediately following the December strikes. In the Krasnik Roller Bearing Plant, strikers were ordered back to work on December 21. Then they all received notices of dismissal, after which the plant started rehiring workers on much worse terms. A similar action was taken at the Predom-Polar Plant in Wroclaw, where a special commission established by the manager and the military commissar issued new passes on December 21. Scores of people did not receive these passes for several days. In this way workers were intimidated by the manager.

Following strikes in the Katowice Foundry on December 28, passes were changed. No striking member of Solidarnosc received a pass;: about 300-400 people were fired for "just

cause." Later, the grounds for dismissal were changed to
"dissolution of the employment contract with no requirement
to work during the dismissal period." Other workers were
dismissed from their positions and transferred to
lower-paying jobs. About 2,000 persons were affected by
these various types of repression at the Katowice Foundry.
In the Ursus Plant, following a strike on December 14 and 15,
1981, about 500 persons were drafted into the Militarized
Factory Security Unit from a list specially prepared for that
purpose. The list contained the names of those suspected of
continuing union activities.

In the Silesian coal mines, all those who remained on
strike for more than three days were fired. In order to be
able to work again, each miner had to submit an application
to the manager requesting re-employment and a declaration
that he acted under duress, having been forced to participate
in the strike. One such application read:

> I am politely requesting to be excused for my
> absence from the 16th to the 23rd of December,
> 1981...I took no part in any protest. I was
> forced to remain in the mine by those leading
> the protest.

In the Piast coal mine, among others, the situation was
similar. Here, as in many other places, the management
resorted to a lock-out. This is an extremeley rare tactic
for a socialist country to use, but it was used repeatedly in
the beginning of the state of war. In the Warski shipyards
in Szczecin, after the strike was broken on the night of

December 14-15, 1981, work resumed on December 16. Since the situation was determined to be "explosive," the military commissar ordered a "suspension of production" on December 21, 1981. On the 28th, passes authorizing entry into the shipyard were changed. On January 4, 1982, the shipyard resumed production, with 1,500-1,600 persons having been fired.

The same procedure was also used in the Gdansk shipyards, where, at the end of December and the beginning of January 1982, production was suspended twice and all passes were changed twice. About 2,000 people lost their jobs. The primary form of repression was termination of employment but denial of bonuses and rewards, as well as transfers to lower paying positions,were also practiced following every protest, strike or demonstration. For instance, in the Ursus Plant, 30 workers were fired for laying flowers on March 17, 1982, at the monument commemorating the victims of the June 1972 strike.

During this period, a new method was invented at the Zremb Works in Warsaw, which would later be used in various factories, especially before a planned strike. After leaflets were distributed, the manager selected persons from each department, stating that they would be fired if leafletting was repeated and those who distributed them were not identified.

On April 28, 1982, the doctrine of "collective responsibility" was introduced in one work place. The militia arrested some employees at the Institute of Steering Systems in Sosnowce. It had been determined that Solidarnosc pamphlets, found on those persons had been printed on the Institute's typographic equipment. As a result, 62 Solidarnosc members were fired.

In March and April of 1982, persecution diminished despite continued protests. The authorities reversed their tactics following May demonstrations, particularly those of May 30. Repression of workers began to equal that of the first days of the state of war. In the Marchlewski Textile Works in Lodz, 35 people were fired following demonstrations on May 13, 1982. Over 260 persons were fired at the Communication Equipment Works in Swidnik. Workers there were summoned individually to the office, their passes were confiscated, and they were escorted from the premises in their work clothes. Middle and lower management, that is, master craftsmen and foremen, were forced to provide the names of those to be fired. Those who refused to do so were fired themselves. No special circumstances were taken into account, such as the fact that someone was close to retirement age or had many years of service in the factory, etc. In the Dolmel Works in Wroclaw, five persons were fired, about 100 received reprimands, and about 50 were denied their bonuses. In the Warsaw Passenger Car Plant, 59 persons were fired while 15 were fired at M.Z.K.

According to official data of the Ministry of Metal and Machine Production, concerning workers in their sector fired following May 13th demonstrations 798 people were fired immediately, with no prior notice; 311 were fired with notice and disciplinary steps were taken against 3,330, including 117 from management.

In May, for the first time, according to our data, repression was used against workers taking part in purely symbolic protests. Dariusz Taran was fired from the Lublin Truck Plant for lighting candles on May 13 in front of a plaque commemorating the events of August 1980. That same day a group of employees at Wola Hospital in Warsaw laid flowers in front of a commemorative stone. One person was fired and about a dozen received reprimands. In Lodz on May 13, Miroslaw Cieslewski, a Solidarnosc chapter member at the Central Institute of Research and Development for the Clothing Industry was fired for placing flowers in front of a display cabinet once used by Solidarnosc. On June 30, the Regional Employment and Social Security Court reinstated him at his job. Following a 15-minute strike at the Institue of Experimental Energy Automation, 70 persons were fired and the institute was "disbanded." In fact, the institute's name was changed and new people hired at lower salaries. Among those fired were people enjoying special protection against loss of employment under the labor laws, including women who were pregnant or on child-care leave. The law did not prevent the administration from deciding to fire them.

A change of tactics followed May 13th. Dismissals intensified in small enterprises and decreased in large ones -the reverse of what happened at the beginning of the state of war. The next major wave of repressions took place in August 1982, in connection with demonstrations commemorating the August 1980 strikes. One hundred workers were fired in Szczecin after demonstrations on August 15. The Communist Party Executive Committee in Szczecin prepared the list of those to be dismissed at a special session. At the meeting, departmental directors and party secretaries used magnifying glasses to identify individual workers in photographs supplied by the secret police.

In the Warsaw Foundry, 8 persons were fired and 80 persons received reprimands for participating in the laying of flowers at a cross located on foundry grounds on August 27, 1982. On August 31, workers at the Gdansk Railroad Repair Shop placed flowers in front of a cross located on railroad property. They said prayers, sung the national anthem and church songs after which they quietly dispersed. Several workers were fired. That same day B. Brzezinski was fired from the Jzestochowa Toy Factory for refusing to remove a Solidarnosc button. In the Wroclaw Hydraulic Factory, two departments were liquidated following protests on October 13.

The work crews were dismissed and had to apply for
re-employment.

About 250 people were fired from the Predom-Polar Works
in Wroclaw following a strike on October 13. A special
commission headed by the military comisar reviewed all
re-employment applications. As a rule, work in worse
positions at lower pay was offered. Some applicants were not
accepted for further employment.

At the Lenin Shipyard in Gdansk about 500 persons were
fired following strikes October 13-14. The shipyard was also
militarized. On November 10, about 100 persons were fired.
Fines were widely employed as well as denial of bonuses and
loss of one day's pay. So-called "performance bonuses" were
introduced for working a specific number of hours without
absence.

According to information available to us, those who were
fired face a bleak situation. It usually takes a long time
to find new work -often several months. The so-called
"wolf's ticket," a denial of employment for political
reasons, is used unofficially.

Those who had been interned are also affected by
repressive measures. Many of them cannot find any kind of
work, let alone work commensurate with their experience and
training. Others are denied employment in their
previously-held position. For example:

On August 24, Anna Walentynowicz was refused a
permanent pass to the Lenin Shipyard,
allegedly because she did not comply with
regulations (probably for refusing to sign a
loyalty oath). It was suggested that "until
the matter is reviewed the citizen will
receive a normal salary without reporting to
work." On August 30, she was arrested and
temporarily detained.

Until the state of war, Anna Kaczynska
was the director of the Social and
Professional Services Center in Torun.
She also held the position of Director of the
Cultural Department at Elana in Torun. She
was interned in December 1981. Following her
release, the only job offered to her was that
of an aide in the Social Services
Department.

We also have information that many former internees, who

had formally retained their employment contracts during the

period of internment, received notices of dismissal

immediately after leaving the interment camps. For instance,

in the Jeljczanski Car Plant, four people were dismissed in

this way in August 1982. These cases continue. Each day we

learn of new dismissals, so it is difficult to fully evaluate

this phenomenon.

Many persons were fired for reasons only indirectly

connected to strikes or protests. If the plant management or

the plant's SB suspected that a worker was continuing union

activity, was somehow engaged in opposition activities, or

could not be relied upon to be fully amenable and loyal to

the authorities, this was grounds for dismissal. This

happened primarily in industrial plants where, unlike

governmental institutions, no formal "verification" was made.

An attempt was made to get rid of inconvenient people either when a strike provided the opportunity, or by methods described above. The official reason for such dismissals was either reorganization, a reduction in the work force or an alleged infraction by the worker.

It is worth noting the role Resolution No. 169 played during the state of war. It was enacted on August 17, 1981, by the Council of Ministers and concerned benefits for workers who changed jobs in the socialized sector. Originally passed for a different reason, during the state of war, the resolution was the grounds for many dismissals for political reasons. A notation in the worker's employment documents of this resolution as the cause for dismissal served as a kind of code indicating the real reason for letting the worker go. In many cases this barred him from other employment opportunities.

D. The Secret Police and the Worker

The workplace in the PRL has always been a site of political confrontation. The authorities regard the political role of the party and the socialist youth organizations at the workplace as important as production. All enterprises, institutions and organizations are areas of operation for the SB. After the declaration of state of war decree, secret police (SB) cells increased their activities at all workplaces with reinforced personnel and supplies.

Their activities were downright ostentatious and, along with the omnipresent army and militia, constituted a "show of force." At some workplaces, people who had been regular workers were called in to work in SB cells, thus showing society that a systematic infiltration had been conducted for a long time from within and from below. For instance, in the October Revolution Polygraphic Plant in Warsaw, a lieutenant who was assigned to the local militia unit turned out to have been a printer's assistant long employed at the plant.

At present we have no exact data regarding this phenomenon, so we will limit ourselves to describing its goals and forms. The chief purpose of SB activity was to maintain constant surveillance at the workplace, particularly over people suspected of working for, or assisting, Solidarnosc.

Typically, SB cell workers are found in all divisions and departments of an institution. They attempt to engage workers in "voluntary" conversations. Searches of work sites, offices, cloak rooms, etc., are also made when necessary. Because these searches do not include "private" areas, they take place regularly without any warrants.

Plant SB and militia cells also conduct individual "talks" with workers whom they suspect are aiding the opposition. "Talks" are also held with those who are potential informers for the SB and militia.

Typically the manager of an enterprise or the worker's

superior orders the worker to go to these "talks" and the
worker cannot refuse.

Having two institutional functions (police and employer)
results in an informal work code for SB and militia agents
working in an enterprise. These agents do not work
officially, unlike the regular militia and SB.

A "citizen" therefore, is called in for a "talk," not a
hearing. He receives no written notice, no explanation and
proper procedures are not followed in the interrogation.
Typically, threats are made to lower wages or bonuses, or
firing or other suitable punishment is implied.

One of the chief functions of the SB and militia cells
is to recruit observers and informers and thus swell their
ranks. All talks, even chance encounters with workers, end
in a proposition to join. These are most often backed by
threats or promises of material gain.

Special methods of recruitment and infiltration in in
the universities have been established since martial law. In
1982, due to martial law, the service for enlisted soldiers
was extended. After leaving the service, a soldier could
enter the university without taking otherwise obligatory
entrance exams. In return, every two weeks the students were
called to militia headquarters and were asked to inform on
the faculty.

Steady pressure is also being applied by the SB
on members and activists of the Communist Party in

order to make them more dynamic in fighting the political
opposition.

The interrelations of the management, the SB and the
Communist Party is difficult to explain without exploring
the complicated problem of power in the Polish People's
Republic.

One thing is certain: the authority of the SB and the
militia at the workplace is enormous. They have a tremendous
influence on the management's policies concerning promotions,
demotions and firings. In personnel decisions, the opinion
of the SB (aside from political criteria) is the main
criterion of judgement.

One of the chief aims of the SB is the uncovering and
preventing independent actions. This is achieved by creating
uncertainty in regard to one's personal status at the work
place by instilling fear of losing work, by fostering
suspicion and enmity among workers, or between workers and
management, creating animosity among various work groups, and
so on.

The object is to hinder mutual assistance, cooperation
and trust. Another way in which this is achieved is by
creating an impression that the SB is omipotent. Repeatedly,
SB agents and militia let it be understood that they are
not bound by legal standards, restrictions, or any other
limitations. This strategy is designed to make the worker
think that his environment is composed of spies, informants,

collaborators, and people who are corrupted or threatened -a
world in which only force prevails.

E.   The Assumption of Secret Police and Militia Functions
     by the Management and Other Professionals

It can be observed that sometimes, the management and
Communist Party units at enterprises assume the repressive
roles of the SB. The principle of cooperation between
ordinary citizens and the for agencies the preservation of
social order in Poland was extended to include not only
informing on criminals, but also on anyone aiding the
opposition.

People connected with the party-government apparatus are
natural allies of the security organs. This is also true of
management people who hold some political clout - political,
economic, and administrative officials, and others who might
benefit from such cooperation.

Supervisory and management functions in factories,
schools, and offices that depend on organization, and
efficiency have been "enriched" with repressive
responsibilities and duties, carried out in normal situations
by specialized servants.

Supervisors on all levels are obliged to inform the
security apparatus about situations at work and the behavior
of particular people. One of the additional duties is the
detection of possible leaders of and prevention of organized

protests through cooperation with the security apparatus.

Information on these modes of operation is obtained from the underground press. Some examples:

> The Regional Appeal Commission in ZMB Sabinow re-employed 13 previously dismissed workers. Management of the enterprise is leading a campaign to enforce the dismissals. Those particuarly active are: Directors Wodzislawski and Noculn. Personnel executive Sliwczynski, and the Communist Party unit secretary.

> On May 13, 1982, Director Kosecki, of the Center of Electronic Projects and Implementation in Warsaw summoned persons wearing Solidarnosc buttons to his office. He locked those who refused to remove their buttons in a room and called for the militia. Later he personally took down names of those who were striking at noon. (Tygodnik Mazowsze No. 15/82).

> On May 11, 1982, Roman Czajkowski, economic director of the Mathematical Machines Institute in Warsaw, along with the SB, conducted talks with employees and threatened them with internment. On May 13, 1982, at 12:00 p.m., Mr. Czajkowski walked out into the corridor and urged people to disperse, in addition to revealing to the SB the identity of one of the employees who engaged in a discussion of issues with him (Mazolsze Weekly No. 15, 1982).

> Kazimierz Witkowski, Vice President of the Ethnographic Museum in Warsaw, interrogated all employees who took part in the May 13, 1982 protest.

It would be a mistake to generalize that the entire managing cadre in our country gave in to pressure and behaved this way. Nevertheless, such pressures continue to be employed. One risks bitter consequences for refusing to yield to pressure:

At Elgel, a foreman was dismissed for refusing to report which of the workers wore Solidarnosc buttons (<u>Conspiracy Action</u> No. 23/32. September 12, 1982).

At the end of November 1982, a militia unit, along with the Communist Party secretary, visited the village of Lawolnicz Naleczow and demanded that all crucifixes be taken down from the walls. The director, upset by the pressure, died at his desk.

Similar incidents occur frequently. Communist Party activists and regular members are asked to play similar repressive roles. They perform these functions out of their own pre-conceived and rationalized notions, for the sake of the "ideological struggle."

F.   Methods of Action, Threat of Punishment

Employees suspected of active or passive sympathy with Solidarnosc, oppositional activists or often plain members of Solidarnosc were interned; party members who turned in their party membership cards and others who might potentially aid the opposition are submitted to various procedures as illustrated below.

a) <u>Threats</u> are used against individuals or groups: On December 12, 1982, in a Bialystok power plant a compulsory meeting took place with an army colonel who informed those present about Soviet army units passing through.   At this meeting,the colonel pointed out that if law and order were preserved (i.e., if there were no protests, bulletins, etc.), there would be no need for the Soviets to pass through.

Thus, besides the security police, the management and party officials, threats are also used by the army. It should be noted, however, that the main target in workplaces are individuals, who are threatened either with established forms of punishment or work-related punishment, either for themselves or their families.

b) Difficult or troublesome employees were often transferred to lower, lesser-paying positions with greater health hazards. Some new workplaces were located far away from their companies' branches. Such occurrances are not frequently mentioned in the underground press. The archives' documentation is also fragmented. Such information, however, is contained, for example in the FAT bulletin (Wroclaw, No. 16, 1982).

> Mr. Grochalik was released from internment and re-employed on December 17, 1981, as an inspector for the work safety division. The position carried a lesser rank and pay than the position he held before his internment.

> In comparison with the deluge of other more "serious" and harsh punishments such forms of repression did not carry much weight.

Nevertheless, financial or hierarchical demotion has a strong influence on peoples' behavior. It creates a constant feeling of fear and insecurity. An added problem was that there was no way to protect oneself from eventual consequences.

c) A more refined form of persecution is to shift an employee from one division to another, or from one position to another. This happened at the Lodz Elgal, where a Solidarnosc member was pressured in such a way to resign his employment.

A similar case took place at a Warsaw power plant, where both a female technical advisor and a male rationalization expert were repeatedly transferred from one building to another, until the man was transferred to one of the more distant divisions.

At some plants, this practice affects large groups of employees, especially those which are suspected centers of opposition. The aim of this practice is not only to create a feeling of insecurity and fear, but also to break down an employee who, like the one in Elgal, finally resigns voluntarily. Such practices are designed to atomize and alienate workers. They disrupt existing ties, disperse informal groups, propagate distrust, and spread beliefs about the prevalance of informers.

d) At some plants, it is made difficult or sometimes impossible for some employees to move around freely on the plant's grounds. At the very beginning of the state of war, many employees who were regarded as "unsafe" received obligatory vacations. Their passes were confiscated to make it impossible for them to enter factory grounds. Solidarnosc activists whose work required movement within the plant were watched particuarly closely.

In one of Lodz's weaving plants, a technician who was an elected Solidarnosc leader was followed by two security agents on plant grounds. They were also employees of the plant.

In Elgal, there is a secret doorman's book with an order from the plant manager forbidding Solidarnosc chairmen from entering the plant on the 13th of every month. Solidarnosc activists were assumed to be the leaders of protest actions at plants, based on the fact that they appeared for work on the 13th.

e) One of the methods of paralyzing Solidarnosc activism in the workplace was reorganization of the personnel, to surround the Solidoarnosc worker with trusted SB agents. Some reorganization took place in order to remove specific persons from managerial positions.

At the October Revolution Printing Plant in Warsaw, two divisions were merged and one foreman's position was eliminated. The foreman also happened to be a Solidarnosc leader.

These practices are the most numerous; at the same time they are the least known to the outside observer. They create the basic reality of life which typically is not worth mentioning when one has to deal with prison sentences, internment and use of firearms against demonstrators.

Long ago, political life in our country became distorted. This is related to the monopolistic position of the Communist Party. Lately, the distortion in political life has increased much more rapidly. Lenin's slogan "each party member - an amateur police agent" has begun to be implemented especially strongly since the imposition of martial law.

As a result, in the consciousness of many Poles, the political struggle is identified with the tracking down and repression of people regarded as enemies or potential enemies.

In this context, the word "struggle" takes on a literal and physical meaning, expecially in the workplace.

CHAPTER XI

REPRESSION OF THE PRESS

Repressions against journalists started on the very day
that martial law was imposed (December 13, 1981). Among the
thousands of people interned the night of December 13, were
over 100 journalists working for Solidarnosc press, for the
state radio, TV and from the Polish Journalists Association.
(SDP). Efforts were made to intern the governing body of SDP;
however, Mr. Maciej Ilowiecki (Vice President of SDP), Mr.
Jacek Kalabinski (President of the Warsaw chapter of SDP),
Mr. Dariusz Fikus (General Secretary) were not arrested,
despite the fact that the warrant to intern them had been
issued. The secretary of SDP, Mr. Krzysztof Klinger, who
suffered from serious heart disease, (he died in 1983) was
interned for a short time (12 days). Several members of the
council of PHA were interned: Mrs. Janina Jankowska (after
her return from abroad in January 1982), Mr. Piotr Zaluski,
Solidarnosc activist in Wroclaw TV, Mr. Piotr Mroczyk and
Mrs. Alicia Maciejowska, Solidarnosc activists at Warsaw TV.
In May, more than 40 journalists were still interned, the
last of them being released in December 1982.

The imposition of martial law brought the closing down
of all press and broadcasting programs except for one radio
program, informational TV broadcasting, two nation-wide newspapers, Trybuna Ludu and Zolnierz Wolnosci, and 17 provincial

-282-

party papers. All other newspapers and periodicals were suspended for several months, and then only gradually allowed to publish after the verification of their personnel. Radio and TV were militarized and their buildings were taken over by the army. Radio broadcasting services were taken over by a "bunker-studio" situated in military barracks in Warsaw and manned with particularly trusted journalists. The majority of the staff was put on leave. They were not admitted to the buildings of radio and TV stations, and they received 75% of their average monthly salaries, but not exceeding 10,000 zlotys, the average wage in the industry.

The verification in radio and TV took place in two phases. First, six-person committees composed of representatives of WRON, the Central Committee of the Party, Voivodship committees of the Party, Ministry of Internal Affairs, local committees of the Party, and the administration of radio and TV interrogated all higher ranking journalists: editor-in-chief, deputy editors and managing editors. In the second phase, three-person committees (composed of the editor-in-chief, a representative of WRON, and a representative of the local party committee) verified all the remaining journalists.

Ad hoc committees in the press comprised representatives of the Security Forces, the army, the party, the management of the publishing houses, and editors-in-chief. This verification had no legal basis. The jurisdiction of these committees was not spelled out in any document. Their

composition was not confirmed by anyone. Their decisions
could not be appealed. Only in the final period of their
work was the possibility for appeal created. The
verification was a de facto interrogation. It took
especially drastic forms in some areas, such as, for
instance, Katowice, Szczecin and Gdansk. In Katowice, the
interrogating committee placed the individual being examined
in a specially prepared room for the cross-questioning (the
committee was sitting on a raised platform around the
"culprit," who was seated in the middle). Questions often
touched on personal matters. For example, one journalist in
Katowice was reproached for having been married in church and
for giving a religious education to his children.
Journalists were forced to testify against their colleagues.
They had to evaluate their own work and to compare it with
that of their colleagues. Standard questions pertained to
assessments of the governing board of SDP, and to evaluations
of SDP and Solidarnosc activists. Journalists were forced to
make confessions, they were humiliated and often insulted.
Not only had the journalists to pass through this
verification procedure, but the members of technical
services, secretaries, and lower personnel of radio and TV as
well. This is described in another chapter. In total,
10,000 people had to participate in this action. The
verification started in January and went on till March. In
those months, some publications began reappearing. Polityka

-284-

resumed publication on February 20, <u>Przekroj</u> on February 21,
and <u>Slowo Powszechne</u> on February 19-21. In consequence of
verification the following penalities and sanctions were
inflicted: dismissal from managerial position (in RSW
"Prasa" 60 editors-in-chief were replaced; in TV, 20
directors were replaced), demotion, prohibition to occupy a
managerial position, prohibition to work in a specific
publishing house or newspaper, prohibition to work on party
papers or on publications of the party publishing house RSW,
and finally, prohibition to work at any publication or in TV.
As a result of the verification about 1,200 journalists were
fired, another 1,000 were demoted or otherwise punished,
moved to new positions, pensioned off, or forced to apply for
early retirement. Taking into account the fact that the
number of journalists in Poland totals about 10,000 (before
December 1981 SDP encompassed about 9,000 journalists), it
means that 20% of the journalists were repressed and 10%
dismissed. In some places the purge went even further. In
Gdansk, where the press employed 156 journalists with an
equal number being employed by TV, 60 people were fired, 20%
of all employed. The situation was similar in Katowice,
Wroclaw and Lodz. It was the greatest purge of journalists
since World War II.

Several dozen of the interned journalists left Poland
with one-way passports, without the right to return to
Poland. Another dozen are waiting for passports. In

principle, this option is open only to former internees and to those who were persecuted.

Besides verifying people, a verification of publications also took place. Some publications were closed down, for example, the very popular weekly Kultura, which resumed publication as a monthly. The weekly Czas, published in Gdansk, which became famous for its coverage of the August strikes was closed down. In some weeklies, the entire staff was changed, for instance, in ITD.

The journalists, exposed to such strong individual pressures, were simultaneously deprived of their legally acting professional organization. SDP was suspended on December 13, 1981, becoming one of the first organizations to be suspended. Suspension meant "oligatory relinquishment of all statutory activities." Security forces interrogated several times the secretaries of SDP urging them to give up all their activities. Seals were put on the SDP offices at 3/5 Foksal Street and they were closed; the assets of SDP were at first administered by a military custodian and then were confiscated. The permanent personnel (more than 60 people) were dismissed and secretaries of SDP, elected and delegated to work at SDP were sent back to the publications where they had worked before. The library of SDP was plundered, all the emigre press collected for many years was confiscated, as was the complete collection of Solidarnosc publications. It was one of the few complete sets of the so-called independent "circulation"

-286-

press, published without being consored.

From the first days of martial law, the activists and the authorities of SDP and especially its president, Stefan Bratkowski, were publicly attacked. This campaign was launched by unknown individuals from Rzeszow who expressed their opinions on TV on December 23, 1981. It was continued in subsequent TV programs by a group of journalists from Poznan. The leadership of SDP were accused of being subordinate to Solidarnosc, of politicking and neglecting the important problems of their members. The same arguments were used in justifying the decision to dissolve the SDP, published in the press on March 19. This decision was preceeded by three months of continuous repressions (internments, arrests, interrogations and searches). For instance, activists of SDP were repeatedly visited at home, the secretaries, Mr. K. Klinger (interned); Mr. Jacek Ratajczak and Mr. Dariusz Filus were interrogated.

The following is an appeal to the members of the SDP:

> We appeal to you in this dramatic moment on behalf of persons in our profession: the decision on dissolving SDP was reached despite our efforts to resume dialogue. This decision follows upon groundless and illegal repressions which have been directed against our profession for several months. The regular channels for public communication have been interrupted, many papers are still suspended, the broadcasting of many reliable programs on the radio has not been resumed, and the journalists are subject to the so-called "verification," which is demeaning and contrary to the law. 'Vigilante courts' deprive journalists of the right to practice

their profession. Especially those who are respected by their colleagues as well as by their readers and listeners, whom they wished to serve. We emphatically protest against the illegal accustion that SDP conducted activities contradictory to the interests of socialist Poland. We did not conduct activities other than those to which we were obligated by the resolutions of the Extra-ordinary Convention of Delegates and our statutory regulations. That Convention decisively pronounced itself in favor of regaining for our profession credibility and public respect. It pronounces itself against the ruthless use of the media for social communication as tools of primitive propaganda, and demanded a guarantee that the slogan 'The press lies' would never again apply to our profession. The governing body of our Association, elected during this Convention, was then obligated to do its best to make every member of our organization observe the Journalists' Code of Ethics.

The decision to dissolve SDP was appealed. In this appeal, attention was also drawn to the fact that the decision violated the regulations of the Code of Administrative Procedures, especially its Article 10 p.1:

SDP was not given a chance to take part in the procedure, in particular, it was not allowed to voice its opinion on the collected materials and evidence;

and Article 61:

SDP was not informed that the administrative procedure had been instituted. The regulations concerning evidential procedure were also violated. No evidence was submitted to support the allegation that SDP did not implement its statutory goals.

The appeal did not bring any result: Minister Kiszczak sustained the contested decision. Neither did we receive any answer to our appeal of the ruling which was submitted to the Main Administrative Court.

Protests against such a treatment of journalists were submitted to General Jaruzelski by many journalists. Protest letters were sent from Warsaw, Cracow, Gdansk and Lodz. They totalled several hundred. Fifty of the 73 elected to the leadership at the Extraordinary Convention protested against the dissolution of SDP.

Two deputies of the Sejm, Karol Malcuzynski and Edmund Osmanczyk posed interpellations on the method of dissolving SDP. Under the pressure of public opinion, the authorities admitted that the method of liquidating the Association had been brutal, but that they had no intention of changing their decision, and they persist in their allegations of antisocialist and enemy activities on the part of SDP.

On the day after the dissolution of SDP, a new organization was created, strictly subordinated to the party, called the Association of Journalists of the Polish People's Republic. By February 1983, this organization had not elected its leadership and its convention is not expected earlier than the middle of 1983. Recruitment to this organization takes place under pressure, and is ordered by editors-in-chief. Thus, it is treated as the last phase of verification.

CHAPTER XII

HIGHER EDUCATION IN POLAND ONE YEAR AFTER THE

IMPOSITION OF MARTIAL LAW

A. Background: Higher Education Between August 1980 and
   December 1981

In September 1980, locals of the new independent trade
unions were established in all the larger universities and
colleges. In October 1980, locals of the Independent
Students' Union were established as well. These unions set
the tone for university life for the next 15 months. In
addition to taking part in national and regional actions
initiated by Solidarnosc, the academic unions worked on
introducing into universities and colleges. The three most
important events from that period are as follows.

1) Drafting and submission to nation-wide discussion
of new higher education bill:

The draft law in the form presented to the ministry by a
committee chaired by Professor Resich was treated as a
binding law by the academic community. The whole of academic
life conformed to it and any deviation from it caused protests in the community (e.g., the procedures in the election
of the president of the Engineering College in Radom caused
lengthy strikes at almost all universities and colleges in
the country).

2) Signing of an agreement in Lodz between striking students and the minister of science and higher and technological education:

The most important elements in that agreement were the changes in the proportional representation of students in collective bodies, increased freedom for universities and colleges in writing their own curricula, the abolition of the compulsory study of Russian and changes in the existing ways of teaching socio-political subjects.

3) Creation and activity of the university presidents' conference:

The Presidents' Conference acted as a governing body for institutions of higher learning. The Conference represented the universities and colleges in dealing with the minister and the government and made decisions concerning intra-mural affairs (the best example was the decision to admit all students of the disbanded Firefighters Academy to technical institutes). It also fulfilled arbitration functions. The Presidents' Conference was dissolved even before the imposition of martial law. By that time, authorities in almost all the universities and colleges, both individuals (presidents, deans, chairmen) and collective bodies (senates, department councils), were democratically elected. The percentage of students in collective bodies was in conformity with the Lodz agreement. Work on new statutes and new curricula was started in all institutions of higher education.

The academic community had achieved until December 1981, new forms of autonomy, self-government, and democracy. Thus the declaration of the state of war had multiple consequences in all aspects of academic life.

Statements made at the seventh plenary session of the communist party central committee on February 24-25, 1982, regarding higher education illustrate the attitude of the authorities towards this issue:

> How should we regard our intelligentsia? The experience of the past few months indicates that many of them sold out to the political opposition. We have many examples of this, for instance, the Congress of Polish Culutre, which the workers called the "witches sabbath," the Conference of University Presidents...(J. Grzesniewski).

> All ambiguous attitudes of superficial loyaly - and we still see this in our schools with regard to the people's state - represent unforgivable harm to the country. So it is necessary, even indispensible, to conduct a review of teachers.... The question has to be asked: will teachers, former Solidarnosc activists, returning to their communities, carry out the tasks of a socialist school? (Z. Gebska)

> Social criticism is not aimed at education as such; it is aimed at the educators who have who have forgotten what their duty is in the socialist Polish state (T. Malichnowski)

> In schools and colleges, intellectual freedom cannot become a screen for anti-government indoctrination. In a socialist country, the university cadre may not be permitted to become a foreign branch of Western, anti-communist institutions. (E. Lukasik)

B. <u>Legal Regulations On Education During the State of War</u>

The December 13, 1981 state of war decree had the
following effects on education:

- All activities of organizations and associations were
  suspended.
- All assemblies were prohibited.
- Many employees and students were arrested or
  interned.

In addition, a Council of Ministers decree suspended
classes in all schools in the country (daytime classes, night
school, and extension courses). Classes were resumed
gradually starting with the extension courses and night
school. Only later were daytime classes resumed in
individual schools. The last to reopen were day classes at
the University of Warsaw, on February 8, 1982. On December
16, 1981, a detailed ministerial directive was sent to
university presidents:

- Employees only, upon presentation of valid ID, are to
  be allowed on school grounds. Others, including
  students, must obtain permission from the appropriate
  organizational units.
- Faculty members are to be assigned to entrances of
  buildings. They are to check everyone who
  enters the building by verifying the name of the
  person entering, the person to be visited, and the
  time of entry and exit.

- Schools are to open at from 8:00 a.m. to 4:00 p.m.
- Offices belonging to unions, societies and
  associations are to be locked and sealed, as were all
  photocopying, reproduction, and amplification
  equipment.

The schools were subjected to these regulations until
the day classes resumed. After that, the January 9, 1982
regulation went into effect, concerning "Functioning of
Schools of Higher Education During the State of War." The
most important features are as follows:

- Higher education was again to be regulated by the
  decree of October 5, 1959.
- Individual, not collective, responsibility for
  governing the school was resumed.
- Faculty senates and departmental councils were to
  have an advisory role only.
- No members of suspended organizations or students
  could participate in meetings of collegiate bodies.
- All academic and scientific papers had to be
  submitted to the censorship office prior to
  publication.
- Educational programming was subject to decisions
  of the Minister of Education prior to the
  beginning of each semester. This included the
  methodology to be used in implementing programs,
  etc.
- the role of self-government and students'

organizations was taken over by representatives
appointed by presidents and deans;
- "Temporary Regulations on Studies" and
  "Temporary Regulations on the Functioning of
  Dormitories" were introduced;
- the re-evaluation of research work was
  recommended;
- work discipline was increased; the president
  obtained the right to assign an employee with
  tasks beyond his duties and to order him to
  work on legal holidays;
- because of the suspension of trade
  unions, all personnel decisions were made
  unilaterally and without consultation;   .
- typographical equipment was operated only with
  permission from the Ministry of Science and
  Higher and Technological Education and under
  the presidents' control;
- employees were allowed on campus during
  working hours only. Students were allowed on
  campus only during classes and library
  business hours.

The provisions of the "Temporary Regulations on Studies
under the Jurisdiction of the Ministry of Science and Higher
and Technological Education" of January 8, 1982, introduced
the following changes:

- attendance at all classes planned as part of
  the curriculum was compulsory; those who
  missed classes without legitimate excuses were
  threatened with sanctions, including
  dismissal;
- for violation of martial law regulations,
  students could be dismissed by the president,
  without disciplinary procedures;
- the number of supplementary exams was reduced
  to one, with an additional exam before a
  professorial body;
- on matters which were not covered by the
  regulations, the ultimate decisions were made
  by president.

Although studies were resumed, security guards at
building entrances continued to be in place. Business hours
at universities and colleges were increased from 8:00 a.m. to
8:00 p.m.

The Independent Students' Union was outlawed by an order
of the Ministry of Science and Higher and Technological
Education. At the same time the activity of the Socialist
Union of Polish Students was resumed. Thus it became the
sole legal representation of students.

The Ministry's order of March 31, 1982, introduced new
"Rules and Procedures for Foreigners' Arrival in the Polish

People's Republic in Matters of Science and Technology under Martial Law." The following are among the most important provisions of that order:

- the number of visits was limited;
- the first criterion was conformity of the visit's purpose "with the state policy's goals and the interest of the PRL;"
- all visits of foreign guests had to be coordinated with the Ministry and applications for visits had to be filed at least two months ahead;
- foreigners who are citizens of the states with which the PRL does not maintain diplomatic relations were allowed to come to international events only;
- these rules did not apply to visits by citizens of socialist states.

On May 4, 1982, the Sejm passed the law on higher education. Its basic content is in accordance with the prior draft but some important changes were introduced. The most important limitations are:

- the functioning of the Council of Higher Education as an advisory, rather than as a legislative body controlling the executive authority (the minister), as the draft suggested;

- the minister's unlimited veto in filling the
  elected university presidents' positions;
- the president's or minister's right - depending on
  the level - to recall elected individuals;
- the minister's power to introduce changes into the
  university and college statute that are not agreed
  upon by the senate.

In early June 1982, orders concerning the verification
of faculty came to institutions of higher learning. This was
an extra-professional re-certification. (Professional
re-certification of personnel is conducted in all
universities and colleges every year and does not apply to
full professors.) The basic criterion was political
attitude, as could be seen from a questionnaire that was
distributed, and in the guidelines for verification. The
verification campaign took various courses in different
universities and colleges. The more renowned academic
institutions were generally less affected. "As a result of
the staunch opposition of the academic community, an
interpellation was even made in the Sejm after which the
Minister of Science and Higher and Technological Education
relented somewhat in his guidelines" (Tygodnik Mazowsza, No.
21, July 14, 1982.) But at the Warsaw Polytechnic, for
example, 38 people were selected for dismissal and 302 were
transferred to other positions or were conditionally retained
(Tygodnik Mazowsza, No. 21).

At Silesian University, the local verification committee prepared 50 dismissal notices, based on lists compiled by Department Councils SB guidelines, included were all the internees, Solidarnosc activists and those who left the United Workers' Party (PUWP). In addition, President S. Klimaszewski unilaterally made a decision on further expulsions. The lists of those fired included about 100 people i.e., about 10 percent of the faculty. At the Silesian Polytechnic, about 200 employees were fired and the Institute of Theoretical Physics was disbanded. Other "rebellious" institutes were deprived of their independent status. All the dismissals were of a political nature. Those expelled were forbidden to work as teachers anywhere in the country. The verification there was directed by Professor M. Starczewski, appointed president in 1983 (Szeptem, July 12, 1982).

The re-certification campaign was intensified in connection with protest actions undertaken at various universities and colleges. In such cases, direct forms of reprisals were applied. On the whole, most President's Committees were able to defend their employees. This was the case, for example, at Warsaw University and in that university's branch in Bialystok.

The highest collective bodies at universities and colleges passed resolutions critically assessing the re-certification campaign.

The removal of inconvenient professors was not only done by the ministry of higher education. It was supported by party cells and military offices at universities and colleges. A document of May 12, 1982, entitled "Long-term Actions," presented at party cells meetings, envisions "the verification of all university and college employees and the assessment of the leading personnel" by "committees adhering to the principle of hierarchy," with the participation of representatives of the military and the Ministry of Science and Higher and Technological Education (by June 25, 1982) and "the assessment of personnel's fulfillment of educational functions" under the leadership of party cells (by August 15, 1982) as well as further changes in the leading personnel at universities and colleges "to ensure such personnel that would guarantee a complete fulfillment of the authorities' policy" (by August 15, 1982). This document was issued after the Sejm had passed the higher education law, May 4, 1982, that ensured basic autonomy for institutions of higher learning.

The verification continued at some academic institutions. of higher learning. As the underground periodical BI Malopolski (No. 29, November 30, 1982) reported, seven more people were fired from Silesian University.

Towards the end of June 1982, the Ministry established rules for admission for the first year of study. They included the provisions that soldiers who had completed three years of service be admitted without entrance examinations. Other rules remained unchanged in comparison with previous years.

On September 1, 1982, the Military Council of National Salvation, reacting to the demonstrations of August 31, 1982, recommended that "the organs of state administrations, particularly ministers of higher education and general education, urgently examine matters connected with unworthy behavior of adults and minors and make appropriate decisions" (Rzeczpospolita, September 2, 1982).

"Resolution No. 189 of the Council of Ministers of August 30, 1982, on Ensuring Public Order in Universities and Colleges" was published in the September 6, 1982 Monitor Polski, No. 21, item 183.

The most important paragraph of that resolution, No. 3, point 1, says: "In the event that a student is sentenced by a court or misdemeanor court for the acts defined in Arts. 46, 47, 48 and 50, par. 1, of the martial law decree, the president is to remove the punished student from the students' register."

Resolution No. 189 requires some commentary:

1. The final clause (par. 4) saying that "The resolution goes into effect on the day of its passing" makes it a retroactive legal act of a repressive nature. Thus the resolution undermines two basic legal principles: nullum

crimen sine lege (no crime without law) and lex retro non agit (law does not apply retroactively). The juxtaposition of the dates mentioned above with the final clause illustrates the repressive nature of the resolution as regards the students who participated in the August 31 demonstration, and who, on that day, could not yet have known the additional punishment introduced by the as yet unpublished resolution. Another quite telling fact was that Resolution No. 189 was prepared only after September 1; as is known from reliable sources, the meeting at which this resolution was passed in its final form, after a motion from the minister of higher education, was held as late as September 6; its original version called for even wider repression.

2. Art. 6, par. 1, and Art. 57 of the December 12, 1981 martial law decree (Legislative Journal, No. 29, item 54) were given as the legal basis for Resolution 189.

Art. 6, par. 1, empowers the Council of Ministers to pass necessary resolutions "in order to protect public order, the state's interest and citizens' rights," i.e., preventive resolutions. Resolution No. 189 does not include any provisions of this type; on the contrary, it includes repressive provisions and delegations, retroactively effective, vis-a-vis participants in the events that already had taken place.

Art. 57 states that "while martial law is in force, all regulations concerning the matters regulated in this decree and in the acts issued on its basis are suspended if they are contrary to the decree. The decree promulgated on December 14, 1981, suspended the regulations issued before that date but it could never suspend the still nonexistent regulations, i.e., the regulations of the law of May 4, 1982, on higher education, (Legislative Journal, No. 14, item 115). The regulations of that law, as a later act, cannot be suspended by an earlier act, i.e., the martial law decree, according to the principle lex posterior derogat prior (a later law abrogates a prior one). This also cannot be done by any act of a lower nature, as the Resolution No. 189 or a ministerial act illegally authorized by it.

3. The Sejm passed the law on higher education in the fifth month of martial law. Thus the Sejm, aware of an emergency situation, passed a law introducing autonomy for schools. In particular, this law does not provide for the president's right to punish students by expelling them for participating in public demonstrations, or to suspend their student rights immediately after penal procedures are started against them (par. 3 of the Resolution refers to suspension for the period while the procedures are pending).

The automatic expulsion imposed by Resolution No. 189 utterly contradicts the provisions of Chapter 3, Art. 106ff of the May 4, 1982 higher education law which went into effect September 1, 1982.

4. In passing Resolution No. 189 without any legal basis (see above, point 2a,b), the Council of Ministers not only violated martial law but, most importantly, violated the May 4, 1982 higher education law. The Sejm, as the supreme organ of authority in the PRL, has been ignored and thus the Executive Branch has usurped the right to cancel provisions of a Sejm law by any arbitrary act.

5. The martial law decree provides for penalties for violation which are defined in detail in Chapter VI. The punishment of a student by penal or administrative means does not constitute, according to Art. 110 of the higher education law, an obstacle in also undertaking disciplinary procedures against him. But, as indicated above, Resolution No. 189 imposes on presidents the duty of applying additional punishments which are not provided for in the martial law decree for specific acts done outside the school The introduction of such punishments violates not only the basic principle of penal law but also the International Covenant on Civil and Political Rights (Art. 101, par. 2) according to which any person accused of committing a crime has the right to be considered innocent until proven guilty by law.

6. Resolution No. 189 contains (par. 1, sect. 2) a delegation of authority to the Minister of Higher Education

to "define detailed rules of activity for universities and colleges during martial law." This delegation is as unlawful as the resolution itself, and it allows the minister arbitrarily to restrict further the higher education law, including Article 15 concerning the maintenance of order and safety on the campus.

Such a threat is contained in the paragraph on "the establishment of conditions for a full completion of provisions of Art. 24 of the martial law decree" concerning the activity of the militia and other bodies destined to protect order.

7. Resolution No. 189, while illegally suspending disciplinary procedures and entrusting presidents with the meting out of extra penalties (point 4), indicates in sect.3, par. 3, that "the procedure of presenting and examining appeals to the minister is regulated by the code of administrative procedure." But this code does not apply to disciplinary matters.

8. The May 4, 1982 higher education law, Art. 217, point 1, and particularly Art. 228, provide that: "Until such time as executive orders provided for in this law are issued, the regulations of the existing legal acts remain in force if they do not contradict the provisions of this law." Resolution No. 189, dated August 30, 1982, basically contradicts the provisions of the law on higher education which had been in force since September 1, and does not have

a legal basis even in the martial law decree (see above, point 2). It does not have legal force from the beginning and can be justifiably defined as an act of lawlessness and terrorism. A similar legal definition must pertain to all executive regulations based on this resolution.

On September 7, 1982, Order No. 28 of the Ministry of Education reached the universities and colleges, reminding them that "Temporary Guidelines" and "Temporary Regulations on Studies" were still in effect.

On November 1, new scholarship regulations came into effect, considerably limiting the access to fellowships and study for people living outside academic centers.

On December 10, the Minister of Science and Higher and Technological Education issued Order No. 255, disbanding all students' organizations and associations and creating the possibility of a new registration of national and local organizations by the minister and the president of a given institution of higher learning. To be registered, first of all an organization must have a statute conforming to the law, in particular "to the constitution of the PRL and must recognize the leading role of the PUWP in building socialism and the principles of the PRL foreign policy."

An order concerning the principles of admission to the universities for 1983 has recently reached academic institutions. It maintains privileges for soldiers who have completed their basic military service.

As can be seen from the above register, there have been a great many regulations in the period of martial law. It is impossible to discuss them in detail. What unites them all is their frequently repressive nature and the fact that they always limit the autonomy of academic institutions. They appeared in a peculiar way - first in the mass media, and then only did they reach the institutions of higher learning. This happened even in the case of establishing the dates of entrance examinations in 1982, which admissions committees learned from newspapers.

C. Unofficial Interference by Authorities in the Life of Academic Institutions

In addition to many official orders, a whole system of unofficial pressures and actions operated during this period. Obviously there are no documents on this subject and it is very difficult to determine exactly the scope and dimension of unofficial actions by the authorities. But it seems important to include in this report the factors that contributed to the atmosphere of the past year in academic institutions.

There were three avenues of pressure: through ministries (first of all the Ministry of Science and Higher and Technological Education), party authorities and the security service of the Ministry of Internal Affairs. Ministerial pressures primarily involved:

- changes of incovenient heads of academic
  institutions i.e., mainly presidents and
  deans whom the ministry tried to persuade
  to quit. At the start of the 1982-1983
  academic year, the total number of
  presidents dismissed was 20, from the
  following institutions: Warsaw
  University, Poznan University, Wroclaw
  University, Gdansk University, Torun
  University, Lublin University, Silesian
  University, Cracow Polytechnic, Wroclaw
  Polytechnic, Szczecin Polytechnic,
  Bialystok Polytechnic, Czestochowa
  Polytechnic, Gliwice Polytechnic,
  Radom Engineering College, Rzeszow
  Engineering College, Poznan Agricultural
  Academy, Wroclaw Agricultural Academy,
  Bydgoszcz Agricultural Academy. Gdansk
  Maritime College, Warsaw Special
  Education College

The president of the Warsaw Academy of Fine Arts died
during martial law.

A whole arsenal of methods was used to force
resignation; the most frequent was the threat to dissolve
whole departments or even institutions.

- the verification as planned by the
  ministry, including distribution of lists
  of people who ought to be dismissed;
- the expelling of students, mainly of
  activists of the autonomous movement and
  the Independent Students' Union.

Party actions were performed through university and
local college party calls. Threats and blackmail were
frequently used. One method was to make announcement of
decisions that were never carried out. For example, at a
meeting of the PUWP Warsaw Committee then First Secretary S.
Kocioek announced that presidents of seven institutions in
Warsaw would go. Of these, four are still holding their
offices.

A separate subject is the activity of the SB. The direct
form of action was internment and arrest (284 employees
and 394 students in 19 institutions). Other overt actions
were:

- the pacification of academic institutions
  during the December 1981 strikes (in
  Gdansk, Lodz, Wroclaw);
- searches on campuses, both in school
  halls and dormitories;
- the appointment of hall proctors by the
  SB;

- operations (using tear gas) on the campus
  during demonstrations.

Besides overt actions, there were activities which are more difficult to register and which are only indicated by protest resolutions from academic communities:

- interrogations and "talks" with employees
  and students, chiefly to intimidate the
  community;
- forcing people to sign collaboration
  pledges through psychological and
  physical pressures, including
  intimidation and beatings;
- provocations in dormitories;
- detention of mostly young people, who
  looked like students, during street
  demonstrations;
- surveillance of individuals and whole groups.

One of the examples of use of force and intimidation was the arrest of Dr. Jan Hutny, a member of the Solidarnosc leadership at the Wroclaw Agricultural Academy, during his tenure hearing in the Senate Hall in front of the president.

D. Education Under Martial Law: Schools

In the schools, methods are used that are designed to create an independently functioning repression system, directed both against teachers and students. The Ministry of

Education issued a recommendation on May 5, 1982, to: (1) remove principals in schools where "illegal" demonstrations of students took place; (2) to suspend and start disciplinary procedures against teachers who took part in such demonstrations or inspired them or who otherwise favored the violation of legal order (3) to penalize students, including through expulsion from school (from Reduta Lordon, No. 15).

The ultimate aim of a repressive system is to create a situation where everyone is afraid of everyone else. The teacher will be held responsible for his students, and if that does not help, the principal will be held accountable for anything that happens in the school. Thus, the higher you are in the bureaucratic structure, the higher the anxiety of having to answer for things you have limited control over. The principal has no choice but to hold the teachers under him responsible for "everything." The teachers, in turn, will do what they can to make the whole class responsible for controlling the acts of each individual.

The principals of all schools in Cracow were advised to evaluate all teaching staff using the following criteria:

1) degree of acceptance of the basic educational goals of a socialist system;

2) teachers' ideological/political and moral behavior;

3) organizational and political activities before August 1980, from August 1980 to October 1981, since October 1981 and how they apply to state of war decrees in practice. (Biuletyn Malpolski, No. 9)

On the other hand, actions are directed towards interposing the teacher into the work of repression outside the school and on the other, the teacher's loyalty is subjected to an additional test. Two examples:

> The Council of National Salvation in Torun Voivodship issued a directive ordering teachers to participate in evening patrols in the company of the militia. They were to check the documents of youth on the streets, visit dorms, and submit reports via the principal to the Board of Education and the militia. Teachers in Torun, protesting against the transformation of schools into a branch of the militia, wrote: "Don't let them press a club into your hand. The tool of our trade is chalk" (Torun, Solidarnosc Information Bulletin, No. 22).

> Universal education under government control is fully subordinate to the state. Because of this, for example, all middle schools in Katowice Voivodship allowed the SB to inspect students' files and if necessary, to appropriate their photographs (Solidarnosc Information Bulletin, No. 53).

> In Cracow on September 9, 1982, at a Principals' Conference, Superintendant Marski threatened to revoke the teaching license of any instructor who participated in a strike. As he put it, the period of November 2-9,

1982, was to be a period of "intensified vigilance in education".

In Lodz, the start of the school year was preceded by pedagogical conferences at which school principals presented an educational program aimed at "deepening political faith" and forming a "socialist attitude" among youth.

Imposing such a system on schools would not have had any effect had it not been compounded by repression against teachers. These ran the gamut from suspension, to transfer to a lower position, through dismissal, all the way to prison sentences.

In May 1982, prior to graduation, B. Dras and L. Plochocka were suspended at the Stefan Batory High school in Warsaw (War Weekly, No. 22).

In Plock Voivodship on June 17, Danuta Palmowska - a teacher in Borowiczki - was dismissed by the verification commission (TS, No. 21).

Piotr Wasilewski, a teacher at the Basic Agricultural School in Klawinowo, was sentenced to three years in prison by the Naval Court in Gdynia for reading a text signed by the Confederation for an Independent Poland (KPN) (TS, No. 19).

The assumption is that after gaining total control of schools, the authorities will aim for even greater control over all youth. It is not difficult to conclude that, in the same way, their aim is to eliminate all alternative institutions and above all, the Church.

It is worth noting the practice of removing crucifixes from schools, for example by the newly-appointed principal of the Technical Schools in Bialystok, Krystyna Hajduk, by

Principal L. Wabel of High School V in Torun, and by

Principal Halat of High School IV in Torun. Ms. Zgierska,

who chairs the Verification Commission in Polk, stated that

"verification is an indispensible means in the plan for

1982-83 for total atheization of education and instruction

(TN, No. 21).

It is evident that the author of the above statement was

telling the truth. At a conference of party activists and

leaders of the Polish Army, held in Warsaw on November 16,

1982, and chaired by Barcikowski, General Siwicki, and

General Baryla, the following theses, among others, were

proposed:

> We will place great emphasis on the patriotic
> re-education of the younger generation into
> fighters for the cause of a socialist
> transformation of life. The secularization of
> education will be a criterion for judging the
> effectiveness of the educational community.
> Let us return to the source, which educated
> the vanguard of those who built socialism to
> education through work in the Service to
> Poland Brigades. The cadre for these Brigades
> will be provided by the Polish Army....

Besides the policy towards the Church, total state

control of students was to be achieved by eliminating any

alternative structures that fall outside of state control.

The history of the eliminiation of the Independent

Students' Association is well known. Less well know is the

fate of Polish scouting.

Within the Polish Scouting Movement (ZHP), a Malkowski Scout Instructors Circle (KIHAM) was formed prior to December 13, 1981. It represented a return to "classical" scouting. On December 17, WRON, the Military Council for National Salvation, did not suspend the Polish Scouting Association. In view of this, KIHAM continued its activities in the hope that the leadership of this Association could continue the process of renewal within the scouting movement in accordance with its bylaws.

In a statement in May, the Consultation Council of KIHAM, as a representative body, drew the attention of the Scouts Supreme Council to the fact that the adopted principles of renewal were abandoned and instructors and members of the KIHAM were harassed. In response, the Supreme Council passed a resolution on June 26 disbanding the Consultation Council and annulling its resolution.

Disciplinary sanctions were applied against members of the Consultation Council for their activities. Less than one quarter of the Supreme Council voted for the resolution. At the same time, the Scouts' administration supported by the strength and administration of the Military Council of National Salvation, started to set up circles loyal to it, but with KIHAM symbols.

E. Repression of High School and University Students in

Connection with Protest Actions

The dictators and their executors alarmingly emphasize the participation of youth in all types of protest. For example, on May 3, 1982, the Minister of Internal Affairs, General Kiszczak, informed the Sejm deputies that 47 students of secondary schools and 54 university students were among the 271 detainees.

Using data from the Prosecutor General's Office and the Ministry of Internal Affairs, the Government Press Office released information that after the demonstrations of August 31, 1982, 4,050 people were detained, of which two thirds were younger than thirty years old.

A special June 28, 1982 supplement to the underground periodical KOS states:

> Since the time of street riots, the mere fact of being young has become sufficient proof of crime justifying the use of violence. There are increasing reports of systematic beating of young people at police stations and cases of particular brutality against minors. A protest against brutal acts of violence in Lublin was signed by 24 priests and 70 students of the Lublin Catholic University.

Among the fatal victims of martial law, young people can be found:

> During a demonstration in Poznan in February 1982, militiamen beat up Wojciech Cieslewicz, a 26-year-old resident of Kynia and a student at the Adam Mickiewicz University. He died

three days afterwards in a coma. During his
funeral the cemetary was surrounded by a
cordon of militia and SB.

Malgorzata Lenartowicz, age 19, died in Warsaw
on May 5, 1982, as a result of injuries,
according to the inscription on her grave in
Powazki Cemetary, quarter 247 (Tygodnik
Mazowsze, No. 15)

Piotr Majchrzak, a student at Gardening
High School in Poznan, age 19, was beaten
up on May 13, 1982, by the ZOMO and died
on May 18. (Biuletyn Wieklopolski, No.
10/82)

The body of Emil Barchanski, age 17,
student of Rey High School in Warsaw, was
fished out of the Vistula River on June
6, 1982. Arrested in February, beaten
during investigation, blackmailed with
alleged statements made by a co-suspect,
he admitted that together with T.
Sokolewicz he participated in the
February action against the Dzierzynski
Monument. Sentenced to being a ward of
the state on March 30, 1982, he said that
he intended to recall the statements
forced from him which provided the basis
for the arrest and sentencing of T.
Sokolewicz (Glos, No. 39, July-August,
1982).

Jarosaw Brejza, 17-year-old student from
Inowroclaw, residing at 41a Jagiellonska
St., committed suicide by hanging
himself.

He had been beaten and harassed during an
interrogation in the Militia
Headquarters. Among other things, he had
to stand with his hands up for six hours.
In a farewell letter to his parents and
friends, he wrote that this was not the
Poland which he was fighting and for
which he wanted to live.

There are many students among political prisoners in
Poland. Many have not yet been sentenced, but one can say

that no lenience is applied to young people. There are four

and five-year sentences. Two examples of high sentences:

> On April 21, 1982, the Pomeranian
> Military District Court sentenced M.
> Debinski, student of Nicholas Copernicus
> University in Torun, to one year in
> prison for possessing and circulating one
> leaflet (Torunski Informator
> Solidarnosci, No. 19).

> Piotr Cichocki, a 17-year-old student of
> Batory High School, was sentenced to one
> and a half years in prison on April 24,
> 1982, for pasting up leaflets in school
> calling for "silent school breaks"
> (Tygodnik Mazowsze, No. 17).

Students of primary schools may also be victims of

beating.

> In Plock, militia men beat children in Primary
> School No. 3 with truncheons. In the local
> pizza parlor, militiamen forced young people
> with Our Lady buttons and resistance symbols
> to stand against the wall with their hands
> raised and beat them with truncheons (Tygodnik
> Mazowsze, No. 21).

In doctor's reports in which the condition of often

anonymous victims of the militia is described one finds, for

example, "L.K., age 21, student and employee of Lenin Steel

Works, deep facial wounds with an open break of the nose bone

and damaged eye socket;" a seven-year-old boy, "kidney injury

by a gas grenade hurled from the distance of a few meters;"

R.N., age 21, student, "hit on the face with a gas grenade, a

vast blood blister on the eyelid and right eye" (Nowa Huta,

August 31, 1982).

> T. Kuligowski, student of the
> Shipbuilding High School in Gdansk, was

detained by ZOMO patrol on October 14,
1982, and beaten up so that his spleen
ruptured.

One of the victims of the beating of
internees in Kwidzyn on August 14, 1982,
was Radoslaw Sarnicki, a 19-year-old
student at a senior high school in
Zamosc. As a result, he was in a coma
and on August 17-18, was transported to a
hospital after the intervention of the
Polish Red Cross. (Tygodnik Mazowsze,
No. 26).

Beating, arrest and imprisonment are the most dangerous,

and immediate forms of repression which also create an

atmosphere of permanent threat. It surrounds not only those

who had the courage to demonstrate in the defense of their

convictions but anyone, anywhere. Any attempt at protesting

is prosecuted and, if the perpetrator is found, severely

punished. If the perpetrator is not found, the principle of

collective responsibility is widely applied:

Tygodnik Mazowsze (No. 8, March 31, 1982)
reported that for example in Lublin 100
people found out from a list in a display
case that they had been removed from the
students' register. (They were
unofficially informed that all those who
who had been detained twice walking while
TV news was broadcast had been
automatically removed.

After the demonstration of students and
employees of Silesian University on May
13, 1982, which consisted of signing M.
Konopnicka's "Oath" and the national
anthem, arrests were made the next day.
From the Department of Chemistry alone,
50 students were detained. (Tygodnik
Mazowsze, No. 16)

After the demonstration of November 11,
1982, classes were suspended at Nicolaus

> Copernicus University in Torun and
> students were ordered to leave the
> dormitories within 24 hours. Rebilleting
> was combined with verification. One of
> the forms of repression was the abolition
> of co-ed and same department
> dormitories.

There are known cases of departments at academic

institutions or of whole high schools being suspended or

closed down. For example, after the demonstration of May 3,

1982 in Lublin, the Zamoyski High School was closed down and

it was announced that anyone detained by the militia would be

expelled from school. In the Fifth High School in Cracow,

one grade was disbanded because its students came dressed in

black on November 10, 1982.

An expelled student received a "wolf ticket," a ban on

school attendance which deprives him of education. For

example, at the start of academic year 1982-83, the Office

for Students' Affairs at Warsaw University sent a letter to

deans reminding them that students expelled from any

institution in the country had no right to apply to Warsaw

University. The list contained 42 names (Tygodnik Mazowsze,

No. 134)

> A student should always openly and
> resolutely reprimand his school mate when
> he acts imprudently and improperly. A
> student has an ill understanding of
> friendship if he does not counteract a
> situation where there is a possibility of
> action which does not conform with the
> existing legal order and principles of
> school discipline or if he remains silent
> about them.

4g. A student determinedly reacts to and immediately reports to his superiors an uncovered crime or attempt to commit it and if a perpetrator is caught red-handed (while painting slogans against the presently reigning legal order, desecrating the state emblem and national flag) he will be reported to prosecuting authorities.

Consequences

2b. The class in which the perpetrator is not uncovered will be reorganized or disbanded and undisciplined pupils or those who have poor grades will be expelled from the school with an appropriate note in their files.

If, in a classroom turned over to another teacher, slogans with anti-state contents attacking the legal order and our alliances are found and the form-master knows this and does not take any preventive measures, his rights as a form-master will be suspended and he will even be disciplinarily dismissed from work.

If it is found that after leaving the classroom, anti-socialist graffiti attacking the legal order or our alliances are inscribed on the walls, the teacher may be disciplinarily dismissed from work or his case may be transferred to prosecuting organs.

SUMMARY

Prior to the introduction of martial law, the last time
when the PRL authorities ordered workers to be shot was in
1970. For 10 years, bloodshed was avoided. This
psychological barrier was broken by the martial law
authorities. The first shots were fired three days after the
imposition of martial law.

The number of fatal victims of martial law is difficult
to establish. It is possible to document 28 cases of
murder.

In February 1983, *Informator Solidarnosci* reported the
death of another victim. On November 26, 1982, Waclaw
Kaminski, age 32, died. He was a worker from the Gdansk o
Shipyard who had been hit on the head with a gas grenade
during the November 11 demonstration and then beaten by the
ZOMO.

The number of those wounded by firearms and severely
beaten in the streets, in prisons, custodies and internment
camps runs into many hundreds.

During the one year of martial law, 10,000 people were
interned. Courts and misdemeanor courts passed more than
30,000 prison sentences in political cases. In Warsaw alone,
1,900 verdicts of this kind were passed.

More than 60,000 people have been fined for
participation in various forms of protest. In Warsaw alone,

2,000 people were fined. Sentencing by misdemeanor courts
was only loosely connected with the activities of the
defendant. Courts passed sentences practically on anybody
who was brought in by the militia, which often caught people
in the street purely by chance.

Tens of thousands of people have been fired from work
for manifesting resistance or sometimes even for mere
membership in Solidarnosc. In Warsaw and its suburbs alone,
at least 5,000 people have been fired. Several hundred
students have been expelled. We can document the dismissal
of at least 200 scholars and scientists for political
reasons.

Even in those branches of industry which suffer manpower
shortage, such as mining, firing for political reasons has
created a sizeable army of unemployed miners and down-graded
foremen. There was a time when it seemed that production in
the Transport Equipment Plant at Swidnik would have to be
suspended because hundreds of highly skilled workers and
engineers were fined for political reasons.

People (particularly employees of state administration)
have been forced to sign loyalty oaths and to leave
Solidarnosc under the threat of dismissal.

Some enterprises have been militarized and people have
been punished for leaving work as for military desertion.
The work schedule can be extended to 12 hours a day and 7
days a week.

Bank accounts have been blocked. Moving in the streets during night hours and leaving places of residence were forbidden for many months. Telephone communications were cut off and when they were restored after a few weeks, monitoring of all conversations was officially introduced. The publication of all newspapers, except two, was forbidden for a certain time. One radio program and one TV program were left. All correspondence was censored.

Finally and most importantly, the activity of labor unions, associations and organizations was suspended. Some of them were later dissolved (labor unions, the Independent Students' Union, the Association of Polish Journalists, etc.) and their property was seized.

By introducing martial law, the PRL authorities violated Art. 4, par. 1, of the International Covenant on Civil and Political Rights, ratified by Poland. They also violate the PRL Constitution. By adopting the law on labor unions in 1982, they violated Convention Nos. 87 and 98 of the International Labor Organization and by adopting the law on handling work shirkers they violated Convention No. 105.

These laws, together with the law on special legal regulations during the period of the suspension of martial law, have created legal foundations for the continuation of terror.

GLOSSARY

KOR or KSS/KOR	Committee for Social Self-Defense
militia	police
PRL	People's Republic of Poland
SB	Secret police or security service
Solidarnosc	Independent Self-Governing Trade Union Solidarity
Voivodship	province
ZOMO	Riot police